THE HISTORY OF ECONOMICS

ECONOMISTS OF THE TWENTIETH CENTURY

General Editors: Mark Perlman, *University Professor of Economics, University of Pittsburgh* and Mark Blaug, *Professor Emeritus, University of London; Professor Emeritus, University of Buckingham; and Visiting Professor, University of Exeter*

This innovative series comprises specially invited collections of articles and papers by economists whose work has made an important contribution to economics in the late twentieth century.

The proliferation of new journals and the ever-increasing number of new articles make it difficult for even the most assiduous economist to keep track of all the important recent advances. By focusing on those economists whose work is generally recognized to be at the forefront of the discipline, the series will be an essential reference point for the different specialisms included.

A list of published and future titles in this series is printed at the end of this volume.

The History of Economics

The Collected Essays of Takashi Negishi
Volume II

Takashi Negishi

Faculty of Economics
University of Tokyo

Edward Elgar

Published by
Edward Elgar Publishing Limited
Gower House
Croft Road
Aldershot
Hants GU11 3HR
England

Edward Elgar Publishing Company
Old Post Road
Brookfield
Vermont 05036
USA

British Library Cataloguing in Publication Data
Negishi, Takashi
  Collected Essays of Takashi Negishi. –
  Vol. 2: History of Economics. –
  (Economists of the Twentieth Century
  Series)
  I. Title   II. Series
  330

Library of Congress Cataloguing in Publication Data
Negishi, Takashi, 1933–
    The history of economics / Takashi Negishi.
      p.   cm. — (Economists of the twentieth century) (The
    collected essays of Takashi Negishi; v. 2)
      Includes indexes.
      1. Economics—History. I. Title. II. Series. III. Series:
    Negishi, Takashi, 1933–   Essays.   Selections; v. 2.
    HB75.N418   1994 vol. 2
    330 s—dc20
    [330'.09]   93–37386
                                                                       CIP

ISBN 1 85278 938 7

Printed in Great Britain at the University Press, Cambridge

Contents

Acknowledgements

The author and publishers wish to thank the following who have kindly given permission for the use of copyright material.

The Academic Press for 'Expenditure Patterns and International Trade in Quesnay's Tableau Economique', in R. Sato and T. Negishi (eds), (1989), *Developments in Japanese Economics*, Academic Press, 85–97.

Blackwell Publishers for 'A Note on Jevons's Law of Indifference and Competitive Equilibrium', *Manchester School* (1982), **50**, 220–30.

The Cambridge University Press for 'Economic Structure and the Theory of Economic Equilibrium', in M. Baranzini and R. Scazzieri (eds), (1990), *The Economic Theory of Structure and Change*, Cambridge University Press, 47–63.

Professor S.B. Dahiya for 'Samuelson, Saigal and Emmanuel's Theory of International Unequal Exchange', in Shri Bhagwan Dahiya (ed.), (1991), *Theoretical Foundations of Development Planning*, **4**, Concept, 37–49.

Editions Dalloz-Sirey for 'F.D. Longe and Refutation of Classical Theory of Capital', *Revue d'économie politique* (1992), **102** (6), 915–24.

Duke University Press for 'The Labor Theory of Value in the Ricardian Theory of International Trade', *History of Political Economy* (1982), **14** (2), 199–210, 'Wicksell's Missing Equation: A Comment', *History of Political Economy* (1982), **14** (3), 310–311, 'Thornton's Criticism of Equilibrium Theory and Mill', *History of Political Economy* (1986), **18** (4), 567–77, 'On Equilibrium and Disequilibrium: A Reply to Ekelund and Thommesen', *History of Political Economy* (1989), **21** (4), 593–600, and 'Comment, Minisymposium, The History of Economics and the History of Science', *History of Political Economy* (1992), **24**, 227–9.

The Economic Society of Osaka University for 'Bertrand's Duopoly Considered as an Edgeworth's Game of Exchange', *Osaka Economic Papers* (1991), **40** (3, 4), 55–62.

Elsevier Science Publishers B.V. (North-Holland) for 'Studies of von Thünen in Japan', *Japan and the World Economy* (1990), **2** (3), 199–209.

The Japan Association of Economics and Econometrics for 'Marx and Böhm-Bawerk', *Economic Studies Quarterly* (1986), **37** (1), 2–10.

Journal of the History of Economic Thought for 'Ricardo and Morishima on Machinery', *Journal of the History of Economic Thought* (1990), **12**, 146–61.

The Macmillan Press Limited and Professor George R. Feiwel for 'Competition and the Number of Participants: Lessons of Edgeworth's Theorem', in G. Feiwel (ed.), (1989), *The Economics of Imperfect Competition and Employment; Joan Robinson and Beyond*, Macmillan, 212–24, (© George R. Feiwel, 1989), 'Non-Walrasian Foundations of Macroeconomics', in G. Feiwel (ed.), (1985), *Issues in Contemporary Macroeconomics and Distribution*, Macmillan, 169–83, (© George R. Feiwel, 1985) and 'On the Non-existence of Equilibrium: From Thornton to Arrow', in G. Feiwel (ed.), (1987), *Arrow and the Ascent of Modern Economic Theory*, Macmillan, 361–74, (© George R. Feiwel, 1987).

The Oxford University Press for 'Comments on Ekelund "Mill's Recantation of the Wages Fund"', *Oxford Economic Papers* (1985), **37**, 148–51.

Presses Universitaires de Grenoble for 'Marx and Böhm-Bawerk in the Theory of Interest', *Économie et Sociétés* (1980), **14**, 287–304.

Seoul Journal of Economics for 'The Role of Demand in Adam Smith's Theory of Natural Price', *Seoul Journal of Economics* (1988), **1** (4), 357–65.

Springer-Verlag, Wien, for 'Wicksell's Missing Equation and Böhm-Bawerk's Three Causes of Interest in a Stationary State', *Zeitschrift für Nationalökonomie* (1982), **42** (2), 161–74.

In addition the author wishes to thank Professors M. Blaug and M. Perlman, Mr E. Elgar and Mrs S. Shailer, Miss J. Rix, Mrs S. Nishimura and Miss M. Hirata.

Introduction

Autobiographical introduction

Born on 2 April 1933, I spent my early days in Tokyo, Shanghai, Kyoto and again in Tokyo. In my high school days, I was an amateur scientist interested in astronomy and meteorology. My major was social sciences, however, when I was admitted to the University of Tokyo in 1952, because I thought that my mathematical ability was not enough to do natural sciences.

My first teacher in economics, Professor Shigeru Aihara, ordered his students in the freshman course of economics to study Adam Smith, Ricardo and Marx, i.e. to read *Wealth of Nations*, *Principles* and *Das Kapital*, in Japanese translation, rather than to study modern textbooks. At the age of sixty, now I can understand that such an introduction to economics is not necessarily unreasonable. But to me as a freshman, it was simply boring to read such books of classical economics. Among classics of economics, however, I found Cournot's *Recherches sur les principes mathématiques de la théorie des richesse* interesting, though it was not recommended by Professor Aihara who is a Marxian economist. From Cournot, I learned that mathematics can be used very productively even in economics, and it is not as difficult as mathematics in natural sciences. I made up my mind to do mathematical economics.

In the 1950s, the faculty of economics was dominated by Marxian economics in the University of Tokyo. But I was very lucky to have Professor Yasuhiko Oishi as my undergraduate adviser, who was one of a few non-Marxians. He suggested that I read Hicks's *Value and Capital* and Keynes's *General Theory* and taught me the theory of linear programming. In his seminar, I wrote an essay entitled 'Macrotheory of Trade Cycles and Non-linear Differential Equations' (in Japanese), which is a survey of Keynesian macro dynamic models and some mathematical exercises based on such models. Being aware of the existence of an active group of Japanese mathematical economists, like Yasui, Morishima, Ichimura, Nikaido, Inada and Uzawa, I decided to undertake graduate study on economic theory, wishing to join the group, if possible.

When admitted to the graduate school of the University of Tokyo in 1956, I was advised by Professor Hiroshi Furuya to study general equilibrium theory. I discussed the existence and optimality of general equilibrium theory and proved the local stability of the gross-substitute case in my essay for a Master's degree. Because of these studies, I was employed on Arrow's project in Stanford as a research assistant (1958–59) and a research associate (1959–60). At Stanford I wrote several articles on general equilibrium, including a joint article on non-tâtonnement stability with Hahn who was at Berkeley. I read a paper on monopolistic competition at the Washington meeting (1959) and a survey paper on stability at the Naples meeting (1960) of the Econometric Society.

ix

I returned to Tokyo in 1960 and finished my graduate study in 1963 with the degree of Keizaigakuhakusi (Ph.D. in economics). Having served as a research associate for two years, I was appointed as an associate professor of economics in 1965, and began to teach at the University of Tokyo. My dissertation was published in 1965 under the title of *Kakaku to Haibun no Riron* (Theories of Price and Allocation). In 1964 I married Aiko Mori, who was an English literature major graduate student (she is now Professor at Bunka Women's University in Tokyo). In 1966, I was elected a Fellow of the Econometric Society.

In 1967–68, I was granted two years' leave from Tokyo, and taught at the University of New South Wales and University of Minnesota. My interest began gradually to shift from the pure theory of general equilibrium to its application to international economics, partly because of M.C. Kemp's influence. While I was away from the University of Tokyo, its graduate school of economics was dissolved by student riots with the result that compulsory courses and Master's degrees were abolished. This is why many good students began to leave for the USA to obtain degrees there.

After writing articles on the theory and applications of the general equilibrium in the 1950s and 1960s, I published my first book in English, *General Equilibrium Theory and International Trade*, in 1972. The book won the Nikkei Prize for Best Books of Economics in 1973. Between 1964 and 1969, I served as an associate editor for the *International Economic Review.*

In 1975 I took a year's leave from Tokyo to give lectures at the London School of Economics. After returning to Tokyo, I was promoted to a professor of economics at the University of Tokyo in 1976. One of the problems I tackled in the 1970s was micro-foundations of macroeconomics, although I had felt already in my undergraduate days that something should be done to connect the world of Hicks's *Value and Capital* and that of Keynes's *General Theory*. Another area I studied in the 1970s was that of public economics, being partly influenced by environmental problems. I wrote articles mainly in these two areas in the 1970s, and published *Microeconomic Foundations of Keynesian Macroeconomics* in 1979.

In 1977, the Matsunaga Science Foundation Prize for Social Science was awarded to me for my studies on the general equilibrium theory. I served as an associate editor for *Econometrica* in 1969–75 and 1979–84, and for the *Journal of International Economics* in 1973–85. In 1973–75, I edited the *Economic Studies Quarterly.*

In 1979 I was hospitalized and operated upon. At the age of 46, I felt I had to shift gear in my life. With my wife, I translated Viner's *The Role of Providence in the Social Order* into Japanese in 1980. It is my pleasant memory that I gave lectures at the International Christian University in Tokyo for several years.

The study of Keynesian economics from the point of view of the general equilibrium theory led me to the strong recognition of the existence of different points of view in current economic theory, each of which has its own origin and predecessors. In the 1980s my main interest was in the history of economic theory. Besides articles on several topics in the history of economic theory, I published two books, *Economic Theories in a Non-Walrasian Tradition* in 1985 and *History of Economic Theory* in 1989. In addition, I wrote *Disequilibrium Trade Theories,* in 1987 with Motoshige Itoh, a former student and now a colleague of mine, who received his degree from Rochester.

Being elected a member of the Science Council of Japan in 1985 and engaged in editing an official report on scientific research in Japan, I found it interesting that Japanese mathematical economists and econometricians do not regard the level of their work highly, although they know their works are internationally known, while Japanese economists of other areas complain that their contributions, which they insist are of a high standard, remain internationally unknown. In 1985, I was also elected President of the Japan Association of Economics and Econometrics. In 1989 the American Economic Association elected me Foreign Honorary Member, while the International Economic Association appointed me as a member of the Executive Committee.

In 1990 I was elected Dean of the Faculty of Economics, and held the office for two years. While I was Dean, the Faculty decided to strengthen our graduate school and to re-introduce Master's degrees and the system of required courses for it. It is twenty years since the student riots that abolished compulsory courses in graduate school. Since 1965, I have been assigned mainly to lectures on price theory in the Faculty. My lecture note was published in Japanese in 1989. I will retire from the University of Tokyo in March 1994. The faculty has already appointed Michihiro Kandori, a former student of mine who took his degree at Stanford, to replace me to give lectures on economic theory.

In 1993, the Japan Academy awarded me for my studies on the history of economic theory. Currently (1994), I am the President of the Econometric Society, and a member of the Executive Commitee of the Japan Society for the History of Economic Thought.

I have published my books and articles in English or in Japanese. Twenty-one essays of mine written in English are collected here in Volume II, in two Parts, i.e. Classical and Marxian Economics and Marginal Revolution and After. Volume I contains forty-seven essays on the theory and application of general equilibrium.

Introduction to essays collected
The essays collected in this volume are concerned with problems of the history of economic theory and economic thoughts. The common feature of these essays is the study of past theories and thoughts in the light of, or from the point of view of, modern economic theory. Why should we carry out such studies?

The answer is obvious: if we follow Lakatos's theory that the history of science has been a history of competing research programmes, or if you prefer, paradigms, but it has not been a succession of periods of the monopolies of a single research programme. Even a currently hibernating research programme can make a triumphal return without changing its core, if some new auxiliary theories are added properly. But, to make such a return possible, however, there must always be some scientists who are seeking to develop it while it is in a state of hibernation. In other words, it is necessary to study theories that are regarded as past ones from the point of view of other reserach programmes (Negishi, 1989, pp. 1–5). Good examples are Sraffa's study of Ricardo and Pasinetti's formulation of a mathematical model of Ricardo's economics, which gave foundations of a neo-Ricardian research programme, one of the most active competitors of mainstream neo-classical study.

Even those who do not believe in Lakatos, furthermore, cannot but admit that the historical development of economic theories is not a uni-directional progression toward the truth and the currently influential theory is not necessarily superior, in every respect, to past theories. In economics it is rather rare that a theory is rejected empirically as a false one by carefully controlled experiments. A new theory often replaces old ones simply because the former seems to be more general, or more elegant or simpler than the latter. Such a progress often means sacrificing something old which is not necessarily useless. To make sure that we are going in the right direction, therefore, it is always necessary to see in the mirror of history whether we have not sacrificed something in error.

To study old theories in the light of modern ones, we often translate old arguments into mathematical models, though they were originally literary or given in terms of numerical examples, at best. This is partly because, as Frisch (1952) admitted, nowadays economists in general are not induced to spend time and trouble discussing problems in theory unless the details of the problems are rigorously formulated in mathematical terms. It cannot be denied that, by studying such mathematical models, we can understand more easily what economists in earlier times really meant, see their historically celebrated and still interesting problems in a new light and using modern techniques solve easily the problems they were unable to solve. But, translation is treason. We must admit that something of the original content is always lost by the mathematical translation of the classical works of past economists. We have, therefore, to study carefully and critically such mathematical models, by always referring to the content of the original literature.

Part I   Classical and Marxian economics

Essay 1, 'Expenditure Patterns and International Trade in Quesnay's Tableau Economique', in R. Sato and T. Negishi (eds), (1989), *Developments in Japanese Economics*, Academic Press, 85–97.

Quesnay's Tableau Economique is the first complete description of economic circulation, in which he considered a country where the agriculture is mostly developed, commercial competition prevails and the ownership of private capital in agriculture is guaranteed. It has a long history of interpretations. It is not easy to interpret simple tables of numbers consistently. Besides, there is a problem whether it can explain the physiocratic theory of growth that expenditure on agricultural products makes the economy grow while that on manufactured goods does not. Essay 1 showed that the recent approach to introducing international trade makes it possible to interpret Tableau Economique consistently, but that the possibility of international trade makes the physiocratic theory of growth entirely untenable. Introduction of the large country assumption does not help, since it merely leads to terms of trade arguments that domestic expenditure on the exportables, not necessarily agricultural products, possibly manufactured goods, makes the economy grow (Negishi, 1989, p. 64).

Besides Essay 1, I have some other works on pre-Smithian economists, Locke, Hume and Quesnay, which were not published in English, but they are summarized in Negishi (1989, pp. 31–59).

Essay 2, 'The Role of Demand in Adam Smith's Theory of Natural Price', *Seoul Journal of Economics* (1988), **1** (4), 357–65.

Natural prices are equilibrium prices which are realized when the suppliers' expectations of demands are correct so that supplies are just equal to demands, while market prices diverge from natural ones and fluctuate around them when suppliers' expectations are not correct. Unlike Ricardo, Adam Smith considered that the natural, not market, price of labour is higher in a growing economy than the subsistence level. Other authors (Hicks, 1965, pp. 37–42; Blaug, 1985, p. 44; Ekelund and Hébert, 1990, p. 115; Eltis, 1975, pp. 437–8), however, have not recognized the significance of Smith's system of natural prices very well. In spite of Hicks's statement that Smith was writing before Malthus (1965, p. 39), Smith clearly argued that 'the reward of labour must necessarily encourage in such a manner the marriage and multiplication of labourers, as may enable them to supply that continually increasing demand by a continually increasing population' (1776, p. 98).

In this article, we construct a small von Neumann-type balanced growth model and confirm that the ratio of the natural wage to the subsistence wage is equal to the rate of growth, that an increase in the labour productivity increases the rate of growth, the natural rate of profit and the natural wage, and that an increase in savings ratio increases the rate of growth and the natural wage and decreases the natural rate of profit. In other words, any shift of demand between consumption goods or unproductive labour and productive labour have effects on the relative prices of commodities through its effects on the natural wage and the natural rate of profit. (Incidentally, in this article, p. 359, line 19, *he footnoted* should read *he mentioned*.)

This balanced growth model with constant labour productivity may also represent Malthus's position, since he emphasized the importance of the regulating principle against the limiting principle in his theory of profit and in his defence of Smith against Ricardo on the falling rate of profit. To do justice to his theory of motives to production, however, we have to regard the labour productivity as an increasing function of the rate of profit. Then we may reply to Malthus's problem of the optimal propensity to consume by choosing the savings ratio which maximizes the rate of growth (Negishi, 1993).

Another possible modification is to consider labour productivity as a function of the level of output. This is either because it is an increasing function of the division of labour, which 'is limited by the extent of the market' (Smith, 1776, p. 31) or because in agriculture the land is a limiting factor of production. With such a modification, unless effects of division of labour and land cancel each other out (Negishi, 1989, p. 88), generally it is impossible to consider the balanced growth of output and labour population. While Reid (1987) suggests disequilibrium models, it is still possible to have a system of natural prices, with the rate of growth of output and that of labour population different. Then, it can be easily shown that, given the current level of output and that of population, the ratio of the natural wage to the subsistence wage is equal to the rate of growth of labour, and that an increase in the savings ratio increases the rate of growth of labour and the real natural wage and decreases the real natural rate of profit.

Essay 3, 'The Labor Theory of Value in the Ricardian Theory of International Trade', *History of Political Economy* (1982), **14** (2), 199–210.

I challenged the neo-classical interpretation of Ricardo's famous numerical example of comparative costs that labour is the single factor of production and that the rate of wage which should be at the subsistence level is lower in the advanced country England than in the less advanced Portugal. Since England has more capital and labour relative to land, the marginal labour productivity is lower even if her technology is not less advanced than Portugal's. If England's subsistence level is not lower than Portugal's, furthermore, it is the rate of profit which is lower in England than in Portugal. I also challenged the view that the terms of trade cannot be determined in Ricardo's model unless, as was suggested by J.S. Mill, the reciprocal demands are taken into consideration. Ricardo as a labour value theorist can determine the international relative price without considering demands, since relative rates of profit are given from the classical implicit assumption of capital mobility through the activity of exporters and importers.

Though Samuelson (1972, p. 679) insisted that the economic geography of Ricardo is odd, what is really odd is the interpretation that in the heyday of England's industrial revolution Ricardo had selected Portugal as the superior of England in every respect, having a greater real per capita GNP. Since a lower marginal productivity of labour implies a greater land rent income, there is no contradiction between Ricardo's numerical example of comparative costs and the fact that England had a larger per head GNP. If you forget the existence of land (Ricardo never did!), Ricardo's numerical examples are interpreted to show the average productivity of labour and are blamed as unrealistic numbers.

Gandolfo (1986, pp. 1–24) referred to this essay's argument that Ricardo can determine the terms of trade without having recourse to demand factors, but only by using the cost–price relation, i.e. by making use of the classical theory of wages, the rate of profit, and the role of exporters and importers. After careful examination, Gandolfo (1986, pp. 1–31) concluded that it will be possible to determine the terms of trade satisfactorily within the context of the Ricardian model, without introducing demand factors, though further studies are necessary on how we can determine the risk premium for foreign investment (i.e. *a* in Essay 3). He even admitted, however, that it may be simply considered as a historico-institutional datum, like the level of subsistence wages.

Burgstaller (1986), who also referred to Essay 3, considered Ricardo's numerical example as the stationary solution of a two-country version of Pasinetti (1960)'s Ricardo model and pointed out that the terms of trade can be determined independently from demands. The difference is that the rates of profit are exogenously given in Burgstaller (1986) as the stationary state with no capital accumulation, while they are endogenously determined in Essay 3 at what Pasinetti (1960) calls natural equilibrium in which population is stationary but capital is not. To limit the consideration of comparative costs only to the stationary state is to make the story unnecessarily uninteresting. For example, it is then impossible to argue, like Ricardo, that the rate of profit is not affected by the foreign trade, unless cheaper wages goods are being imported.

The lesson from this study on Ricardo's theory of comparative costs is that the study of the classical theory from the point of view of modern theory should not be a cutting or stretching of the former theory in a Procrustean Bed of the latter theory. It should be a mirror in which the modern theory can find the importance of what it did not inherit from the classical theory, in this case, the role of exporters and importers in international trade and investment. One example of how to learn this lesson was given in Essay 46 in Volume I.

Essay 4, 'Ricardo and Morishima on Machinery', *Journal of the History of Economic Thought*, (1990) **12**, 146–61.

This article was developed from my review of Morishima's *Ricardo's Economics*, although the latter was published later than the former. '*Ricardo's Economics* is the newest version of Morishima's economics. ... As a book on Ricardo himself, furthermore, the book is also highly worth reading since the author grasped the essence of Ricardo firmly and suggested several new and useful interpretations of Ricardo, which mediocre historians of economic thoughts could never imagine. ... This does not mean, however, that the author is always right in his new interpretations of Ricardo. An example of such possible misinterpretation is perhaps the case of Ricardo's famous chapter on machinery' (Negishi, 1991). I think that Morishima considered his own problem which is different from the one Ricardo had in mind. Nevertheless, I am highly grateful to Morishima for letting me pay attention to Ricardo's numerical examples, behind which Ricardo intuitively worked out general equilibrium problems beautifully.

Perhaps I may take advantage of this occasion to make the following change in the article: *production of the raw materials* should read *gross products* on p. 155, line 19 up. This is a part of my quotation from Mangoldt, which I wrote originally in German, since I thought readers of a journal of the history of economic thoughts can, at least, read German. A member of the editorial staff of the journal was, however, kind enough to translate it into English but unfortunately I was not informed of it before publication. German *Roherzeugnisse* can be translated in most cases as 'production of the raw materials', but in this context it should be 'gross products', which is related to the demand for labour. German *Roh* has the meaning of gross as well as raw, crude, etc. The editor of the journal was kind enough to publish a note of correction in one of the subsequent issues (Vol. 15, 1993, p. 173). You might think that it is a very minor point for my article. In the Western world, perhaps you are right. In Japan, however, where translation has been regarded as a job for qualified scholars, such a mistranslation is considered as a shame. Many scholars have been discredited by mistranslations. This is the reason for the above correction.

Essay 5, 'Comments on Ekelund "Mill's Recantation of the Wages Fund"', *Oxford Economic Papers* (1985), **37**, 148–51.

While the long-run wage theory of classical economics is that of the natural wage, i.e. the subsistence wage adjusted by the rate of growth, its short-run wage theory is the wages fund doctrine to explain market wages. Wages fund doctrine is also the essence of the classical theory of capital, as we can see in Ricardo's consideration of the machinery problem and his theory of economic growth (Pasinetti, 1960; Findlay, 1974). In Mill's *Principles*, we can confirm this, i.e. 'Demand for commodities is not demand for labor', and wages 'depend mainly upon the demand and supply of labor; or, as it is often expressed, on proportion between population and capital' (Mill, 1848, pp. 79, 343). Mill (1869), however, recanted this cornerstone of classical economics. It is generally believed that it shook the foundations of classical theoretical system and is an important factor in explaining the decline and fall of classical economics (Ekelund and Hébert, 1990, pp. 190, 197).

If this is so, we should consider under what conditions we can find 'the wage-fund doctrine, properly stated, not "wrong" logically' (Schumpeter, 1954, p. 669) and which of such conditions is abandoned by Mill in his recantation. A set of assumptions which are sufficient conditions for the unitary elasticity of demand curve for labour is given by Ekelund (1976)'s short-run model of wages fund. Two assumptions which may be called, respectively, the annual harvest assumption and the wage good assumption are the most important necessary conditions for the unitary elasticity of labour demand and it is the latter assumption which was abandoned by Mill in his recantation to admit that the elasticity may be zero.

Since these two statements are given in this essay as comments on Ekelund (1976), however, there is a reply to them from Ekelund (1985).

As for the first point that the annual harvest assumption is unnecessary for wages fund doctrine by Ekelund (1976, p. 74), Ekelund (1985) replied that it was made clear on p. 79 of his original paper (1976), where he clearly stated that harvest discontinuity is not required for the short-run determinancy of a wages fund. If harvest (output) is continuous and there is a finite period of production, however, input is also continuous. Then, as I showed in my essay, wages fund cannot be predetermined, since capitalists may let a part of their capital remain idle when the rate of wages is high.

Ekelund (1985) seems to admit the second point that Mill's recantation of the wages fund doctrine may have stemmed from the abandonment of the wage good assumption. But he still insists what is more likely is that it stemmed from 'a failure to work out and utilize the full ramifications of the classical dichotomy'. He is right if the wage good assumption was not abandoned. What seems most likely, however, is Mill abandoned the assumption and skilfully utilized the dichotomy of real and monetary economies to discuss in monetary terms the allocation of real funds.

It might be argued that the annual harvest assumption and the wage good assumption, prerequisites for the predetermined wages fund, are not very unrealistic in a certain stage of economy where agriculture is predominant and the rate of wage is at a level not far from that of subsistence. It might also be argued that these assumptions have lost their relevance as the economy developed, so that manufacturing predominates over agriculture, agriculture itself is highly artificialized, and distinct consumption patterns between classes are not observed. Wages fund doctrine surely played some historical roles, but now it almost played them out.

In his recantation, Mill not only denied the predetermined wages fund but also argued that the rate of wage may be indeterminate. This is a strong case 'in which there is nothing to restrain competition; no hindrance to it either in the nature of the case or in artificial obstacles; yet in which the result is not determined by competition, but by custom or usage; competition … producing its effect in quite a different manner from that which is ordinarily assumed to be natural to it' (Mill, 1848, p. 239). The wage once raised by a well-organized strike remains unchanged even if labourers returned thereafter to competitive suppliers. The wage changed exogenously is supported by endogenous decisions of competitive demanders and suppliers.

Essay 6, 'Thornton's Criticism of Equilibrium Theory and Mill', *History of Political Economy* (1986), **18** (4), 567–77.
Essay 7, 'On Equilibrium and Disequilibrium', *History of Political Economy* (1989), **21** (4), 593–600.
Essay 8, 'F.D. Longe and Refutation of Classical Theory of Capital', *Revue d'économie politique* (1992), **102** (6), 915–24.

Mill's recantation of the wages fund doctrine constitutes one of the most difficult problems in the history of economics, since he did not revise his *Principles* in this respect, after he recanted the doctrine in his review (Mill, 1869) of a book by Thornton, *On Labour* (1869). Thornton attacked the equilibrium theory in general, and the wages fund doctrine in particular, by using several examples. In his recantation, Mill interpreted one such example that demand cannot be increased by the reduction of the price so that there is no unique equilibrium price which equates demand with the given supply. Mill admitted that such a case may be conceivable in the labour market, and wages fund doctrine is wrong, as we discussed in Essay 5.

In Essay 6, we tried to solve the question why Mill left the doctrine of wages fund unchanged in his 1871 edition of his *Principles*, by referring to a hitherto unnoticed fact that, in the second edition of his *On Labour* (1870), Thornton denied Mill's interpretation of his example in 1869. Thornton did not assume an inelastic demand in his example and insisted not on the possibility of the indeterminacy of equilibrium price but the fact that the bulk of the goods is sold at disequilibrium prices. Certainly Mill recognized in 1871 that his interpretation of Thornton's example, on which his recantation in 1869 was based, was wrong and that Thornton's attack on equilibrium theory was based on the possibility of trades carried out at disequilibrium prices. While Mill was ready to admit the possibility of multiple equilibria and to deny the validity of the classical doctrine of wages fund in 1869, it is impossible for Mill the equilibrium theorist to accept Thornton's disequilibrium theory, since the latter is a theory of an entirely different paradigm, which was still immature as was pointed out in the preface to the 1871 edition of Mill's *Principles* (Mill, 1871, p. xciv).

This essay seems to have succeeded, at least, to remind the profession that Mill, in the 1871 edition of the *Principles*, retracted some of his earlier enthusiasm for Thornton, and in effect rejected the idea that disequilibrium trades in any way undermine the importance of the principle of the equality of demand and supply, and cautioned that it was too early to adduce any firm conclusions from the discussion engendered by Thornton's book (de Marchi, 1988, p. 157).

Essay 7 is my reply to comments of Ekelund and Thommesen (1989) on my disequilibrium interpretations of Thornton in Essay 5.

After all, how should John S. Mill the equilibrium economist have replied to W.T. Thornton the disequilibrium economist, who argued that the equilibrium theory is a truth of small significance since it does not explain disequilibrium prices at which the bulk of the goods offered for sale are actually sold? J.S. Mill the classical economist could not but express his hope that only a small portion of goods may be sold at disequilibrium. After the marginal revolution, however, we can reply to Thornton that the equilibrium theory is of great significance even if only a small portion of goods are sold at the equilibrium price which is finally established after the bulk of goods are sold at disequilibrium. This is because the marginal rates of substitution are equalized among buyers and sellers through such trades at equilibrium price so that a Pareto efficient allocation of goods is established. The effect of disequilibrium transactions is limited to changes in income distribution among buyers and sellers.

As a matter of fact, it was Longe (1866) who was the first to refute wages fund theory, though he was ignored by both Thornton and Mill. In Essay 8, we found that Longe refuted not only wages fund theory, but also the essence of the classical theory of capital that wages must be advanced by capitalists. It is no wonder that the name of Longe was not mentioned by Thornton and J.S. Mill. They never dreamed of denying the existence of the wages fund itself. Whether it is a fixed fund or not was their concern. In this respect, Longe is the predecessor not to Thornton, but to Walras (Eagly, 1974, pp. 7–8).

Essay 9, 'Marx and Böhm-Bawerk in the Theory of Interest', *Économie et Sociétés* (1980), **14**, 287–304.
Essay 10, 'Marx and Böhm-Bawerk', *Economic Studies Quarterly* (1986), **37** (1), 2–10.
Essay 11, 'Samuelson, Saigal and Emmanuel's Theory of International Unequal Exchange', in Shri Bhagwan Dahiya (ed.), (1991), *Theoretical Foundations of Development Planning*, **4**, Concept, 37–49.

Although a Western economist can proudly insist that 'without Marx economic theory would be as it is now' (Krelle, 1991), Marx is still an important figure in Japan where Marxian economics is the strongest competitor of neo-classical economics. As a non-Marxian economist, I feel I have to explain why I cannot accept Marx, and at the same time I am willing and ready to learn from my Marxian colleagues if possible.

Essay 9 is the oldest one collected in this volume. Here 'interest' should be understood rather as profit, since it is the translation of the German word *Kapitalzins*. The crux of Marxian economics is to explore the social relation between those who exploit and those who are exploited. Marx's theory does not, however, make sense so far as it is concerned with the exploitation of labour by capital, since, as was pointed out by Böhm-Bawerk, it is based on an unwarranted supposition that the embodied labour value of an output can be compared with that of an input without any discounting, even though they are located at different times. Unless labour is mobile through time, a larger value of output in terms of labour in the future compared with a smaller labour value of wages paid in the past does not necessarily imply that those who advanced wage costs exploit wage earners.

Marx also argued, however, that a rich country exploits a poor one through the exchange of one day's labour of the former and three days' labour of the latter. As is argued in the first half of Essay 10, this argument of Marx does make sense, even though labour is not mobile internationally, since in Marxian economics labour is an intermediate good produced by the consumption of consumers' goods, which are, directly or indirectly, mobile internationally, so that we can compare labours of different countries. As for the second half of Essay 10, which is concerned with Böhm-Bawerk's theory of interest, see the explanation of Essay 18 below.

According to Marx's plan of economics, only a small part of the first part of the plan is covered by *Das Kapital*, and many important problems including that of international trade are located in the second part of the plan and left to be done by his successors. In view of the north–south economic relations of the present world, what is most interesting to us may perhaps be the problem of international value, which is the foundation of Marxian theory of international trade and international exploitation. Essay 11 is a critical review of some recent theories of international trade of neo-Marxian economics, a competing research paradigm of neo-classical economics.

As for Marx, I have several other points which I discussed in my essays written in Japanese. They are (1) the dichotomy between Volume I and Volume III of *Das Kapital*, (2) the falling rate of profit, and (3) market values, which are summarized in Negishi (1989, pp. 213–37).

Part II   Marginal revolution and after

Essay 12, 'Studies of von Thünen in Japan,' *Japan and the World Economy* (1990), **2** (3), 199–209.

It is difficult to decide whether this essay should be placed in Part I, or Part II of this volume. Von Thünen is, of course, a pioneer of the marginal revolution, who first utilized the concept of marginal productivity extensively in his writings. He is, however, a very faithful follower of Adam Smith in all other respects. This essay surveyed studies of von Thünen in Japan and proved his famous formula of the natural wage (the geometric mean of the marginal productivity of labour and the subsistence wage). The lesson from this essay is that it is difficult to understand von Thünen fully unless one notes firmly that von Thünen is basically a classical economist. It is no wonder that one fails to derive the natural wage formula as the optimal wage in the sense of neo-classical economics.

Essay 13, 'A Note on Jevons's Law of Indifference and Competitive Equilibrium', *Manchester School* (1982), **50**, 220–30.
Essay 14, 'Competition and the Number of Participants: Lessons of Edgeworth's Theorem', in G. Feiwel (ed.), (1989), *The Economics of Imperfect Competition and Employment; Joan Robinson and Beyond*, Macmillan, 212–24.
Essay 15, 'Bertrand's Duopoly Considered as an Edgeworth's Game of Exchange, *Osaka Economic Papers* (1991), **40** (3, 4), 55–62.

These three essays are studies based on a famous theorem of Edgeworth. As is emphasized in Essay 13, Jevons's view of market equilibrium is quite different from that of Cournot and Walras, though the outcome is shown to be equivalent by Edgeworth in the case of a large economy where the number of participants is infinitely large. While Cournot and Walras presuppose the existence of a single market price for each single commodity and consider the equality of supply and demand as the equilibrium condition, it is the law of indifference (one price for one commodity) that plays the role of the equilibrium condition for Jevons and Edgeworth. Demand equals supply trivially, since the quantity of a commodity given by a person A is equal to the quantity received by another person B. From the point of view of emphasizing the significance of the law of indifference, a slight attempt is made to extend Edgeworth's theorem.

Essays 14 and 15 considered the possibility of a duopoly model which is different from Cournot's model. In the latter model, only firms are active players of the game and consumers are passive as a part of the environment of the game. Edgeworth's theorem can be applied if not only two firms but also infinitely many consumers are active players of the game of exchange. It is shown in Essay 14 that such a game can be considered as the so-called Bertrand's duopoly, although recently Magnan de Bornier (1992) objected to call such a duopoly as Bertrand's.

Essay 16, 'Non-Walrasian Foundations of Macroeconomics', G. Feiwel (ed.), (1985), *Issues in Contemporary Macroeconomics and Distribution*, Macmillan, 169–83.

One might wonder why this essay is not placed in Part VI of Volume I, judging from the title of the essay. The reason why it is here is that it contains my study of Menger as one of the first non-Walrasian economists. Menger's theory of the marketability of commodities is a first attempt at non-Walrasian economics. While Walras assumed well organized markets where all commodities have high marketability, Menger considered the theory of commodity for which the market is poorly organized and for which marketability is not high. From the point of view of the short-side principle, it may be said that a commodity is highly marketable when its suppliers are on the short-side of the relevant market and it is not so marketable when they are on the long-side of the market. Menger explains the origin of money on the basis of his theory of the marketability of commodities. Money is the commodity which has the highest marketability. It is no wonder the role of money is limited in Walrasian economics, since money as a medium of exchange presupposes the low marketability of other commodities. This confirms the conclusion of Essay 19 and Essay 47 of Volume I.

Essay 17, 'Wicksell's Missing Equation: A Comment', *History of Political Economy* (1982), **14** (3), 310–311.
Essay 18, 'Wicksell's Missing Equation and Böhm-Bawerk's Three Causes of Interest in a Stationary State', *Zeitschrift für Nationalökonomie* (1982), **42** (2), 161–74.

Wicksell, following Böhm-Bawerk, developed a stationary state model in which the existence of a positive rate of interest is explained by the marginal productivity of the period of production. In such a one-sided productivity model, however, there is one equation missing. Sandelin (1980) suggested that the model can be made closed by the introduction of a variable return production function. As was pointed out in Negishi (1985, p. 104), however, there must be an implicit factor of production besides labour, say, land, if the production function is not linear with respect to labour. Because of a new unknown variable, say, land rent, then an equation is still missing. Essay 17 is a comment on Sandelin (1980) and argues that such an equation should be supplied from a theory of saving behaviour.

A recent challenge to the missing equation problem is Kompas (1992, pp. 13, 92) who insists that Wicksell 'recognized the need and set out the required conditions, in terms of savings behavior or intertemporal preferences, to close all of his systems of equations properly', against the common 'belief that Wicksell treats the aggregate value of capital as a datum'. Even so, however, as Kompas (1992, pp. 137, 154) himself admitted, Wicksell (1934, pp. 209–218) could not make the rate of interest positive in a stationary economy, since he considered the second ground of Böhm-Bawerk as inappropriate in a stationary economy. In other words, in spite of Kompas, we can still say that an equation is missing in Wicksell's model of a stationary economy, which closes the model so as to make the rate of interest positive.

Essay 18 argues that the missing equation should be supplied by the consideration of the first cause among Böhm-Bawerk's three causes of interest and shows the possibility of the positive interest by the use of a stationary two-period life-cycle model in which younger savers can have larger consumptions when they are old. In the case of such a circulating capital model as the one used in this essay, however, we have to assume stringent conditions on the relation between the period of production and the life span of individuals, and on the pattern of consumptions of individuals. While a more roundabout method of production implies a longer period of production in the circulating capital model, it implies, among others, a higher capital–labour ratio in the case of fixed capitals, as in Böhm-Bawerk's examples of the use of a boat and net in fishing and of a sewing machine in tailoring. The fixed capital model used in the second half of Essay 10 above, therefore, needs less stringent assumptions to explain the positive interest by the first cause, since the durability of capital alone is not related to the roundabout method of production.

Essay 19, 'Economic Structure and the Theory of Economic Equilibrium', in M. Baranzini and R. Scazzieri (eds), (1990), *The Economic Theory of Structure and Change*, Cambridge University Press, 47–63.

The neo-classical economic theory that is currently predominant should, to be precise, be referred to as Walrasian or neo-Walrasian economic theory, to distinguish it from the Marshallian tradition that was originally designated neo-classical economics. Though Walrasian and Marshallian approaches are different in many respects, they share an identical view of the market contrary to the Jevons–Edgeworth approach.

Essay 19 is a comparative study of structures of equilibrium theory of Walras, Marshall and Edgeworth. While the comparison of Walras and Marshall follows the standard view, our original view on Marshall's equilibrium of industry with disequilibrium firms is emphasized through the construction of the life-cycle theory of firms. It also emphasizes the difference in the communication structure between the Walras–Marshall model of non-co-operative market games and the Jevons–Edgeworth model of co-operative market games.

As for Marshall, I have an article on Marshallian tax-bounty policies which cannot be included in this volume, since its publication in a *festschrift* is being delayed. Marshall's proposition is that diminishing returns industries should be taxed and increased returns industries should be subsidized. It has been misunderstood by modern scholars that Marshall forgot to consider the changes in producers' surplus. This is partly due to their failure to see that variable returns are considered by Marshall to be caused by external economies and diseconomies and to their confusion of particular expense curves and supply curves, which Marshall correctly distinguished.

Essay 20, 'On the Non-existence of Equilibrium: From Thornton to Arrow', in G. Feiwel (ed.), (1987), *Arrow and the Ascent of Modern Economic Theory*, Macmillan, 361–74.

This essay plays the role of a bridge between the two volumes of collections of my essays. It reviews the other side of the history of the problem of the existence of an equilibrium, the problem with which some essays in Part I of Volume I are concerned. Thornton, whose attack on equilibrium theory was discussed in Essays 6 and 7, also gave some examples of the case where no equilibrium of demand and supply is possible. Arrow plays, of course, the central role in the modern proofs of the existence of a general equilibrium. Arrow's comment on this essay is as follows.

Negishi offers a small but important history of examples of non-existence of equilibrium going back to W.T. Thornton, in 1869. Thornton, as is well known, had a great influence on John Stuart Mill in one of his last essays. The examples are, of course, all characterized by discontinuous demand curves; as is well known, continuous demand and supply curves, with Walras' law, must inevitably lead to the existence of equilibrium. Negishi has an interesting wrinkle: he points out that exchange out of equilibrium can frequently converge to a determinate conclusion which nevertheless is not an equilibrium in the strict sense. (Feiwel, 1987, p. 685)

Essay 21, 'Comment, Minisymposium, The History of Economics and the History of Science', *History of Political Economy* (1992), **24**, 227–9.

This is a comment in a symposium on Schabas (1992) who insists that historians of economics should break free from economics and belong to the history of science in general. The point is, I think, that the history of economics should be studied by both historians of sciences and economic theorists.

References

Blaug, M. (1985), *Economic Theory in Retrospect*, Cambridge: Cambridge University Press.

Burgstaller, A. (1986), 'Unifying Ricardo's Theories of Growth and Comparative Advantage', *Economica*, **53**, 467–81.

de Marchi, N. (1988), 'John Stuart Mill Interpretation Since Schumpeter', in W.O. Thweatt (ed.), *Classical Political Economy*, Boston: Kluwer.

Eagly, R.V. (1974), *The Structure of Classical Economic Theory*, Oxford: Oxford University Press.

Ekelund, R.B. (1976), 'A Short-Run Classical Model of Capital and Wages: Mill's Recantation of the Wages Fund', *Oxford Economic Papers*, **28**, 66–85.

Ekelund, R.B. (1985), 'Mill's Recantation Once Again: Reply to Professor Negishi', *Oxford Economic Papers*, **37**, 152–3.

Ekelund, R.B. Jr., and R.F. Hébert (1990), *A History of Economic Theory and Method*, New York: McGraw-Hill.

Ekelund, R.B. and S. Thommesen (1989), 'Disequilibrium Theory and Thornton's Assault on the Laws of Supply and Demand', *History of Political Economy*, **21**, 567–92.

Eltis, W.A. (1975), 'Adam Smith's Theory of Economic Growth', in A.S. Skinner and T. Wilson (eds), *Essays on Adam Smith*, Oxford: Oxford University Press.

Feiwel, G. (ed.), (1987), *Arrow and the Ascent of Modern Economic Theory*, London: Macmillan.

Findlay, R. (1974), 'Relative Prices, Growth and Trade in a Simple Ricardian System', *Economica*, **41**, 1–13.

Frisch, R. (1952), 'Wicksell', in H.W. Spiegel (ed.), *The Development of Economic Thought*, New York: John Wiley.

Gandolfo, G. (1986), *International Economics*, Berlin: Springer-Verlag.

Hicks, J.R. (1965), *Capital and Growth*, Oxford: Oxford University Press.

Kompas, T. (1992), *Studies in the History of Long-Run Equilibrium Theory*, Manchester: Manchester University Press.

Krelle, W. (1991), 'Review, T. Negishi, *History of Economic Theory*', *Zeitschrift für Nationalökonomie*, **53**, 96–104.

Longe, F.D. (1866), *A Refutation of the Wage-Fund Theory*, Baltimore: Johns Hopkins Press, 1903.

Magnan de Bornier, J. (1992), 'The "Cournot-Bertrand Debate": A Historical Perspective', *History of Political Economy*, **24**, 623–56.

Mill, J.S. (1848, 1871), *Principles of Political Economy*, Toronto: University of Toronto Press, 1965.

Mill, J.S. (1869), 'Thornton on Labour and Its Claim', in *Essays on Economics and Society*, Toronto: University of Toronto Press.

Negishi, T. (1985), *Economic Theories in a Non-Walrasian Tradition*, Cambridge: Cambridge University Press.

Negishi, T. (1989), *History of Economic Theory*, Amsterdam: North-Holland.

Negishi, T. (1991), 'Review, M. Morishima, *Ricardo's Economics: A General Equilibrium Theory of Distribution and Growth*', *Economic Studies Quarterly*, **42**, 82–4.

Negishi, T. (1993), 'A Smithian Growth Model and Malthus's Optimal Propensity to Save', *The European Journal of the History of Economic Thought*, **1**, forthcoming.

Pasinetti, L. (1960), 'A Mathematical Formulation of the Ricardian System', *Review of Economic Studies*, **27**, 78–98.

Reid, G.C. (1987), 'Disequilibrium and Increasing Returns in Adam Smith's Analysis of Growth and Accumulation', *History of Political Economy*, **19**, 87–106.

Samuelson, P.A. (1972), 'The Way of an Economist', in R.C. Merton (ed.), *The Collected Scientific Papers of Paul A. Samuelson*, 3, Cambridge: MIT Press.

Sandelin, B. (1980), 'Wicksell's Missing Equation; The Production Function and Wicksell Effect', *History of Political Economy*, **12**, 29–40.

Schabas, M. (1992), 'Breaking Away: History of Economics as History of Science', *History of Political Economy*, **24**, 187–203.

Schumpeter, J.A. (1954), *History of Economic Analysis*, Oxford: Oxford University Press.

Smith, Adam (1776), *An Inquiry into the Nature and Causes of the Wealth of the Nations*, The Glasgow Edition of the Works and Correspondence of Adam Smith, Vol. II, 1976.

Thornton, W. (1869, 1870), *On Labour*, London: Macmillan.

Wicksell, K. (1934), *Lectures on Political Economy*, 1, London: Routledge.

PART I

CLASSICAL AND MARXIAN ECONOMICS

5

Expenditure Patterns and International Trade in Quesnay's Tableau Economique

TAKASHI NEGISHI

Department of Economics
The University of Tokyo
Hongo Bunkyo-ku, Tokyo
Japan

1.

The traditional interpretation of the simplified form or the final version of Quesnay's tableau economique was based on suppositions that landowners spend half their rent income on agricultural and half on manufactured products, while workers both in agriculture and manufacturing spend their whole wage income on food (agricultural products), and that the fixed capital (the original advance) of agriculture (the productive sector) consists entirely of the products of manufacture (the unproductive sector).[1] This interpretation suffers from some weaknesses. Firstly, the supposition of different expenditure patterns between landowners and workers is not consistent with Quesnay's assumption of the identical expenditure pattern of all the classes in his original tableau with zigzags. Secondly, it is more natural to consider that the fixed capital of agriculture consists entirely of the agricultural products, since it mainly consists of horses and other animals.[2]

[1] Blaug [1978], p. 27; Eagly [1974], p. 23. See also Engels [1878], p. 234.
[2] Apart from the problem of what Quesnay really meant, the traditional supposition in this respect may be defended purely logically, since in the tableau agriculture is defined not as agriculture in general but as a sector which can yield rent, represented by grain farming with the most efficient horse-drawn plough technique, and all other activities, which may include cattle breeding, are called manufacturing.

DEVELOPMENTS IN
JAPANESE ECONOMICS

85

Meek [1962], Barna [1975, 1976], and Eltis [1975a, 1975b] insist, however, that all the problems and apparent inconsistencies in the interpretations of Quesnay's tableau economique are solved when Quesnay's published works including *L'Ami des hommes* and *Philosophie rurale* are read as a whole. According to this new interpretation, the fixed capital of agriculture consists entirely of the agricultural products and international trade, i.e., export of food and import of manufactured products is emphasized so as to make an identical expenditure pattern between landowners and workers possible. It is, however, one thing to accept the new interpretation as superior to the traditional one, and it is quite another to follow uncritically all the conclusions derived by Quesnay by using the tableau economique. The introduction of international trade, particularly, makes the following argument of Quesnay entirely untenable.

It can be seen from the distribution delineated in the tableau that if a nation's expenditure went more to the sterile expenditure side than to the productive expenditure side, revenue would fall proportionally, and this fall would increase in the same progression from year to year successively. It follows that a high level of expenditure on luxury in the way of ornamentation and conspicuous consumption is ruinous. If, on the other hand, a nation's expenditure goes to the productive expenditure side, revenue will rise, and this rise will in the same way increase successively from year to year. Thus, it is not true that the type of expenditure is a matter of indifference.[3]

The type of expenditure is actually a matter of indifference, however, since any change in it can always be adjusted by a corresponding change in international trade so that there are no changes in the production and the revenue (rent) of the nation.[4] We shall demonstrate this by using the final version of the tableau in Section 2 and by using the original version of the tableau after a critical review of Eltis' [1975b] arguments to support Quesnay in Section 3. It should be emphasized that not merely changes in the expenditure pattern but changes in capital accumulation, if any, induced by it are relevant for economic growth or decline. While changes in expenditure pattern are entirely absorbed in changes in trade, and no changes in accumulation are induced under the new interpretation of the tableau, the expenditure pattern does matter for capital accumulation, somewhat ironically, under the traditional interpretation which assumes autarky, as will be shown in Section 4.

---

[3] Kuczynski-Meek [1972], p. 12 and Eltis [1975b].

[4] Samuelson [1982] is also against Quesnay in this respect but argued that expenditure patterns have effects on the level of output of different sectors, without paying attention to international trade.

2.

Consider Table 1, the final version of the tableau economique, though somewhat modified.[5] Each year agriculture advances £1 billion, i.e., 500 million in agricultural products and 500 million in manufactured products, for workers and produces £2.5 billion in agricultural products; while manufacturing advances £1 billion, i.e., 500 in agricultural products for raw materials and 250 million in agricultural products and 250 million in manufactured products for workers, and produces £1 billion in manufactured products. Landowners spend their rent income of £1 billion, half on agricultural products and half on manufactured products, so that the first 500 million in agricultural products and the first 500 million in manufactured products are sold out. Manufacturing buys the second 500 million in agricultural products using the £500 million received from landowners, and agriculture buys the second 500 million in manufactured products in return. Finally, manufacturing buys the third 500 million in agricultural products with the £500 million received from agriculture for the second 500 in manufactured products. Now £1 billion in money, 500 million in manufactured products, and 1 billion in agricultural products are in the hands of agriculture. Agriculture pays £1 billion rent to landowners, replaces annual advances of 500 million in agricultural products and 500 million in manufactured products, and covers the depreciation of the fixed capital, the so-called "interest" cost of agriculture (to replace

TABLE 1.

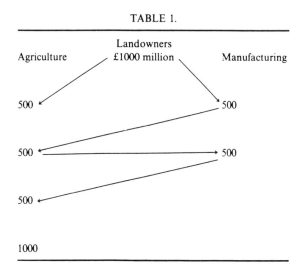

[5] Bauer [1895] and Eagly [1969].

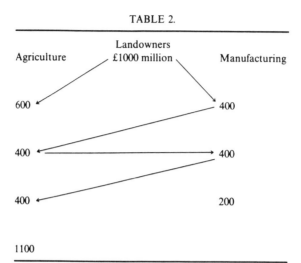

TABLE 2.

horses, etc.) by the remaining 500 million in agricultural products. Manufacturing, having 1 billion in agricultural products, exports 250 million in agricultural products and imports 250 million in manufactured products, so
that annual advances of 750 million in agricultural products and 250 million
in manufactured products are replaced. The economy can continue, therefore, to produce 2.5 billion in agricultural products and 1 billion in manufactured products.

Suppose the propensity to consume agricultural products changes from 0.5
to 0.6 not only for landowners but also for workers in agriculture and
manufacturing. The tableau shifts from Table 1 to Table 2, though identical
outputs, 2.5 billion in agricultural products and 1 billion in manufactured
products, are already produced from the annual advances made before the
propensity to consume has changed. Now landowners spend £600 million on
agricultural products and £400 million on manufactured products, so that the
first 600 in agricultural products and the first 400 in manufactured products
are sold out. Manufacturing then buys 400 in agricultural products with the
£400 million received from landowners, and agriculture in return buys the
second 400 in manufactured products. Finally, manufacturing buys a further
400 in agricultural products with the £400 million received from agriculture.
Now, 1 billion livres in money, 400 million in manufactured products, and
1.1 billion in agricultural products are in the hands of agriculture, so that it
can pay £1 billion to landowners as rent, advance 600 million in agricultural
products and 400 million in manufactured products to workers, and cover
the interest cost with the remaining 500 million in agricultural products.

Having now 800 million in agricultural products and 200 in unsold manufactured products, manufacturing can replace advances for raw materials (500 in agricultural products) and advance 300 in agricultural products and 200 in manufactured products for workers. Changes in propensity to consume are entirely absorbed in changes in international trade, and the economy can continue to produce the unchanged outputs (2.5 billion in agricultural products and 1 billion in manufactured products), under the changed patterns of expenditure.

Similarly, Table 3 shows the case where the propensity to consume agricultural products changes from 0.5 to 0.4. Landowners spend £400 million on agricultural products and £600 million on manufactured products, so that the first 400 in agricultural products and the first 600 in manufactured products are sold out. Manufacturing then buys 600 in agricultural products with the £600 million received from landowners, and agriculture buys 400 in manufactured products with the £400 million received from landowners. The next step for manufacturing is to export 500 in agricultural products to be able to import 500 in manufactured products, which implies that manufacturing can supply 1.5 billion in manufactured products in all, i.e., 1 billion produced and already sold and 500 million imported and circled in Table 3. Agriculture then buys 200 million in imported manufactured products from manufacturing with £200 million, i.e., a part of the money already received from manufacturing when 600 in agricultural products are sold. Finally, manufacturing uses this £200 million and £400 million already

TABLE 3.

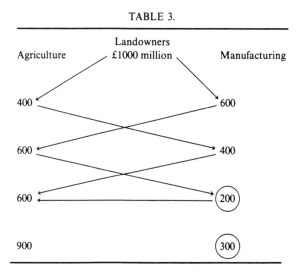

received when 400 in manufactured products are sold to agriculture to buy a further 600 in agricultural products. Since £400 million are left unused, out of £600 million received from manufacturing when the first 600 of agricultural products are sold, agriculture now has £1 billion to pay rent. Also 600 million in manufactured products and 900 million in agricultural products are in the hands of agriculture, so as to advance 400 in agricultural products and 600 in manufactured products for workers and to cover interest with the remaining 500 in agricultural products. Having bought 1.2 billion in agricultural products and exported 500 million, manufacturing has 700 million in agricultural products and 300 in unsold manufactured products, just enough to replace the advanced raw materials (500 in agricultural products) and to advance 200 in agricultural products and 300 in manufactured products for workers. The economy can continue, therefore, to produce 2.5 billion in agricultural products and 1 billion in manufactured products under the -new patterns of expenditure.

Changing expenditure patterns make neither growth nor decline in output possible. There must be something wrong in Quesnay's reasoning which led him to the conclusion cited in Section 1.

3.

According to Eltis [1975b], accounts of the effect of the propensity to consume agricultural products on the rate of growth are found in *Philosophie rurale* and *L'Ami des hommes*, written by Quesnay and Mirabeau, and can best be analyzed by using the original Tableau with zigzags and by focusing attention on the financial receipts of the agricultural producers.[6]

The original Tableau economique with zigzags is given in Table 4 when the propensity to consume agricultural products is q and rent or revenue is R.[7] Landowners spend qR on agricultural products and $(1-q)R$ on manufactured products. Agriculture then spends $(1-q)qR$ on manufactured products out of qR received from landowners, while manufacturing spends $q(1-q)R$ on agricultural products out of $(1-q)R$ received from landowners. Agriculture further spends $(1-q)q(1-q)R$ on manufactured products out of $q(1-q)R$ just received from manufacturing, while manufacturing spends $q(1-q)qR$ on agricultural products out of $(1-q)qR$ just received from agriculture. In this way, agriculture ends up with the total receipt of money

---

[6] We cannot, however, understand Eltis' explanation of why the final tableau cannot be used to consider the effect of variable expenditure patterns. As we shall see, the original version is rather inconvenient for this purpose.

[7] Table 4 is originally due to Hishiyama [1960] and reproduced in Eltis [1975a].

TABLE 4.

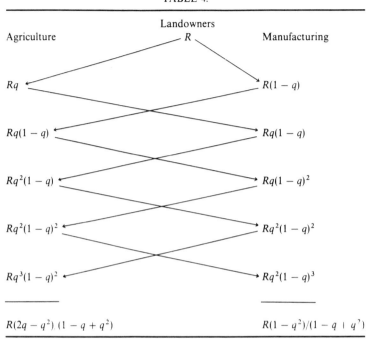

$$R(2q - q^2)/(1 - q + q^2)$$, while manufacturing ends up with the total receipt of $R(1 - q^2)/(1 - q + q^2)$.

Suppose agriculture advances annually £1 billion and pays rent of £1 billion, and the propensity to consume agricultural products is 0.5. In the Tableau's zigzags, both agriculture and manufacturing receive £1 billion and spend £500 million on the products of the other sector, while manufacturing uses the other £500 million as advances for raw materials which are bought from agriculture at the end of the year. Thus, the economy's whole stock of money, £1 billion, will reach agriculture by the end of the year. Since agriculture is assumed to produce £2 billion in products from £1 billion in annual advances, it is left with £1 billion in money, £500 million in manufactured products, and £500 million in agricultural products, so that it can pay again £1 billion in rent and advance again £1 billion in agricultural and manufactured products for workers. Manufacturing is left with £500 million in raw materials and £500 million in other agricultural products, half of which are assumed to be exported in order to be able to import manufactured products. The economy can continue, therefore, to produce £2 billion in agricultural products and £1 billion in manufactured products.

Eltis [1975b] insists, however, that things will be quite different when q is not equal to 0.5, say when $q = 0.4$. The Tableau's zigzags bring £842 million (obtained by substituting $q = 0.4$ into $1000(2q - q^2)/(1 - q + q^2)$) instead of £1 billion to agriculture and £1.105 billion (obtained from $1000(1 - q^2)/(1 - q + q^2)$) instead of £1 billion to manufacturing. Agriculture receives a further £552.5 million from manufacturing for sales of raw materials at the end of the year, since half of the £1.105 billion that manufacturing receives is assumed to be put aside by manufacturing for its advances. However, agriculture spends six-tenths of £842 million it receives from the zigzags (or £505 million) on manufactured products and has to pay £1 billion on rent. Agriculture therefore has a financial deficit of £110.5 million (i.e., 842 + 552.5 − 505 − 1000). Following Quesnay and Mirabeau, Eltis assumes that half the deficiency is met by landowners who accept lower rents than those previously agreed. Then half of £110.5 million has to be met by a fall in the annual advance in agriculture from £1 billion to £945 million, since Eltis considers that agriculture must sell its advance for the next year to get enough money to pay rent. The economy has to start next year with £945 million in agricultural advances and the same amount of rent, which implies that agricultural products are only £1.89 billion. It can be shown, in this way, that the economy eventually declines at a rate of 5.5 percent per annum.

Naturally, questions may arise with regard to the above arguments of Eltis concerning Quesnay's theory of economic growth and decline. When $q = 0.4$, the Tableau's zigzags bring £1.105 billion to manufacturing and manufacturing spends four-tenths of it or £442 million on agricultural products in zigzags, so that at the end of the year manufacturing has £663 million in money. Why does manufacturing not spend the whole £663 million instead of only £552.5 million on agricultural products at the end of the year? Since manufacturing need not pay rent to landowners, it is of no use for it to keep money unutilized.[8] Eltis insists that a part of the annual advances in agriculture has to be sold, i.e., capital must be expended in agriculture when agriculture has a financial deficit. Since a financial deficit means that agriculture has unsold products which were originally intended to be sold, however, it implies the accumulation of an unintended stock of products, and not necessarily the decline in capital to be advanced. To get enough money to pay rent, therefore, it is enough to sell those products originally intended to be sold, and it is not necessary to sell products which were intended to be advanced.

As a matter of fact, agriculture receives $R(2q - q^2)/(1 - q + q^2)$ from the Tableau's zigzags and manufacturing receives, similarly, $R(1 - q^2)/$

[8] Hoarding is not the problem here. Eltis himself must admit that manufacturing is willing to buy more than £552.5 million in agricultural products at the end of the year, since he argued. as we just saw, that agriculture must sell its advances for the next year to get enough money to pay rent, which of course can be bought only by manufacturing.

$(1 - q + q^2)$, i.e., 842 and 1105 respectively if $R = 1000$ and $q = 0.4$. If manufacturing spends on agricultural products all the money that it does not spend in zigzags, i.e., $(1 - q)R(1 - q^2)/(1 - q + q^2)$ or 663, agriculture can pay rent R or 1000 after it spends $(1 - q)R(2q - q^2)/(1 - q + q^2)$ or 505 on manufactured products in zigzags, since we have generally

$$R(2q - q^2)/(1 - q + q^2) + R(1 - q)(1 - q^2)/(1 - q + q^2)$$
$$- R(1 - q)(2q - q^2)/(1 - q + q^2) = R,$$

or $842 + 663 - 505 = 1000$. A propensity to consume agricultural products that is lower than 0.5 does not cause any financial deficit for agriculture, and the economy can continue to produce unchanged amounts of agricultural and manufactured products. Incidentally, manufacturing has to sell £1105 million in manufactured products in zigzags, while it produces only £1000 million in manufactured products if $R = 1,000$ and $q = 0.4$. In the course of zigzags, therefore, manufacturing has to export some of the agricultural products it bought so as to be able to import the additional manufactured products necessary to carry on the zigzags. This was already pointed out in our consideration of Table 3 in Section 2.

Similarly, we cannot accept Eltis' argument that agriculture has a financial surplus and the economy grows eventually at 4.2 per cent when $q = 0.6$. Eltis considered that agriculture receives £1.105 billion in the Tableau's zigzags, spends there £442 million on manufactured products, and receives £421 million from manufacturing at the end of the year. In the course of zigzags, manufacturing receives merely £842 million and spends there £505 million, however. How can manufacturing spend £421 million at the end of the year? If manufacturing spends all the money it has, i.e., £337 million (obtained by 842×0.4), on agricultural products at the end of the year, agriculture has neither surplus nor deficit, since $1105 + 337 - 442 = 1000$. Manufacturing need not buy more than £337 million agriculture at the end of the year, since it has already bought enough agricultural products in the course of zigzags so as to advance raw materials (500) and feed workers (300), since $500 + 300 < 505 + 337$. Actually, we have to understand that manufacturing sold back £42 million in agricultural products to buy back £42 million in manufactured products in the course of the Tableau's zigzags. Similarly, agriculture has to sell £42 million in manufactured products to buy back £42 million in agricultural products in zigzags, since otherwise it sold £1.442 billion $(1105 + 337)$ in agricultural products and the remaining £558 million $(2000 - 1442)$ in agricultural products are not enough to advance £600 million in agricultural products to workers. We have to say that the original Tableau with zigzags is in this respect clumsy, inconvenient, and likely to confuse even such an eminent scholar as Eltis.

We have to conclude that Quesnay's theory of economic growth is not a successful one so far as it is related to the effects of expenditure patterns on economic growth. As Eltis [1975b] pointed out, many developing countries today face precisely the same conditions which Quesnay used to analyze the problems involved in achieving economic growth. However, we cannot blame these countries for adopting policies of favoring manufacturing at the expense of agriculture on the basis of Quesnay's theory of economic growth.

4.

It may be interesting to see that different expenditure patterns may induce economic growth or decline in the traditional interpretation of the final version of the tableau economique. Table 1 is interpreted such that each year agriculture advances £1 billion in agricultural products for workers while manufacturing advances £500 million in agricultural products for raw materials and £500 million in agricultural products for workers, the fixed capital of agriculture consists entirely of manufactured products, and there is no possibility for international trade. Landowners spend their £1 billion half on agricultural and half on manufactured products. Agriculture buys 500 in manufactured products to cover the depreciation of the fixed capital, and manufacturing buys 500 in agricultural products to replace the advances for raw materials and another 500 in agricultural products to replace advances to workers. Agriculture ends up with £1 billion in money to pay rent and £1 billion in unsold agricultural products to replace advances to workers. The economy can continue, therefore, to produce 2.5 billion in agricultural products and 1 billion in manufactured products.

If the expenditure pattern of landowners is changed and they spend £600 million on agricultural and £400 million on manufactured products, manufacturing ends up, as before, with 1 billion in agricultural products, just enough to replace advances, while agriculture has £1 billion in money to pay rent, £600 million in manufactured products as gross investment to the fixed capital or £100 million in manufactured products as net investment to the fixed capital, and £900 million in agricultural products, which means a £100 million decline in annual advances to workers, as is shown in Table 5. Since manufacturing can continue to produce £1 billion in manufactured products, therefore, agricultural products grow or decline depending on the relative marginal productivity of the fixed and circulating capitals. Table 6 shows similarly the case where landowners spend £400 million on agricultural products and £600 million on manufactured products. The fixed capital declines by £100 million and circulating capital increases by £100 million. The economy grows, in the case of Table 6, if it declines in the case of Table 5, and vice versa.

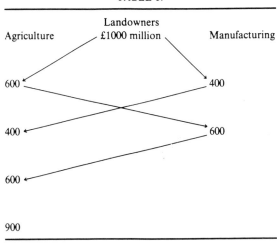

TABLE 5.

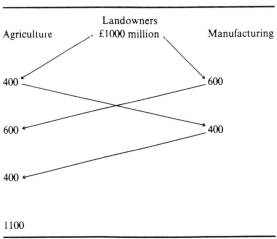

TABLE 6.

The point is that changes in expenditure patterns are relevant for economic growth or decline only if they induce changes in the composition of capital such that productivity changes. Higher propensity towards consuming agricultural products leads to economic growth only if manufactured products which are saved are more productive as capital than as agricultural products which are dissaved. This seems to have more relevance for developing countries than the physiocratic dogma that agriculture itself has something to do with economic growth. Larger consumption of agricultural products itself has nothing to do with economic growth, even if agriculture is more productive than manufacturing in the sense that agriculture alone can yield rent. We can admit that "the rate of growth can be a function of what is consumed rather than the rate of investment to consumption," in a way different from Eltis' [1975b] argument.

5.

On the occasion of the publishing of our comments on Eltis' studies of Quesnay in a volume entitled *Recent Developments in Japanese Economics*, it is our pleasant duty to acknowledge my indebtedness to the Japanese tradition of studies in the history of political economy. As an importer of economic sciences in the past, intensive studies have been made in Japan on mercantilism, physiocrasy, classical economics, and Marxian economics. Results of such studies were, unfortunately, published chiefly in Japanese and consequently were not well known internationally. The case of Hishiyama [1960], which was published in English, is a rare exception. It should be emphasized, however, that what Japan can export is not limited to the area of mathematical and quantitative economics.

In as early as 1956, K. Shibata, a famous economic theorist known for the so-called "Shibata-Okishio theorem" on the falling rate of profit, argued that expenditure pattern of landowners and workers in manufacturing is a matter of indifference (see p. 86) for the original tableau economique with zigzags, if it is rationally interpreted as a model of reproduction. T. Watanabe, an historian of early economic thought, supported the conclusion of Shibata's study, though his reason was somewhat different from Shibata's. According to Watanabe [1961], the original tableau economique is a model designed to express Quesnay's view on the importance of the expenditure pattern of landowners, which was influenced by Cantillon and is incomplete as a model of reproduction so that it cannot be interpreted rationally.[9] These studies were made, however, before the publication of Meek [1962] and therefore international trade was not taken into consideration. Our conclusion in this article is that expenditure patterns are a matter of indifference even if international trade is introduced following Meek [1962] in the interpretation of the tableau economique.

---

[9] See Shibata [1946] and Watanabe [1961, p. 341–398]. The latter also contains a useful survey of Japanese literature on Quesnay. For the Shibata-Okishio theorem, which denies Marx's law of falling rate of profit, see Shibata [1934] and Okishio [1961].

References

Barna. T., Quesnay's tableau in modern guise, *Economic Journal*, Vol. 85, p. 485–496, 1975.

Barna. T., Quesnay's model of economic development, *European Economic Review*, Vol. 8, p. 315–338, 1976.

Bauer, S., Tableau economique, *Economic Journal*, Vol. 5, p. 1–21, 1895.

Blaug. M., *Economic Theory in Retrospect* (3rd ed.). Cambridge: Cambridge University Press, 1978.

Eagly, R. V., A physiocratic model of dynamic equilibrium, *Journal of Political Economy*, Vol. 77, p. 66–84, 1969.

Eagly, R. V., *The Structure of Classical Economic Theory*, Oxford: Oxford University Press, 1974.

Eltis. W. A., Francois Quesnay: A reinterpretation 1. The tableau economique, *Oxford Economic Papers*, Vol. 27, p. 167–200, 1975a.

Eltis, W. A., Francois Quesnay: A reinterpretation 2. The theory of economic growth, *Oxford Economic Papers*, Vol. 27, p. 327–351, 1975b.

Engels, F., Herrn Eugen Dührings Umwälzung der Wissenschaft, 1878, in: *Karl Marx Friedrich Engels Werke*, 20, Berlin: Dietz Verlag, pp. 1–303, 1962.

Hishiyama, I., The tableu economique of Quesnay, *Kyoto University Economic Review*, Vol. 30(1), p. 1–45, 1960.

Kuczynski, M., and R. L. Meek. (ed.), *Quesnay's Tableau Economique*. London: Macmillan, 1972.

Meek. R. L., *The Economics of Physiocracy*. London: Allen and Unwin, 1962.

Okishio, N., Technical changes and rate of profit, *Kobe University Economic Review*, Vol. 7, p. 85–99, 1961.

Samuelson, P. A., Quesnay's tableau economique as a theorist would formulate it today, in: I. Brandley and M. Howard (eds). *Classical and Marxian Political Economy*, London: Macmillan p. 45–78, 1982.

Shibata. K., Quesnay no keizaihyo no nazo nitsuite (On the mystery of Quesnay's Tableau Economique), *Yamaguchi Journal of Economics*, Vol. 7 (5, 6), p. 1–10, 1956.

Shibata. K., On the law of decline in the rate of profit, *Kyoto University Economic Review*, Vol. 9(1), p. 61–75, 1934.

Watanable, T., *Sosetsusha no Keizaigaku (Economics of Founders)*. Tokyo: Miraisha, 1961.

[2]

The Role of Demand in Adam Smith's Theory of Natural Price

Takashi Negishi

University of Tokyo

By the use of a simple growth model, it is shown that prices are not determined purely by technological or cost considerations and the role of demand in the determination of prices is properly recognized in Adam Smith's theory of natural prices, in which the natural rate of wage is considered to be higher in an economy with a higher rate of growth and the higher wage and the higher rate of profit can coexist. Smith's theory of falling rate of profit is defended from Ricardo's criticism.

I

It has often been argued that the prices are determined purely by technological or cost considerations in the classical economics and the role of demand in the determination of prices is essentially disregarded by the classical school initiated by Adam Smith and followed by Ricado, J. S. Mill, and Marx, among others. While this may be correct as far as Ricardo is concerned,[1] it is not so in the case of Adam Smith's theory of the natural price, as I suggested elsewhere. "Natural prices are by no means independent of demands, since the natural rate of wage, for example, is higher in a growing economy, such as that of new colonies where demands expand rapidly, than in a stationary economy or in a declining one."[2] The purpose of this article is to develop this point fully, by the use of a Smithian growth model which I constructed in Negishi(1988, pp. 83-9).

The Section II sketches the theory of natural prices, which Adam Smith(1723-1790) developed in *The Wealth of Nations*(1776). A simple Smithian growth model of Negishi(1988), in which capitalists

---

[1] This is, of course, so as far as natural prices are concerned, as will be seen in the section V below. See Casarosa(1978) for market prices in Ricardian system.

[2] Negishi(1988, p. 13). See also Negishi(1985, p. 25).

[Seoul Journal of Economics 1988, Vol. 1, No. 4]

are assumed only to save and invest and not to consume, is extended in the Section III so that they can also consume labour products as well as labour services in their households. This extension of the model is necessary, since our aim is not only to explain the relations among the natural rate of wage, the natural rate of profit and the rate of growth, but also to consider the role of demand in the determination of natural prices. By the use of this model, then, it is argued in the Section IV that Smith's theory of the falling rate of profit, which does not advert to the diminishing returns in agriculture, can be defended, in spite of the famous criticism of Ricardo's. Finally, the Section V is devoted to show the role played by demand in our model of Smith's theory of natural prices.

II

Smith started in Chapter VI, Book I, of *The Wealth of Nations*, "Of the Component Parts of the Prices of Commodities", with the famous example of the deer and the beavers in the early and rude state of society which precedes both the accumulation of capital and the appropriation of land (Smith 1976, p. 65). But the consideration of the early and rude state is not very interesting, since there is no possibility of economic growth (Smith 1976, pp. 82-3). Economic growth is possible if and only if the net capital accumulation is caused by the existence of the positive rate of profit. If the rate of profit is positive, however, Smith argues that embodied labour theory of value does not hold.

In this state of things, the whole produce of labour does not always belong to the labourer. He must in most cases share it with the owner of the stock which employs him. Neither is the quantity of labour commonly employed in acquiring or producing any commodity, the only circumstance which can regulate the quantity which it ought commonly to purchase, command, or exchange for. An additional quantity, it is evident, must be due for the profits of the stock which advanced the wages and furnished the materials of that labour(Smith 1976, p. 67).

If we ignore the land and the land rent,[3] therefore, Smith's natural price of a commodity is defined as the sum of wages and profit,

---

[3] See Hollander(1980) for Smith's neglect of the implication of land scarcity in economic growth.

both at the natural rate, which is defined as follows.[4]

> There is in every society or neighbourhood an ordinary or average
> rate both of wages and profit in every different employment of labour
> and stock. This rate is naturally regulated ⋯ partly by the general
> circumstances of the society, their riches or poverty, their advancing,
> stationary, or declining condition: and partly by the particular nature
> of each employment. ⋯ These ordinary or average rates may be called
> the natural rate of wages, profit. ⋯ (Smith 1976, p. 72).

> The liberal reward of labour, therefore, as it is the necessary effect,
> so it is the natural symptom of increasing national wealth. The scanty
> maintenance of the labouring poor, on the other hand, is the natural
> symptom that things are at a stand, and their starving condition that
> they are going fast backwards (Simth 1976, p. 91).

This argument of Smith should not be interpreted that the market
rate of wage, which can deviate temporarily from the natural rate, is
higher in a growing economy. When Smith defined the natural rate
of wages and profit in Chapter VII, Book I, of *The Wealth of Nations,* "Of the Natural and Market Price of Commodities" (Smith
1976, p. 72), he footnoted that the natural rate of wage is shown, in
Chapter VIII, Book I, "Of the Wages of Labour" (Smith 1976, pp.
82–104), to be different according to whether the economy is
advancing, stationary or declining. Smith considered, therefore, that
the natural rate of real wage or the equilibrium rate of real wage is
high in an economy with a high rate of growth. Since the natural
rate of wage must be at the subsistence level in a stationary economy so as to keep the population unchanged, then, the wage at the
natural rate is higher than the subsistence wage in growing economies. Not only the natural rate of wage, furthermore, but also the
natural rate of profit are considered by Smith to be higher in a
growing economy than in a stationary economy.

> The rise and fall in the profits of stock depend upon the same
> causes with the rise and fall in the wages of labour, the increasing or
> declining state of the wealth of the society (Smith 1976, p. 105).

> In a country which had acquired that full complement of riches which
> the nature of its soil and climate, and its situation with respect to
> other countries allowed it to acquire; which could, therefore, advance
> no further, and which was not going backwards, both the wages of

---

[4] See Smith(1976, pp. 72–81) for the definition of natural prices as long-run equilibrium prices. "The natural price, therefore, is, as it were, the central price, to which the
prices of all commodities are continually gravitating" (Smith 1976, p. 75).

labour and the profits of stock would probably be very low. ⋯ In a country fully stocked in proportion to all the business it had to transact, as great a quantity of stock would be employed in every particular branch as the nature and extent of trade would admit. The competition, therefore, would everywhere be as great, and consequently the ordinary profit as low as possible (Smith 1976, p. 111).

We may conclude, therefore, that a high natural rate of wage and a high natural rate of profit coexist in an economy with a high rate of growth, as Smith argued that "in our North America and West Indian colonies, not only the wages of labour, but the interest of money, and consequently the profits of stock, are higher than in England"(Smith 1976, p. 109).

III

Let us make an extension of a Smithian growth model, which is given in Negishi(1988, pp. 83-9), so that capitalist households can now consume labour products as well as labour services (labour power). Suppose that the period necessary for the reproduction of labour (power) in laborers' households is identical to the period of production of labour products and that a units of labour must be expended one period before to produce one unit of product and b units of the labour product must be consumed in households one period before to produce one unit of labour. Let us denote the capitalists' aggregate stock of the product at time t by $X(t)$ and the labour population at time t by $L(t)$. Then, from definitions of coefficients a and b,. we have

$$eX(t) = bL(t+1) \tag{1}$$

and

$$cL(t) = aX(t+1) \tag{2}$$

where $0 < e < 1$, $0 < c < 1$, and capitalists are assumed to use e of their stock of products to employ labour and to use $(1-c)$ of their employees in the households as unproductive labour. In other words, they consume $(1-e)$ of the stock of products and capitalists' rate of saving is ec while laborers are assumed not to save.

To consider a balanced growth solution of our model (1) and (2) in which both $X(t)$ and $L(t)$ grow at the common rate of g, substitute

$X(t+1)=(1+g)X(t)$ and $L(t+1) = (1+g)L(t)$ into (1) and (2). It can be easily seen that the rate of growth g and the given coefficients must satisfy the condition

$$ab(1+g)^2 = ec. \tag{3}$$

Particularly, the given coefficients must satisfy the condition $ec > ab$ to assure the positive rate of growth. The rate of growth g is higher, if the rate of saving ec and the labour productivity $1/a$ are higher, or the real rate of subsistence wage b is lower.

Since equilibrium relative prices remain unchanged through time on such a balanced growth path of the economy, let us denote the natural price of the product by p and the natural rate of wage by w. According to Smith, then,

$$p = (1+r)aw \tag{4}$$

and

$$w = (1+s)bp, \tag{5}$$

where r is the natural rate of profit, and r and s are assumed to be positive if g is positive. In other words, the natural price of the product is the sum of the wage aw and profit raw at their natural rates, since we assume away the land rent, and in a growing economy the natural rate of wage is higher than the subsistence wage bp, which is the wage at the natural rate in a stationary economy. From (4) and (5), it can be easily seen that

$$1 = (1+s)(1+r)ab \tag{6}$$

must be satisfied by s and r.

From the definition of e,

$$wL(t) = epX(t). \tag{7}$$

By substituting $L(t+1, = (1+g)L(t)$ and (7) into (1), we have

$$w = (1+g)bp. \tag{8}$$

Smith's assumption that s is positive when g is positive is justified, therefore, in the balanced growth path of our model, since $s = g$ from (5) and (8).

Similarly, by substituting $X(t+1)=(1+g)X(t)$ and (7) into (2), we have

$$ecp=(1+g)aw. \tag{9}$$

As Smith assumed, therefore, r is higher if g is higher, since (4) and (9) imply that $ec(1+r)=(1+g)$. In view of the fact that $s = g$, then, both s and r can be higher, if g is higher, provided that the rate of saving ec remains constant. In other words, the coexistence of high profit and high real wage is possible, if the labor productivity $1/a$ is high so that the rate of growth is high.

IV

If the rate of saving is increased either through an increase in e or through an increase in c, there is an increase in the rate of growth g, as is seen in (3). This increases s and the real wage w/p in (5), since $s = g$ as we saw in the above. The increased s implies that the rate of profit r decreases from (6). As far as the balanced growth path is concerned, therefore, the analysis of our Smithian growth model would confirm the following argument insisted by Adam Smith in *The Wealth of Nations*.

> The rise and fall in the profits of stock depend upon the same causes with the rise and fall in the wages of labour, the increasing or declining state of the wealth of the society; but those causes affect the one and the other very differently. The increase of stock, which raises wages, tends to lower profit. When the stocks of many rich merchants are turned into the same trade, their mutual competition naturally tends to lower its profit; and when there is a like increase of stock in all the different trades carried on in the same society, the same competition must produce the same effect in them all (Smith 1976, p. 105).

This argument of Smith was, however, criticized severely by Ricardo. He insisted that the rate of profit falls as capital accumulated, only through the diminished labour productivity in agriculture, as a result of the capital accumulation on the limited land, an effect which we assumed away in our Smithian growth model.

> [N]o accumulation of capital will permanently lower profits, unless there be some permanent cause for the rise of wages. If the funds for the maintenance of labour were doubled, trebled, or quadrupled, there would not long be any difficulty in procuring the requisite number of hands, to be employed by those funds; but owing to the increased difficulty of making constant additions to the food of the country, funds of the same value would probably not maintain the same quantity of labour. If the necessaries of the workman could be constantly increased with the same facility, there could be no permanent alternation

in the rate of profits or wages, to whatever amount capital might be accumulated. Adam Smith, however, uniformly ascribes the fall of profits to accumulation of capital, and to the competition which will result from it, without ever adverting to the increasing difficulty of providing food for the additional number of labourers which the additional capital will employ (Ricardo 1951, p. 289).

The difference between Smith and Ricardo arises from the different definitions of the natural rate of wage. For Ricardo, the natural wage is a constant real wage at the subsistence level. "The natural price of labour is that price which is necessary to enable the labourers, one with another, to subsist and to perpetuate their race, without either increase or diminution" (Ricardo 1951, p. 93). It cannot, therefore, rise as the real wage, i.e., the wage in terms of food. It can rise only in the sense that the embodied labour value of the subsistence wage rises. In our notations in the previous section, the real subsistence wage is b while its labour value is ba, which rises when a, i.e., the difficulty of providing food, is increased. According to Ricardo, it is the market wage or the market price of labour that can be higher than the subsistence wage, when the labour is scarce and the population is increasing.

For Adam Smith, as we saw, the natural, not the market, rate of real wage is higher, when the rate of saving is higher, even if the difficulty of providing food remains unchanged. In spite of Ricardo, this rise in wage is not "a temporary rise, proceeding from increased funds before the population is increased" (Ricardo 1951, p. 289). As a matter of fact, the natural rate of wage is reduced, rather than increased, by the increasing difficulty of providing food itself, since higher a implies lower g from (3), and lower g implies lower w/p from (8).

V

Let us now consider the role of demand in the determination of natural prices of commodities by using the model which was developed in the Section III. There are two consumers' goods in this simple model, the labour service which is consumed in the capitalists' households, and the labour product which is consumed by both capitalists and labourers. Smith considered that the former good is produced by what he called unproductive labour and simultaneously consumed by consumers. "His services generally perish in the very instant of their performance" (Smith 1976, p. 330). The latter is, on the other hand, produced by what Smith called productive labour which, unlike unproductive one, needs a period of production to be produced but yields positive profits to what is advanced by capitalists. "Thus the labour of a manufacturer adds, generally, to the value of the materials which he works upon, that of his own maintenance, and of his master's profit" (Smith 1976, p. 330).

The natural price of the latter good is defined as the sum of wages and the profit, both at the natural rate, i.e.,

$$p=(1+r)aw \tag{4}$$

while the natural price of the former good is the natural rate of wage itself, i.e.,

$$w=(1+s)bp, \tag{5}$$

as was considered in the Section III.

As was seen in the Section IV, Ricardo considered that the natural wage is the subsistence wage, so that $s=0$ and $w=bp$ in (5). From (4) and (5), then,

$$(1+r)=1/ab, \ w/p=b \tag{10}$$

in Ricardo's natural equilibrium.[5] Since a and b are technological parameters, we can say that natural prices (including natural rate of profit) are determined by purely technological or cost consideration in Ricardian economics and the role of demand is essentially disregarded by Ricardo.

In the case of Smith's theory of natural prices, however, $s=g$ as we saw in the Section III so that w/p depends on g from (5). Since g is dependent on demand parameters e and c as well as on technological parameters a and b as we saw in (3) in the Section III, the role of demand is definitely taken into consideration in the determination of relative price of two consumers' goods. Any changes in c and e, which increases (decreases) the rate of saving ec, and therefore the rate of growth g, increases (decreases) the real wage w/p, i.e., the relative price of a good with the zero period of production to a good with a positive period of production. The rate of profit is, of course, reduced (raised) by an increase (a decrease) in ec. Although there are only two goods in our model, it requires little stretch of

---

[5] See Pasinetti(1960) for Ricardo's natural equilibrium, in which capital is accumulating while population is stationary.

imagination to suppose that generally the high real wage and the low rate of profit, caused by the high rate of saving, make the relative price of a good with a longer period of production cheaper.[6]

References

Casarosa, C. "A New Formulation of the Ricardian System." *Oxford Economic Papers* 30 (March 1978) : 38–63.

Hollander, S. "On Professor Samuelson's Canonical Classical Model of Political Economy." *Journal of Economic Literatures* XVIII (June 1980) : 559–74.

Negishi, Takashi. *A History of Economics* (in Korean). Suk-Tai Suh(tr.), Seoul: Bum Moon Sa, 1985.

——————. *History of Economic Theory.* Amsterdam: North-Holland Publishing Co., 1988.

Pasinetti, L. "A Mathematical Formulation of the Ricardian System." *Review of Economic Studies* 27 (February 1960) : 78–98.

Ricardo, David. *On the Principles of Political Economy and Taxation.* (1821) Cambridge: Cambridge University Press, 1951.

Smith, Adam. *An Inquiry into the Nature and Causes of the Wealth of Nations.* (1776) London: Oxford University Press, 1976.

[6] Our Smithian model of growth disregards the possibility of not only diminishing returns but also of increasing returns. Unlike the former possibility, however, Smith emphasized the latter one in his theory of the division of labour. See Negishi (1988, pp. 89–95) for the role of demand for the determination of prices in Smith's theory of the division of labour.

[3]

History of Political Economy 14:2
© 1982 by Duke University Press

The labor theory of value in the Ricardian theory of international trade

Takashi Negishi

I

The labor theory of value fails as a theory of international trade if one regards it simply as the theory that the relative prices are proportional to the quantities of labor embodied. Thus Ricardo admitted that "the same rule which regulates the relative value of commodities in one country does not regulate the relative value of the commodities exchanged between two or more countries" (Ricardo, p. 81). According to Schumpeter, this is very serious for the Ricardian theory of value:

> We may look upon the comparative cost principle as an exception from the labor quantity law, for it describes a case where commodities no longer exchange according to this law. This exception is the more serious because it covers not only international values but also, in all cases of less than perfect mobility of labor, domestic values. In fact, together with all the other exceptions and qualifications that Ricardo was forced to make, it really rips up the entire fabric of Ricardo's theory of Value [p. 612].

In the standard theory of international trade, therefore, the theory of international value is that of reciprocal demand developed by Mill (p. 584), who insists that we have to fall back upon an antecedent law, that of supply and demand, when the law of cost of production is not applicable.

The essence of the labor theory of value lies, however, not so much in the proportionality of relative values and quantities of labor embodied as in the explanation of the profit created not in the process of circulation but in the process of production.[1] In other words, what is important is the fact that relative prices and the rate of profit are determined independently of the demand situations. From such a point of view, the following statement of Morita is very interesting:

Correspondence for the author may be sent to Professor Takashi Negishi, Department of Economics, University of Tokyo, Bunkyo-Ku, Tokyo, JAPAN.

1. This is the point insisted on by Hilferding against the criticism given by Böhm-Bawerk. See Negishi, "Marx and Böhm-Bawerk."

200   *History of Political Economy 14:2 (1982)*

Since the day of J. S. Mill the standard interpretation of Ricardo has been that there is no theory in Ricardo to determine the terms of trade and therefore demand factors must be introduced so as to supplement Ricardo in this respect. This interpretation is clearly wrong. By combining the comparative cost principle and theory of international distribution of gold, Ricardo presented a mechanism which can uniquely determine terms of trade (international prices) by the conditions in production without having recourse to demand factors [Morita 1977].

We shall show that Ricardian theory can determine the terms of trade without having recourse to demand factors, though the theory of international distribution of gold suggested by Morita in his ingenious paper cannot unfortunately help us in this respect. What are relevant here are the classical theories of wages, the rate of profit, and the role of exporters and importers, which have been missing in the standard interpretation of the classical theory of international trade.

II

Ricardo's numerical example of the comparative-cost principle is as follows. Suppose one unit of cloth made in England is being exchanged against one unit of wine made in Portugal:[2]

> England may be so circumstanced that to produce the cloth may require the labour of 100 men for one year, and if she attempted to make wine, it might require the labour of 120 men for the same time. England would therefore find it her interest to import wine, and to purchase it by the exportation of cloth. To produce the wine in Portugal might require only the labour of 80 men for one year, and to produce the cloth in the same country might require the labour of 90 men for the same time. It would therefore be advantageous for her to export wine in exchange for cloth [Ricardo, p. 82].

This exchange takes place notwithstanding that the commodity imported by Portugal could be produced there with less labor than in England and that England gives the produce of the labor of 100 men for the produce of the labor of 80. The reason is, of course, the difficulty with which capital moves from one country to another.

> Experience, however, shows that the fancied or real insecurity of capital, when not under the immediate control of its owner, together with the natural disinclination which every man has to quit the country of his birth and connections, and intrust himself, with

2. This interpretation of Ricardo that the terms of trade are one-to-one is due to Yukizawa, "Ricardo."

all his habits fixed, to a strange government and new laws, check the emigration of capital. These feelings, which I should be sorry to see weakened, induce most men of property to be satisfied with a low rate of profits in their own country, rather than seek a more advantageous employment for their wealth in foreign nations [Ricardo, p. 83].

Let us note three points.

(i) Here Ricardo emphasized the difficulty of international capital movement rather than that of labor movement between countries to explain the unequal exchange of labor between countries, and he discussed the difference in the rate of profit rather than that in the rate of wages between countries. In the modern interpretations of Ricardian theory of international trade, however, it is assumed that labor is the sole factor of production requiring remuneration, and the capital and land are assumed away, with the result that there is no rate of profit nor rent for land use.[3] In such interpretations, wages are explained as the quasi-rent for labor whose available amount in each country is assumed constant. In other words, wages are derived from the value of products on the basis of productivity of labor. This is an Austrian rather than a classical concept of wages, and it suggests that the true model of Ricardian theory of international trade is quite different from that of modern interpretations.

(ii) In the above numerical example, Ricardo assumed that labor productivity is generally, i.e., in both the cloth and the wine industries, lower in England, which seems to be the more advanced country, than in Portugal, which seems to be the less developed country. Although it is not inconsistent with Ricardian theory of economic development, as will be shown below, this assumption seemed strange to some economists. Thus, Akamatsu (Kinoshita 1960, p. 79) concluded that Portugal is the more advanced country and England is the less developed country in Ricardo's example. Nishikawa (p. 154) explained this alleged paradox by the fact that Ricardo was a polite Englishman so that he paid his respects to the foreign country. Joan Robinson (1974), on the other hand, speculated that Ricardo used an example as extreme as possible so that he could attack the vulgar arguments for protection most vigorously. All of these arguments are based on a quite un-Ricardian but popular supposition that labor productivity is highest in the most developed country.

(iii) Ricardo assumed that one unit of cloth is exchanged internationally against one unit of wine, which implies that the labor of 100

---

3. For the modern interpretations of Ricardian theory of international trade, see Caves and Jones, pp. 119–37, and Helpman and Razin, pp. 5–12, which are a few examples among many textbooks on the theory of international trade.

Englishmen is exchanged for the labor of 80 Portuguese. From the point of view of the theory of reciprocal demands, the commodity terms of trade can be anything, depending on the conditions of demand, between two domestic price ratios, i.e., 120/100 and 80/90, and there is no reason why it should be 1 irrespective of demand conditions. Morita (1977) admitted that the question whether Ricardo's assumption is arbitrary remains unresolved. He suggests that Ricardo's supposition that terms of trade are determined without consideration of demand is justified if we supplement the argument of the comparative-cost principle by the theory of international distribution of gold. As a matter of fact, this suggestion is not entirely new. For example, Kojima (p. 77) seems to insist that Ricardo has his own theory of international equilibrium based on the principle of the cost of production, which is entirely different from Mill's principle of demand, and that Ricardo's argument on international value and that on the transfer mechanism should be considered jointly.

III

It seems difficult, however, to follow these suggestions. The Ricardian argument concerning the international distribution of gold may be interpreted as the theory of the redistribution of a given amount of gold through the trade balance, i.e., the theory of the specie-flow mechanism. As such it is above all an argument concerning the adjustment of the terms of trade in disequilibrium rather than the theory of the determination of the equilibrium terms of trade. The adjustment process is, of course, not independent of the conditions of demand. The question is whether the resulting terms of trade after adjustment are independent of demand. But Ricardo (pp. 83–84) states that "gold and silver having been chosen for the general medium of circulation, they are, by the competition of commerce, distributed in such proportions amongst the different countries of the world as to accommodate themselves to the natural traffic which would take place if no such metals existed, and the trade between countries were purely a trade of barter." In other words, the system is completely dichotomized so that real variables are unchanged by the introduction of monetary factors.[4] If the terms of trade are not determined independently of demand in the case of pure barter trade, they cannot be so determined by the introduction of gold as the general medium of circulation.

The above argument is based on the interpretation that the amount of gold is constant and the value of gold is determined according to the quantity of money. One might consider, however, that the amount of

4. For the classical dichotomy of real and monetary theories, see Negishi, *General Equilibrium Theory*, pp. 247–77.

gold in circulation is not constant and its value is determined by the cost of production in gold mines. If gold is actually being produced in both Portugal and England, and the constant labor productivity in gold production in England is 80 percent of that in Portugal, Ricardo's assumption that the labor of 100 Englishmen and that of 80 Portuguese are exchanged can be justified by the international flow of gold. This justification has, however, several difficulties. Firstly, as argued by Yukizawa, we need an unwarranted assumption that gold is located between cloth and wine from the point of view of comparative cost.[5] Secondly, even so, it depends on the demand condition that gold is actually produced in both countries, though cloth production in England and wine production in Portugal are independent of demand. Finally, if there is a country with no gold mine, it does not work.

With respect to this last point, one should not be misled by following statements by Ricardo and Senior, which are themselves correct, into the incorrect belief that the labor value of gold in a country without gold mines is determined by the physical productivity of the export industries:

> When any particular country excels in manufactures, so as to occasion an influx of money towards it, the value of money will be lower, and the prices of corn and labor will be relatively higher in that country than in any other [Ricardo, p. 90].

> The mine worked by England is the general market of the world, the miners are those who produce those commodities by the exportation of which the precious metals are obtained [Senior, p. 15].

Mill (p. 609) criticized Senior to the effect that not only the great efficiency of English labor but also the great demand in foreign countries for the staple commodities of England are causes why the precious metals are of less value in England. Bowley (p. 223) defended Senior, but she did it correctly only by pointing out that Senior implied value productivity of labor, which of course depends on demand.

If there is a commodity, not necessarily gold, which is actually being produced in both of the two countries, the terms of trade between such countries is determined by the ratio of constant labor productivity in the production of such a common commodity. In a many-good, many-country case, the possibility for it might be great, as was recognized by Mangoldt and emphasized by Graham in the idea of linked competition.[6] The trouble is, however, that we cannot tell whether

5. Yukizawa 1957, p. 254, which criticized Kinoshita, p. 167.
6. Mangoldt, p. 188, and Graham. See also Yukizawa 1957, p. 256, and Nawa, p. 164.

such a common commodity exists, without knowing the demand conditions. It cannot work, furthermore, in the Ricardian two-country, two-good case of complete specialization.

IV

To justify our supposition that the terms of trade are determined independently of demand in Ricardian theory, we have to take into consideration the classical theories of wages, the rate of profit, and the roles of exporters and importers which have been missing in the standard interpretation of the classical theory of international trade.

Let us start with the theory of wages. As we pointed out in Section II above, the wage rate in the modern interpretation of the classical theory of international trade is the quasi-rent imputed to the given supply of labor. This is quite un-Ricardian:

> The natural price of labour is that price which is necessary to enable the labourers, one with another, to subsist and to perpetuate their race, without either increase or diminution. The power of the labourer to support himself and the family which may be necessary to keep up the number of labourers, does not depend on the quantity of money which he may receive for wages, but on the quantity of food, necessaries, and conveniences become essential to him from habit which that money will purchase. The natural price of labour, therefore, depends on the price of the food, necessaries, and conveniences required for the support of the labourer and his family. . . . The market price of labour is the price which is really paid for it, from the natural operation of the proportion of the supply to the demand; labour is dear when it is scarce and cheap when it is plentiful. However much the market price of labour may deviate from its natural price, it has, like commodities, a tendency to conform to it [Ricardo, pp. 52–53].

It is impressive to see that this point is well recognized in modern mathematical reformulations, not of Ricardo's theory of international trade but of his economic theory in general, i.e., those of Brems (1970), Pasinetti (pp. 1–28) and Samuelson (1959). In the Ricardian system which is a typical classical system in this respect, the supply of labor is variable and is adjusted so that the market wage is equal to the natural wage, which is given in terms of commodities.

In the Ricardian two-commodity model, therefore, the wage rate is given by

$$w = c_1 + p_1 + c_2 p_2 \qquad (1)$$

where c_1 and c_2 are positive constants, w is the wage rate, p_1 is the price of cloth, p_2 is that of wine, and w and the p_i's are measured in terms of an abstract unit of account. This implies that the market wage is equal to the natural wage which covers just the cost of living or the cost of reproduction of labor power and purchases just the given specified amount of each commodity, i.e., c_1 and c_2. Unlike in the neoclassical framework, where substitution among goods in consumption and in production is the main feature of the theory, substitution is excluded in Ricardian analysis.[7] Being unable to do otherwise, we simply assume that c_1 and c_2 are identical for different countries.

Let us next consider the numerical values of labor productivity given by Ricardo, which we noted in Section II above. In spite of some economists' wonder, it is quite natural for Ricardo to assume a lower labor productivity in England, i.e., an advanced country:

> If the profits of capital employed in Yorkshire should exceed those of capital employed in London, capital would speedily move from London to Yorkshire, and an equality of profits would be effected; but if in consequence of the diminished rate of production in the lands of England from the increase of capital and population wages should rise and profits fall, it would not follow that capital and population would necessarily move from England to Holland, or Spain, or Russia, where profits might be higher [Ricardo, pp. 81–82].

Labor productivity in England is lower both in cloth and in wine than that in Portugal, because English lands are more densely populated and more heavily invested than Portuguese lands. One may perhaps consider that in the Ricardian macro production function the marginal rate of substitution between cloth and wine is constant and the marginal productivity of labor is diminishing because of the existence of land as a fixed factor of production, i.e.:

$$C + sV = F(N), \quad F'(N) > 0, \quad F''(N) < 0, \tag{2}$$

where C, V, and N are respectively the output of cloth, that of wine, and labor input, and s is a constant.[8] Of course s is different for different countries, i.e., the comparative advantage. To employ N labor, furthermore, wN amount of capital has to be advanced. "Capital consists entirely of the wage-bill, in other words, it is only circulating capital which takes one year to be re-integrated."[9]

---

7. Equation (1) here corresponds to the last equation in (10) of Samuelson, p. 14. See also Pasinetti, p. 18 n.37, for the argument that substitution is excluded in a Ricardian type of analysis.

8. See Pasinetti, p. 7, for the case of no-joint output.

9. Pasinetti, p. 7. See also Samuelson, p. 219.

In the Ricardian numerical example, in which cloth and wine require respectively 100 and 120 units of labor in England, the rate of profit and prices in England before trade are determined by

$$p_1 = (1 + r)100(c_1p_1 + c_2p_2) \tag{3}$$

and

$$p_2 = (1 + r)120(c_1p_1 + c_2p_2) \tag{4}$$

where r is the rate of profit. This implies that at the margin where there is no land rent, the price of a product must be equal to the sum of the wage bill advanced and the profit earned on it. By multiplying (3) and (4) by c_1 and c_2 respectively, and adding them, we have

$$1/(1 + r) = 100c_1 + 120c_2 \tag{5}$$

since $(c_1p_1 + c_2p_2)$, assumed to be non-zero, can be canceled out.

Similarly, we have for Portugal

$$p_1 = (1 + r')90(c_1p_1 + c_2p_2) \tag{6}$$

and

$$p_2 = (1 + r')80(c_1p_1 + c_2p_2) \tag{7}$$

from which we conclude that

$$1/(1 + r') = 90c_1 + 80c_2, \tag{8}$$

where r' is the rate of profit in Portugal. As is seen in (5) and (8), the rate of profit is higher in Portugal than in England before trade.

Cloth is relatively cheaper in England and wine is relatively cheaper in Portugal before trade. After trade begins, the prices of cloth and wine are the same in the two countries.[10] This implies that money wages are equalized between the two countries, in addition to the assumed equality of real wages, i.e., c_1 and c_2. For the balance of trade to be established between the two countries, each country must produce at least one commodity. Then it is certain that cloth is produced in England and wine is produced in Portugal, while it is not certain whether wine (cloth) is produced in England (Portugal). We have, therefore,

$$p_1 = (1 + r)100(c_1p_1 + c_2p_2) \tag{9}$$
$$p_2 = (1 + r')80(c_1p_1 + c_2p_2) \tag{10}$$
$$p_1 \leqslant (1 + r')90(c_1p_1 + c_2p_2) \tag{11}$$

and

$$p_2 \leqslant (1 + r)120(c_1p_1 + c_2p_2), \tag{12}$$

10. Strictly speaking, labor productivity in each country might be changed before and after trade because of the changes in population and capital in each country. We ignore this possibility by assuming that marginal productivity of labor does not change

where r is the profit rate in England and r' is the profit rate in Portugal. From (9) and (10), we must have

$$RR' - 100c_1R' - 80c_2R = 0,\qquad 13)$$

where $R = 1/(1 + r)$ and $R' = 1/(1 + r')$.[11]

The relationship between r and r' depends on the possibility of capital movement between countries. In classical economic theory, the role of capital is mainly to advance wage costs until the product is sold to consumers. An aspect of the role of the capital of foreign trade merchants is, furthermore, to replace the capital of foreign as well as domestic producers. This is most clearly stated by Adam Smith:

> The capital employed in purchasing foreign goods for home consumption when this purchase is made with the produce of domestic industry, replaces too, by every such operation, two distinct capitals, but one of them only is employed in supporting domestic industry. The capital which sends British goods to Portugal, and brings back Portuguese goods to Great Britain, replaces by every such operation only one British capital. The other is a Portuguese one [Smith, I, 329].

When there is a profit rate differential between countries, therefore, capital moves from the lower-rate country to the higher-rate one by shifting from the domestic production of the former country to the import-export business, so as to share the higher profit rate of the latter country. The result is narrowing down of the profit rate differential, since the output of the lower-rate country is decreased while that of the higher-rate country is increased by the accelerated turnover of capital.

In view of factors which, Ricardo emphasized, induce most men of property to be satisfied with a low rate of profits in their own country rather than to seek a higher rate in foreign nations,[12] r and r' are not equalized. Let us define the rate of conversion a (<1) by which English capitalists discount r' when it is higher than r by

$$R' = aR. \qquad (14)$$

Then (13) reduces to

$$R = 100c_1 + (80/a)c_2. \qquad (15)$$

---

continuously, but changes in stepwise fashion, and remains unchanged for the changes in population and capital under consideration.

11. Conditions (11) and (12) in strict inequalities imply that a commodity is not produced when the price cannot cover the cost including profit. Equation (13) is obtained from (9) and (10) in a similar way as (5) was obtained from (3) and (4).

12. See Section II above for the quotation from Ricardo, p. 83.

By substituting (14) into (9)–(12), it can be seen that the possible range of a satisfying (9)–(12) is

$$80/120 \leqslant a \leqslant 90/100. \text{[13]} \tag{16}$$

Comparison of (5), (8), and (15) shows that trade does not decrease the profit rates, while specialization—i.e., when strict inequalities apply in (16)—always increases the profit rates. Ricardo's numerical example is the case of $a = 0.8$, so that $p_1 = p_2$ in (9) and (10).

V

We have shown that in Ricardian theory an international difference in labor productivity results, not in wage differentials, but in the difference in the rate of profit between countries. Ricardo argued that home capitalists are satisfied with a rate of profit lower than that in the foreign country, taking risk and uncertainty into consideration. By specifying the rate of conversion by which home capitalists discount a higher rate of profit in the foreign country, then,[14] Ricardian theory can determine the terms of trade on the basis of cost-price relations without having recourse to reciprocal demands.[15] Modern interpretations of Ricardian theory of international trade cited in Section II failed to see this and concluded that Ricardian comparative cost merely sets the limits for the possible range of the terms of trade and that one must introduce demand factors to determine the equilibrium terms of trade. This is due to the facts that such interpretations assumed away the capital and the rate of profit on which Ricardo put so much emphasis and that they explain the wage rate in a quite un-Ricardian way, i.e., not by the reproduction cost of labor but by the productivity of labor.

As is seen in Equation (15), the rate of profit r in England is higher if the rate of conversion a by which English capitalists discount a higher rate of profit r' in Portugal and in foreign trade with Portugal is higher. On the other hand, in view of Equation (14), r' is lower if a is higher. In spite of Ricardo's being sorry to see it, therefore, a weakening of the feelings of English capitalists causing them to discount a higher foreign rate of profit is favorable to British capitalists themselves. As a matter

13. In view of (5) and (8), it can be seen that the ratio of R' to R before trade satisfies condition (16).

14. Given the psychology of capitalists and cultural and social backgrounds, we assume that this rate of conversion is exogenously given. Ricardo seems to consider that there is a tendency for this rate to increase, since he was sorry to see risk aversion of capitalists weakened. See Ricardo, p. 83.

15. The terms of trade depend, of course, on the given subsistence bundle which we assumed equal in the two countries. Ricardo (pp. 54–55) admitted, however, that the natural price of labor "depends on the habits and customs of the people." The terms of trade are, therefore, not independent of demand from wage income, though independent of demand from profit and rent income.

of fact, Ricardo rather doubted whether a higher profit rate in foreign trade would have a favorable effect on the domestic profit rate. His argument is, however, based on the reason that "in all cases the demand for foreign and home commodities together, as far as regards value, is limited by the revenue and capital of the country. If one increases the other must diminish" (Ricardo, p. 78). This clearly shows that here Ricardo was not considering the possibility that the capital of the country diminishes through the shift to a profitable export and import business which replaces the capital of foreign producers. On the basis of this possibility, however, he should have agreed that

> it has been said, by high authority [i.e., A. Smith], that less capital being necessarily devoted to the growth of corn, to the manufacture of cloth, hats, shoes, etc., while the demand continues the same, the price of these commodities will be so increased, that the farmer, hatter, clothier, and shoemaker will have an increase of profits as well as the foreign merchant. [Ricardo, pp. 77–78].

The author is grateful to anonymous referees for comments.

References

Bowley, M., *Nassau Senior*. London, 1937.

Brems, H., "Ricardo's Long-Run Equilibrium." *History of Political Economy* 2(1970): 225–45.

Caves, R. E., and R. W. Jones. *World Trade and Payments*. Boston, 1973.

Graham, F. D. "The Theory of International Values." *Quarterly Journal of Economics* 46(1932): 581–616.

Helpman, E., and A. Razin. *A Theory of International Trade under Uncertainty*, New York, 1978.

Kinoshita, E. *Ronso-Kokusaikachiron* (Readings in the Theory of International Value). Tokyo, 1960.

———. *Shihonshugi to Gaikokuboeki* (Capitalism and International Trade). Tokyo, 1963.

Kojima, K. *Kokusaikeizairiron no Kenkyu* (Studies in the Theory of International Economics). Tokyo, 1952.

Mangoldt, H. *Grundriss der Volkswirtschaftslehre*. Stuttgart, 1963.

Mill, J. S. *Principles of Political Economy*. London, 1921.

Morita, K. "Kotenha Kokusaibungyoron Saiko." *Keizaigakuronshu* (Tokyo University Journal of Economics) 43, no. 3(1977): 2–20.

Nawa, T. *Kokusaikachiron Kenkyu* (Studies on the Theory of International Value). Tokyo, 1949.

Negishi, T. *General Equilibrium Theory and International Trade*. Amsterdam. 1972.

———. "Marx and Böhm-Bawerk in the Theory of Interest." *Economies et Sociétés*, 14(1980): 287–304.

Nishikawa, J. *Keizaihatten no Riron* (Theory of Economic Growth). Tokyo, 1976.

Pasinetti, L.L. *Growth and Income Distribution*. Cambridge, 1974.

Ricardo, D. *The Principles of Political Economy and Taxation*. Everyman's Library ed. London. 1976.

Robinson, J. *Reflections on the Theory of International Trade*. Manchester, 1974.

Samuelson, P. A. "A Modern Treatment of the Ricardian Economy." *Quarterly Journal of Economics* 73(1959): 1–35, 217–31.

Schumpeter, J. A. *History of Economic Analysis*. Oxford, 1954.

Senior, N. W. *Three Lectures on the Cost of Obtaining Money*. London, 1830.

Smith, A. *Wealth of Nations*, 1776–78. Everyman's Library ed. London, 1950.

Yukizawa, K. *Kokusaikeizaigaku Josetsu* (Introduction to International Economics). Kyoto, 1957.

———. "Ricardo Hikakuseisanhisetsu no Genkeirikai to Henkeirikai." *Shogakuronsan* (Chuo University Journal of Commerce), 15, no. 6 (1974): 25–51.

[4]

RICARDO AND MORISHIMA
ON MACHINERY

BY

TAKASHI NEGISHI

I

Following the appearance of John Barton's *Condition of the Labouring Classes of Society* (1817), David Ricardo admitted, in the third edition (1821) of his *Principles*, that the process of mechanization may prove injurious to the working class.[1] Michio Morishima claims, however, that he "carefully investigates Ricardo's chapter on machinery and shows that the introduction of machinery does not create unemployment" (Morishima 1989, p. 14). In view of the importance of Ricardo's machinery problem in the history of economic thought,[2] as well as its applicability in past and current cases of rapid industrialization,[3] it is worthwhile to scrutinize Morishima's criticism of Ricardo carefully.

Ricardo derives his conclusion from two numerical examples, which are explained in detail in section II below. Then we present our interpretations of Ricardo's first example in section III and of Morishima's corrected version of it in section IV. Section V is devoted to considering Morishima's thesis. Our interpretation of Ricardo's second example will be given in section VI, while Morishima's argument on it will be considered in section VII. Section VII refers also to the question of unproductive labor. Finally, section VIII concludes our study.

As for Ricardo's first example, it will be shown that his result remains unchanged even if his partial equilibrium analysis with the assumption of no depreciation of fixed capital is replaced by a general equilibrium analysis with Morishima's assumption about the depreciation of capital. It is true that the *existence* of machines as such does not prevent the economy from achieving full employment, as is clearly shown by Morishima's own

University of Tokyo. The author is grateful to two referees for useful comments and to Mr. Ken Mizuta of Hosei University for his comments on section IV. This study is supported by a Grant-in-Aid for Scientific Research by the Japanese Ministry of Education, Science and Culture.

1. See Barton 1934 and Ricardo 1821, pp. 386-97.
2. See, for example, Blaug 1958, pp. 64-79; David 1989; Hollander 1979, pp. 346-75; Marx 1954, p. 384; Marx 1968, pp. 550-81; Mazane 1959. pp. 17-18, 146; and Samuelson 1988, 1989.
3. See Hicks 1977, p. 185. These cases may include not only that of the Industrial Revolution in England but also those of some socialist countries.

Journal of the History of Economic Thought, 12. Fall 1990.
© 1990 by the History of Economics Society.

general equilibrium analysis. This is. however, a problem in Ricardo's theory of value. a problem different from the one which concerned Ricardo in his machinery chapter. i.e., whether an *introduction* of machines hurts labor through a decrease in the wages fund. Similarly, it will be shown that different problems are discussed by Ricardo and Morishima in the case of Ricardo's second example. While Ricardo considered only the service of unproductive labor to be instantaneous. Morishima assumed instantaneous production of commodities to discuss the effects of changes in the pattern of demand on the employment. Naturally they arrived at different results. but the assumption of instantaneous production is inconsistent with the classical theory of capital. Finally, as will be seen in the last section where we examine Morishima's criticism of Ricardo, Morishima rightly emphasizes that Ricardo assumed Say's law in the machinery chapter. This does not necessarily imply, however, that there can be no unemployment of labor, even though investment is identically equalized to saving and there is always sufficient demand for commodities, since the demand for commodities is not the demand for labor in Ricardo's classical economics. Ricardo is right, therefore, regarding the world of the classical wages fund doctrine.

II

In Chapter 31 on machinery in the third edition of his *Principles*. Ricardo gave two numerical examples concerning the effects of the employment of machinery on the demand for labor. The first example is concerned with the application of machinery in the wage goods industry, while the second is on the employment of machinery in a non-wage goods industry. The first is regarded by Ricardo as the most simple case which he could select (Ricardo 1821, p. 390) and is described as follows:

> A capitalist we will suppose employs a capital of the value of £20,000 and that he carried on the joint business of farmer, and a manufacturer of necessaries. We will further suppose, that £7,000 of this capital is invested in fixed capital, viz. in buildings, implements. &c. &c. and that the remaining £13,000 is employed as circulating capital in the support of labour. Let us suppose, too, that profits are 10 per cent., and consequently that the capitalist's capital is every year put into its original state of efficiency, and yields a profit of £2,000 (ibid., p. 388).
> ·Each year the capitalist begins his operations, by having food and necessaries in his possession of the value of £13,000, all of which he sells in the course of the year to his own workmen for that sum of money, and, during the same period, he pays them the like amount of money for wages: at the end of the year they replace in his possession food and necessaries of the value of £15,000, £2,000 of which he consumes himself, or disposes of as

may best suit his pleasure and gratification. As far as the products are concerned, the gross produce for that year is £15,000,
and the net produce £2,000. Suppose now, that the following
year the capitalist employs half his men in constructing a machine, and the other half in producing food and necessaries as
usual. During that year he would pay the sum of £13,000 in
wages as usual, and would sell food and necessaries to the same
amount to his workmen; but what would be the case the following year? (ibid., pp. 388-89).

While the machine was being made, only one-half of the usual
quantity of food and necessaries would be obtained, and they
would be only one-half the value of the quantity which was produced before. The machine would be worth £7,500 and the food
and necessaries £7,500, and, therefore, the capital of the capitalist would be as great as before; for he would have besides these
two values, his fixed capital worth £7,000, making in the whole
£20,000 capital, and £2,000 profit. After deducting this latter sum
for his own expenses, he would have a no greater circulating
capital than £5,500 with which to carry on his subsequent operation; and, therefore, his means of employing labour, would be
reduced in proportion of £13,000 to £5,500, and, consequently,
all the labour which was before employed by £7,500, would become redundant (ibid., p. 389).

Compared with the first example, which was called the most simple
case, the second example would be more complicated. While the first was
described in some detail by Ricardo, as shown above, only an abstract
and rather vague sketch was given by him in the second case, possibly
because "it would make no difference in the result, if we supposed that
the machinery was applied to the trade of any manufacturer—that of a
clothier, for example, or of a cotton manufacturer" (ibid., pp. 390-91).

If in the trade of a clothier, less cloth would be produced after
the introduction of machinery; for a part of that quantity which is
disposed of for the purpose of paying a large body of workmen,
would not be reqired by their employer. In consequence of using
the machine, it would be necessary for him to reproduce a value,
only equal to the value consumed, together with the profits on
the whole capital. £7,500 might do this as effectually as £15,000
did before, the case differing in no respect from the former instance. It may be said, however, that the demand for cloth would
be as great as before, and it may be asked from whence would
this supply come? But by whom would the cloth be demanded?
By the farmers and the other producers of necessaries, who employed their capitals in producing these necessaries as a means of
obtaining cloth: they gave corn and necessaries to the clothier for
cloth, and he bestowed them on his workmen for the cloth which
their work afforded him (ibid., p. 391).

This trade would now cease; the clothier would not want the food and clothing, having fewer men to employ and having less cloth to dispose of. The farmers and other, who only produced necessaries as means to an end could no longer obtain cloth by such an application of their capitals, and therefore, they would either themselves employ their capitals in producing cloth, or would lend them to others, in order that the commodity really wanted might be furnished; and that for which no one had the means of paying, or for which there was no demand, might cease to be produced. This, then, leads us to the same result; the demand for labour would diminish, and the commodities necessary to the support of labour would not be produced in the same abundance (ibid.).

III

In spite of Morishima's assertion that we can find a general equilibrium system concealed within Ricardo's economics (Morishima 1989, p. 3), Ricardo confined himself to partial equilibrium analysis, at least in the discussion of the case of the wage goods industry in the first example quoted in section II. What enables him to do so is the assumption that the fixed capital does not depreciate so that it need not to be replaced although it yields profit at the same rate as the circulating capital does. This is because otherwise repercussions to non-wage goods industries have to be taken into consideration and general equilibrium analysis has to be applied, unless fixed capital consists all of wage goods in the wage goods industry. Of course, the assumption is stringent, but it can be defended if fixed capital consists of capital goods which are by nature highly durable and do not depreciate very much, or if the consideration is confined to the effects in the very short run.

In this respect, the assumption is made clearer in the example considered by J.S. Mill to the same effect:

Suppose that a person farms his own land, with a capital of two thousand quarters of corn, employed in maintaining labourers during one year (for simplicity we omit the consideration of seed and tools), whose labour produces him annually two thousand four hundred quarters, being a profit of twenty per cent . . . . Let us now suppose that by the expenditure of half his capital he effects a permanent improvement of his land, which is executed by half his labourers, and occupies them for a year . . . . At the end of the year . . ., the improver has not, as before, a capital of two thousand quarters of corn. Only one thousand quarters of his capital have been reproduced in the usual way; he has now only those thousand quarters and his improvement (Mill 1871, p. 94).

The fixed capital and machinery of Ricardo's example are changed into the land and its permanent improvement.

Returning to Ricardo's first example, we have the accounting equation of the wage goods (food and necessaries) industry:

	Gross produce	Circulating capital		Total capital		Rate of Profit
(1)	15,000 =	13,000	+	20,000	×	0.1

in view of the assumption that fixed capital (7,000) does not depreciate. Since profits are assumed to be consumed, we have a stationary state or simple reproduction in which there are neither savings nor capital accumulation. Each year the same number of laborers are employed with a circulating capital of 13,000, which is reproduced with profits of 2,000 and the same process repeats forever.

Suppose now that the industry is divided into two sectors. In sector I, food and necessaries are produced as usual but with only half the capital, i.e., a fixed capital of 3,500 and a circulating capital of 6,500, while a machine is constructed in sector II, with the remaining capital 10,000, i.e., fixed capital 3,500 and circulating capital 6,500. The equations of the two sectors are:

	Wage goods	Circulating capital		Total capital		Rate of Profit
(2)	7,500 −	6,500	+	10,000	×	0.1

and

	Machine	Circulating capital		Total capital		Rate of Profit
(3)	7,500 =	6,500	+	10,000	×	0.1

The result is that the industry has food and necessaries of 7,500, a machine worth 7,500 and a fixed capital of 7,000 at the end of the year.

Since profits of 2,000 are consumed on food and necessaries in the following year the industry starts unchanged with a total capital of 20,000, the composition of which is now a fixed capital of 7,000, a machine worth 75,000 and a circulating capital (food and necessaries) of only 5,500. Demand for labor is reduced from 13,000 to 5,500. Equation (1) is now replaced by

	Gross produce	Circulating capital		Total capital		Rate of Profit
(4)	7,500 =	5,500	+	20,000	×	0.1

if the rate of profit remains unchanged. "The reduced quantity of labour which the capitalist can employ, must, indeed, with the assistance of the machine, and after deductions for its repairs, produce a value equal to £7,500, it must replace the circulating capital with a profit of £2,000 on the whole capital" (Ricardo 1821, p. 389).

So far we assumed that the profits of the wage goods industry are entirely consumed on its produce, i.e., food and necessaries. If they are consumed entirely on a different, non-wage good, however, we have to consider that there is another industry which produces such a good. Assuming that the ratio of fixed and circulating capitals is identical to that in the wage-goods industry before the introduction of machinery, the accounting equation of the non-wage good industry is

	Gross produce	Circulating capital	Total capital		Rate of Profit
(5)	2307 =	2000 +	3073	×	0.1

since its fixed capital is 1,073. The profit of 307 is consumed on its own produce while its circulating capital is replaced through the exchange with the wage goods industry, i.e., by the consumption of the profits of the latter industry. Proving that the profits of the wage goods industry remain unchanged, therefore, the employment of machinery there does not have any repercussions on this non-wage good industry. In other words, there is still no need for general-equilibrium or inter-industry analysis.[4]

IV

Morishima starts his criticism of Ricardo by correcting the latter's numerical example (the first example) so that the accounting equation (1) is changed into

	Gross produce	Fixed capital	Circulating capital		Profits
(6)	22,000 =	7,000 +	13,000	+	2,000

and insists that the difference between the two gross products, i.e., 22,000 in (6) versus 15,000 in (1), is not a matter of definition, but arises from Ricardo's incorrect methods of accounting (Morishima 1989, p. 171). We agree that the difference is not a matter of definition, but consider that it arises, not from Ricardo's error, but from the difference in assumptions. While Ricardo assumed that fixed capital does not depreciate, Morishima assumes that it depreciates entirely in a single period. As we admitted that Ricardo's assumption is a stringent one in section III, it is certainly worthwhile to consider an alternative assumption, even though it is equally stringent.

If we follow Morishima in assuming that the fixed capital depreciates entirely in a single period, there must be an industry producing fixed capital goods which has the accounting equation

	Gross produce	Fixed capital	Circulating capital		Profits
(7)	$10,266(\frac{2}{3})$ =	$3,266(\frac{2}{3})$ +	$6,066(\frac{2}{3})$	+	$933(\frac{1}{3})$

though Morishima does not give (7) explicitly. It is assumed that two industries have identical ratios between fixed and circulation capitals, and the rate of profit is 10 percent. If the profits are assumed to be consumed on food and necessaries, the condition of an inter-industry equilibrium is that the fixed capital depreciated in the food and necessaries industry is

---

4. If the rate of profit rises, which is very likely, the non-wage good industry must be expanded and there should be a further reduction in the demand for labor.

equal to the sum of circulating capital and profits in the fixed capital goods industry, which is satisfied in (6) and (7), since
(8) $7,000 = 6,066(\frac{2}{3}) + 933(\frac{1}{3})$.
Both fixed and circulating capitals are replaced in two industries and the stationary state or simple reproduction can be maintained.

Suppose now that the food and necessaries (wage goods) industry is divided into two sectors. In sector I, food and necessaries are produced as usual but with only half of the capital, 10,000, i.e., a fixed capital of 3,500 and a circulating capital of 6,500, while a machine is constructed in sector II with the remaining capital of 10,000 i.e., fixed capital of 3,500 and circulating capital of 6,500. The equations of the two sectors are, instead of (2) and (3),

	Wage goods		Fixed capital		Circulating capital		Profits
(9)	11,000	=	3,500	+	6,500	+	1,000

and

	Machine		Fixed capital		Circulating capital		Profits
(10)	11,000	=	3,500	+	6,500	+	1,000

with the result that the industry has a machine worth 11,000, a fixed capital of 7,000 and a circulating capital of 2,000 at the end of the year. This is because, out of a gross produce of 11,000 of food and necessaries, 7,000 are exchanged against fixed capital goods, and 2,000 are consumed by capitalists. Total capital is maintained at 20,000 but the demand for labor in the following year is reduced from 13,000 to 2,000.[5]

If we consider that the original intention of Ricardo in his first example is to construct a machine value of 7,500, rather than to employ a half of the capital (and labor) to construct a machine, the accounting equations (9) and (10) of the wage goods industry have to be modified as follows.

	Wage goods		Fixed capital		Circulating capital		Profits
(11)	14,500	=	4,614	+	8,568	+	1,318

and

	Machine		Fixed capital		Circulating capital		Profits
(12)	7,500	=	2,386	+	4,431	+	682

where the industry's total gross produce of 22,000 ($= 14,500 + 7,500$), fixed capital of 7,000 ($= 4,614 + 2,386$), circulating capital of 13,000 ($+ 8,568 + 4,431$) and profits of 2,000 ($+ 1,318 + 682$) are kept unchanged from those in (9) and (10). At the end of the year, the industry now has a machine worth 7,500, fixed capital of 7,000 and circulating capital of 5,500. This is because, out of gross produce of food and necessaries worth

5. The total demand for labor of two industries together is also reduced by the same amount. i.e., from $19,066(\frac{2}{3})$ to $8,066(\frac{2}{3})$, even if the food and necessaries industry does not demand 7,000 fixed capital goods after the mechanization. I owe this point to Mr. K. Mizuta.

14,500, 7,000 are exchanged against fixed capital goods, and 2,000 are consumed by capitalists. Total capital is maintained at 20,000 but the demand for labor in the following year is reduced from 13,000 to 5,500.

Thus, the implication of Ricardo's first example remains unchanged, even if his assumption on fixed capital is substituted by Morishima's assumption. Particularly, the demand for labor is reduced, by the construction of a machine with a value of 7,500, in the proportion of 13,000 to 5,500, in the cases of both Ricardo's and Morishima's assumptions. Ricardo's assumption does work, therefore, as a simplifying assumption to consider the immediate effects of construction and employment of machinery in a stationary economy, since it can dispense with an application of general-equilibrium or inter-industry analysis.

V

In the previous section, we showed that an introduction of labor saving machines would create unemployment of labor, even if we accept Morishima's "correction" of Ricardo's numerical example. Morishima, however, derives different results from his corrected numerical example. "The demand for labour after the production of machines will be the same as before such an operation was commenced; thus, it does not cause unemployment" (Morishima 1989, p. 174).

Morishima begins with correcting Ricardo's numerical example and gives the accounting equation of "a capitalist who carries on the joint business of producing food (corn) and manufactured necessaries"

	Gross produce	Fixed capital		Circulating capital		Profits
(6)	22,000 =	7,000	+	13,000	+	2,000

which we discussed in section IV. "There exists the produce worth £22,000, a part of which, worth £13,000, is bought by the worker of that business, another part worth £2,000 is bought by the capitalist himself and the remaining part (£7,000) by the workers and capitalists of the industry producing fixed capital goods" (ibid., p. 171). Thus, Morishima recognizes the existence of the fixed-capital goods industry, though the accounting equation of the former industry is not explicitly given. (i.e., equation (7) in section IV).

Now following Ricardo, the food and necessaries industry is divided into two sectors, the food-necessaries sector (sector I) and the machine sector (sector II), with

Sector I:	Gross produce	Fixed capital		Circulating capital		Profits
	11,000 =	3,500	+	6,500		+1,000

and

Sector II:	Gross produce	Fixed capital		Circulating capital		Profits
	11,000 =	3,500	+	6,500	+	1,000

being the accounting equations for sector I and II respectively (Morishima 1989, pp. 171-72). These two equations are equations (9) and (10) we considered in section IV. Morishima seems to forget, however, the existence of the fixed capital goods industry when he argues that "after deducting the total profits (£2,000) for the capitalists' consumption from the gross output of food and necessaries, there would remain £9,000 of circulating capital, with which the subsequent operation could be carried out. The wage fund would then be reduced from £13,000 to £9,000" (ibid., p. 172). As we argued in section IV, the wage fund should be reduced to £2,000, if we take into consideration the existence of the industry which has been supplying £7,000 of fixed capital goods to the food and necessaries industry.

Morishima rather considers that this two-sector industry is a self-sufficing one, in which the fixed capital of sector I is to be replaced by the supply from sector II. Then, it turns out that the inter-sector equilibrium condition (fixed capital of sector I = circulating capital of sector II + profits of sector II) is not satisified and there are £4,000 of excess demand for food and necessaries and £4,000 of excess supply of machines (fixed capital goods), if both sectors produce £11,000 gross produce. "We have obtained this state of disequilibrium because Ricardo arbitrarily assumed that half the workers were employed in the production of machines" (ibid., p. 173.)

If two sectors' accounting equations are

	Food and necessaries		Fixed capital		Circulating capital		Profits
(13)	15,000	=	4,773	+	8,864	+	1,364

and

	Machines		Fixed capital		Circulating capital		Profits
(14)	7,000	=	2,227	+	4,136	+	637

the inter-sector equilibrium condition is satisifed, since 4,773 = 4,136 + 637. From (13) and (14), Morishima concludes that "the demand for labour after the production of machines will be the same as before such an operation was commenced; thus, it does not cause unemployment. In Ricardo's example unemployment is generated because the labour force is distributed between the two sectors in the wrong proportions" (ibid., p. 174).

Morishima is right to consider that Ricardo "included machines, as well as other capital goods such as implements, tools and buildings" in his definition of fixed capital, and that "Ricardo obviously allowed for machines in his theory of value" (ibid., p. 170). It is also true that Ricardo maintained full employment in his theory of value. What Morishima shows us by the use of (13) and (14) is, then, that a full employment stationary equilibrium is possible if initially there exists a sufficient wages fund (food and necessaries) to employ all the labor at the natural wage (so that there is no change in the population), and if the initial ratio of fixed and circulating capitals is at its equilibrium (i.e., 7/13). The existence of machines as such in the fixed capital does not prevent the economy from achieving the full employment.

The problem solved by Morishima is, however, the problem of Ricardo's theory of value, and not the problem of his machinery chapter. In the former, not only the total capital, but also the proportion between fixed and circulating capitals are kept unchanged. The fixed capital of 7,000 can be machines, but they are merely replaced and not increased. In the latter, on the other hand, machinery is newly and suddenly introduced, or machines are increased, at the expense of the reproduction of wages fund, though the total capital is kept unchanged. As was shown in section IV, fixed capital including machines increased from 7,000 to 14,500 while circulating capital is reduced from 13,000 to 5,500. The two problems are clearly different ones. As far as Ricardo's first example is concerned, therefore, Morishima's criticism of Ricardo seems to miss the mark.

VI

Let us now consider the second numerical example of Ricardo (see section II above). It is concerned with the introduction of machinery in a non-wage goods industry. This interpretation can be confirmed by the following elucidation given by H. Mangoldt: "The result does not turn out to be different if the change concerns an enterprise which produces other goods rather than the ones desired directly by the workers. In the silk manufacturing industry, for example, the introduction of machines was accompanied by a decrease of gross products" (Mangoldt 1868, p. 169). Following Mangoldt, let us call the industry in question the silk industry and assume that all the profits are spent on silk.

The accounting equation of the silk industry is

	Gross produce	Circulating capital	Profits
(15)	15,000 =	13,000 +	2,000

in view of Ricardo's assumption that fixed capital (7,000) does not depreciate. To replace the circulating capital of the silk industry, the profits of other industries should also be 13,000. If the wage goods (food and necessaries) industry represents other industries, its accounting equation should be

	Gross produce	Circulating capital	Profits
(16)	97,500 =	84,500 +	13,000

since it has a fixed capital of 45,500, the ratio of fixed and circulating capital is 7/13 and the rate of profit is 10 percent.

As in the case of the wage goods industry in the first example, the capitalists of the silk industry introduce machinery by constructing a

machine with half of their men. The silk industry is now divided into two
sectors and their accounting equations are

	Silk		Circulating capital		Profits
(17)					
	7,500	=	6,500	+	1,000

and

	Machine		Circulating capital		Profits
(18)					
	7,500	=	6,500	+	1,000

so that the gross produce of silk is reduced from 15,000 to 7, 500. At the
end of the year, the total capital of the silk industry is still 20,000 but its
composition is a fixed capital of 7,000, a machine worth 7,500 and a
circulating capital of 5,500, since the industry could sell only 5,500 to the
wage goods industry after the consumption of its profits 2,000 on its own
product.

In the following year, the accounting equation of the silk industry is

	Silk		Circulating capital		Profits
(19)					
	7,500	=	5,500	+	2,000 ·

if we assume that the machine does not depreciate. In comparision with
(15) and (19), the gross produce, which is necessary to reproduce capital
with profits, is reduced from 15,000 to 7,500 by the introduction of machinery, as was correctly anticipated by Ricardo. "£75,000 might do this
as effectually as £15,000 did before, the case differing in no respect from
the former instance" (Ricardo 1821, p. 391).

In view of (16), however, there remains an unsatisfied demand of 7,500
(= 13,000 − 5,500) for silk, since the silk industry can now supply only
5,500 to the wage goods industry after its profits of 2,000 are spent on
silk. To satisfy their demand for silk, capitalists in the wage goods industry would themselves employ their capital to produce silk, with the result
that wage goods industry is now divided into two sectors, having accounting equations

	Silk		Circulating capital		Profits
(20)					
	7,500	=	6,500	+	1,000

and

	Wage Goods		Circulating capital		Profits
(21)					
	90,000	=	78,000	+	12,000

in which fixed capital 3,500 is used for silk production and 42,000 for
wage goods production.

The assumption that the rate of profit remains unchanged can be justified in the case of the second example, since the method of production is
changed only in a non-wage goods industry, i.e., the silk industry while
the rate of profit is determined in the production of wage goods, where
input and output are identical commodities. With unchanged total capital

150,000 (52,500 fixed capital and 97,500 circulating capital), then, total profits and demand for silk remains unchanged. Demand for labor to produce silk is, however, reduced from 13,000 to 12,000 (= 5,500 + 6,500) in spite of the following statement of Mangoldt to the contrary.[6] "It is possible that when this changed application of circulating capital to the production of silk products occurs, it may no longer be used as a means of subsistence. The laid-off silk workers will find other employment, but a corresponding number of workers who have been producing the means of subsistence will lose theirs" (Mangoldt 1868, p. 170). The reason is, of course, the introduction of machinery in the original silk industry. Demand for labor in the production of wage goods is also reduced from 84,500 to 78,000. Total reduction in the demand for labor is, of course, equal to the reduction of the production of wage goods, i.e., 7,500.

VII

Morishima's interpretation of the second example of Ricardo is very different from ours in section VI. "Next, Ricardo was concerned with the case of mechanization undertaken by manufacturers such as clothiers or cotton manufacturers, which resulted in a substitution between fixed and circulating capitals in favour of the former . . . . Let us suppose that those who mechanize their own production process, like Ricardo's clothier and cotton manufacturer, belong to the food and necessaries producing sector (sector I). Suppose the proportion of fixed to circulating capital of sector I was, for example, 7/13 before the mechanization and is increased to 3 as the result of it" (Morishima 1989, p. 178). This is rather close to our interpretation of Ricardo's first example, in which the proportion of fixed and circulating capitals is 7,000/13,000 before the mechanization and is increased to 14,500/5,500 as the result of it in the wage goods (food and necessaries) industry.

Morishima describes the stationary equilibrium before the mechanization by

(13)   Gross   Fixed   Circulating   Profits
Sector I produce   capital   capital
          15,000 =   4,773   +   8,864   +   1,364

and

(14)   Gross   Fixed   Circulating   Profits
Sector II produce   capital   capital
          7,000   =   2,227   +   4,136   +   637

where sector I produces food and necessaries and sector II produces fixed capital goods (machines). After the mechanization of sector I, according to Morishima (ibid., p. 179), these two equations have to be changed respectively to

6. This was pointed out by Shibata in his criticism of Mangoldt. See Shibata 1935, p. 317.

	Gross produce		Fixed capital		Circulating capital		Profits
(22)	15,888	=	10.833	+	3,611	+	1,444

and

	Gross produce		Fixed capital		Circulating capital		Profits
(23)	15,888	=	5,055	+	9,389	+	1,444

in which total circulating capital of 13,000 remains unchanged from that in (13) and (14) in spite of the mechanization in sector I.

As a result of mechanization, total fixed capital is increased from 7,000 in (13) and (14) to 15,888 in (22) and (23), though total circulating capital remains unchanged and profits are entirely consumed. This is the story in the Land of Cockaigne (Koopmans 1951, pp. 49-50). What Morishima shows is that mechanization can be easily done without reducing demand for labor and without making saving from profits, if machines are freely available like manna, or if they are given free by foreign countries. Again, Morishima's problem is clearly different from Ricardo's. Morishima seems to consider that Ricardo explained unemployment by the existence of unused wages fund (Morishima 1989, p. 179). As we have explained, however, Ricardo's problem is different. There is not enough wages fund, since its replacement is sacrificed for the mechanization.[7]

Finally, Morishima criticizes the following argument of Ricardo's. "If a landlord, or a capitalist, expands his revenue in the manner of an ancient baron, in the support of a great number of retainers, or menial servants, he will give employment to much more labour than if he expanded it on fine clothes, or costly furniture; on carriages, on horses, or in the purchase of any other luxuries" (Ricardo 1821, p. 393). A general equilibrium model is constructed, with the assumption that "it takes one period to produce agricultural products (food), while production is assumed to be instantaneous for all other commodities" (Morishima 1989, p. 180). Then, it is shown that "a change in the consumption pattern has no effect upon the employment of labour" (ibid.). Morishima concludes, therefore, that "the demand for labour will be as great as before, even if a capitalist diverts his revenue from expenditure on a luxury good to another good" (ibid., pp. 181-82).

Morishima's general equilibrium model is, unfortunately, quite non-Ricardian. In the classical economics in general, and in Ricardian economics in particular, production cannot be assumed instantaneous, not only for food, but also for all other commodities. Otherwise, profits cannot accrue to circulating capital, since it is defined as advancement of wages fund to labor to produce commodities. Suppose instead it takes one period to produce any commodity, and the wages fund (stock of food) is given. Then, Morishima is right to argue that "the demand for

7. "Ricardo's result . . . has not the slightest reason to invoke a disequilibrium level of unemployment" (Samuelson 1989, p. 54).

labour will be as great as before, even if a capitalist diverts his revenue from expenditure on a luxury good to another good," as far as the demand for productive labor is concerned. Productive labor is, of course, supported by the wages fund and reproduces it with profits in the production of commodities.

What Ricardo had in mind is not, however, that "a capitalist diverts his expenditures on a luxury good to another good," but that he diverts his expenditure on a luxury good to, say, the employment of "menial servants." The labor of menial servants is called unproductive labor, since it is employed not by capital (wages fund) but by revenue, and no profits accrue to the employers of such a labor. This is, of course, because the production of the service of menial servants is instantaneous. If expenditure is diverted from a luxury commodity to the employment of unproductive labour, the production of the luxury commodity is reduced and that of food is increased, so that not only the given wages fund is reproduced but also it is possible to supply for the demand from the unproductive laborers, certainly the total employment of labor is increased by the employment of such unproductive laborers as menial servants.[8]

                                    VIII

Let us conclude by considering why Morishima tries to criticize Ricardo's theory of machinery. "Ricardo is well known as a strong believer in Say's law of markets" (ibid., p. 154). "There is no obstacle to full employment whenever Say's law prevails" (ibid., p. 151). "Ricardo assumed Say's law in the machinery chapter of the third edition as well as in all the other chapters" (ibid., pp. 169-70). "Ricardo mistakenly concluded that mechanization in one of the sectors would give rise to the unemployment of labour, because he forgot that Say's law prevails in his economy" (ibid., pp. 179-80)[9]

Morishima is certainly right to say that Ricardo assumed Say's law in the machinery chapter, since, as we saw, the aggregate investment, I, is identically equalized to the aggregate savings, S, though the composition of the gross investment (i.e., the reproduction of fixed and circulating capitals) is considered to change. If $I = S$, then, there always exists a sufficient demand for aggregate commodities produced, $Y = C + S$, since $Y = C + I$. This is exactly the point by which Ricardo distinguished himself from Malthus. "Malthus' objection to machinery is that it adds so much to the gross produce of the country that commodities produced cannot be consumed—that there is no demand for them: mine, on the contrary, is that the use of machinery often diminishes the quantity of gross produce" (Ricardo 1821, p. 387).

8. See Samuelson 1988, p. 279 for a graphical exposition.
9. "Labor is indeed hurt by the invention even when we and Ricardo obey Say's law" (Samuelson 1988, p. 280).

If there always is sufficient demand for commodities, then, why is the demand for labor reduced? It is because the demand for commodities is not demand for labor (Mill 1871, pp. 79, 96-97) in the classical economics in general, and, of course, in Ricardo's economics. Demand for labor is determined by the wages fund, which is reproduced by the gross produce. It is reduced, then, if the use of machinery diminishes the quantity of gross produce. Demand and supply are equalized for commodities produced, but there exists an excess supply of labor and there exists an excess demand for wage goods. The existence of an excess supply of one thing and an excess demand for another is not inconsistent with Say's law, since it merely implies that demand and supply are equalized for commodities produced, or that an excess supply cannot exist for everything.

Unemployment in Ricardo's machinery chapter is, therefore, not due to an insufficient demand for commodities produced, but due to a shortage of the supply of capital. The wages fund (circulating capital) is not enough to support all the labor. Nor is it necessary to employ all the laborers, since the machinery (fixed capital) that is introduced requires few laborers to be operated. As a matter of fact, in his *The Economics of Industrial Society* (Morishima 1984, pp. 195, 197), Morishima clearly recognized the existence of Marxian unemployment due to a deficiency in capital, along with Keynesian unemployment due to a deficiency in effective demand. In *Ricardo's Economics*, however, Morishima assumed it away before he began the discussion of the machinery problem. "The thesis claiming that full employment would prevail under Say's law tacitly assumes that the economy is provided with an amount of capital which is enough to employ the whole of the labour force" (ibid., pp. 153-54). That assumption is fatal.

REFERENCES

Barton, J. 1934. *Condition of the Labouring Classes of Society,* Johns Hopkins Press, Baltimore.

Blaug, M. 1958. *Ricardian Economics,* Yale University Press, New Haven.

Davis, J.B. 1989. "Distribution in Ricardo's Machinery Chapter," *History of Political Economy, 21,* 457-80.

Hicks, J. 1977. *Economic Perspectives,* Clarendon Press, Oxford.

Hollander, S. 1979. *The Economics of David Ricardo,* University of Toronto Press, Toronto, Buffalo.

Koopmans, T.C. 1951. *Activity Analysis of Production and Allocation,* John Wiley, New York.

Mangoldt, H.K.E. von. 1868. *Volkswirtschaftslehre,* Julius Maier, Stuttgart.

Marx, K. 1954. *Capital, 1,* Progress Publishers, Los Angeles.

_____. 1968. *Theories of Surplus-Value. 2,* Progress Publishers, Los Angeles.

Mazane, K. 1959. *Kikai to Shitsugyou, (Machinery and Unemployment)*, Rironsha, Tokyo.

Mill, J.S. 1871. *Principles of Political Economy*, Longmans, Green, Reader and Dyer, London, 1909.

Morishima, M. 1984. *The Economics of Industrial Society*, translated by D. Anthony, J. Clark, and J. Hunter, Cambridge University Press, Cambridge.

———. 1989. *Ricardo's Economics*, Cambridge University Press, Cambridge.

Ricardo, D. 1821. *On the Principles of Political Economy and Taxation*, 3d ed., Cambridge University Press, Cambridge, 1951.

———. 1952. *Letters 1819-June 1821*, Cambridge University Press, Cambridge.

Samuelson, P.A. 1988. "Mathematical Vindication of Ricardo on Machinery," *Journal of Political Economy*, 96, April, 274-82.

———. 1989. "Ricardo Was Right!" *Scandinavian Journal of Economics*, 91, no. 1, 47-62.

Shibata, K. 1935. *Rironkeizaigaku (Theoretical Economics)*, Kobundo, Tokyo.

[5]

Oxford Economic Papers 37 (1985), 148–151

COMMENTS ON EKELUND "MILL'S RECANTATION OF THE WAGES FUND"

By TAKASHI NEGISHI[1]

1

EKELUND [1] considered skillfully a set of sufficient conditions for the wages fund doctrine, i.e., the unitary elasticity of the demand for labor with respect to wage, and correctly argued that Mill's recantation of the doctrine (i.e., complete inelasticity of demand for labor) was a matter of analytical error. The aim of this note is twofold. We shall argue firstly that the annual harvest assumption is necessary for the doctrine, though Ekelund insisted not ([1], p. 74). In spite of Ekelund's argument ([1], p. 73), secondly, Mill's treatment of capitalists' decision process can be interpreted as endogenous, if Ekelund's model is extended by discarding the wage good assumption that laborers consume only wage goods which are not consumed by capitalists.[2]

2

The annual harvest assumption implies not only that the period of production, i.e., the time interval between an input and the resulted output is given, but also that the period of production is identical to the time interval between successive inputs and also to the time interval between successive outputs. Since to make input means to purchase labor (with wage goods) and output has to be sold, we may say that the annual harvest assumption implies that the period of production is identical to the market interval.

It is because of this implication of the annual harvest assumption that makes capitalists "never allowing capital to be idle" (Schumpeter [3], p. 666). Suppose that the market is open each year on the first of April and that this year the rate of wage is higher than the level a capitalist expects as normal. Even though the rate of profit is lower than the level the capitalist expects as normal, however, it is not wise for him to postpone the start of production and to let the capital to be idle. Since the next market to be opened is on the first of April next year, and by that time the production started this year will be completed and the capital advanced will be replaced, it never pays to let capital to be idle in one period of production, even though the rate of profit in this period is lower than the level expected in the subsequent periods of production. All the stock of wage goods existing has,

---

[1] I am grateful to Professor R. B. Ekelund, a referee and the editor of the journal for useful comments on earlier drafts.

[2] Ekelund's assumption that there are no crossovers between capitalist and worker consumables, which corresponds no crossovers between landlords and workers in Pasinetti–Findley models, is called the wage good assumption in the below. Ekelund ([1], pp. 76–77) correctly recognized that the wage fund could be affected by discarding the wage good assumption or his assumption of fixed composition of capitalist consumption.

therefore, to be expended to employ labor on the first of April this year. This is why the wages fund is predetermined.

This suggests that the implication of the annual harvest assumption essential to the wages fund doctrine is not that the period of production is a year but that the market interval is identical to the period of production. Abandonment of the annual harvest assumption is, therefore, not to make the period of production shorter as Ekelund seemed to do, but to make the market interval shorter than the period of production.

Suppose the period of production is still a year but the market interval is now a month. Let the rate of real wage (in terms of wage goods) on the first of April this year be w_1 and the normal rate of real wage expected by a capitalist in wage good industry to prevail on the first of May this year and on be w. Having a stock of wage goods at hand, the capitalist has two alternatives on the first of April this year, either to exchange his wages fund with labor now at the rate of w_1, and start production immediately so that output for sale is available on the first of April next year, or to wait until the first of May this year and then to exchange, at the rate of w, his wages fund with labor to start production with the result that output for sale is not available until the first of May next year.

Note that the period of production is a year for both alternatives but the period of investment is thirteen months for the second alternative, since capital is left idle for the first market interval, i.e., in April this year. Even so, the capitalist will choose the second alternative and will not expend his stock of wage goods to employ labor on the first of this April, if expected w is inelastic with respect to current w_1 and w_1 gets sufficiently higher, since the internal rate of return per month for the second alternative is higher than that of the first.

Since different capitalists have different expectations, we can say that more and more capitalists will choose second alternative as the current rate of wage gets higher. Aggregate wages fund offered to be exchanged against labor is not predetermined but a decreasing function of the current real wage, given the distribution of expected wage. Since the demand for labor is of unitary elasticity when the wages fund is predetermined, the elasticity of demand for labor is now larger than one. This is the result of the abandonment of the annual harvest assumption. It cannot be said, therefore, that the annual harvest assumption is not essential for the wages fund doctrine, in spite of the argument of Ekelund to the contrary.

In his recantation Mill argued in terms of monetary funds that capitalists can change rather freely the allocation between wages fund and their private expenses. As was pointed out by Ekelund, however, this merely changes the prices of wage goods and non-wage goods and the real wages fund remains unchanged under the wage good assumption. There are, of course, arguments against the plausibility of the wage good assumption in the classical economics (Hollander [2], p. 332). Setting this big problem aside, however, we can at least say that Mill's recantation was reasonable, if the wage good assumption happens to be discarded. This is because money is merely a veil in the classical dichotomy of real and monetary economies and changes in the allocation of monetary fund may then cause changes in the real wages fund.

Suppose the capitalist has been in stationary conditions up to the time t_1. A given stock of the consumables Y is in the hands of the capitalist at t_1, which can be either consumed by himself or advanced to employ laborers, i.e.,

$$Y = wL + c_1 \tag{1}$$

where w, L and c_1 signify respectively the real rate of wage, the level of employment, i.e., the demand for labor, and the level of capitalist's consumption, all at time t_1. Let us denote the average product of labor by a which is considered as technologically given. Then after the period of production $t_1 t_2$ which is technologically given under the annual harvest assumption, a stock of the consumables aL is available, which can again be either consumed or advanced as wages fund at t_2, i.e.,

$$aL = wL' + c_2 \tag{2}$$

where L' and c_2 denote respectively the demand for labor and the level of capitalist's consumption, all at t_2, and the rate of wage is expected to be still at w in t_2.

As the result of the maximization of the utility, which is a function of c_1 and c_2, under the conditions (1) and (2), then, we have the following familiar condition,

$$U_1 = (1+r)U_2 \tag{3}$$

where U_1 is the marginal utility of current consumption c_1 at t_1, U_2 is the marginal utility of the next period consumption c_2 at t_2, and r is the rate of profit defined by $(a/w) - 1$.

As for the demand for labor at t_2, i.e., L', let us suppose that the capitalist expects the economy to return to the stationary condition in which it has been up to t_1, after a short-run variation in the rate of wage at t_1 and t_2, and plans to employ such a number of laborers at t_2 as is sufficient to rebuild his stock of the consumables Y at t_3, i.e., after the given period of production $t_2 t_3 = t_1 t_2$. With unchanged productivity of labor, this requires that L' should be Y/a. If L' is given in this way, we have now 3 conditions (1)–(3) to determine c_1, c_2 and L as functions of w. As is easily seen, however, the demand for labor is, in general, not completely inelastic with respect to the rate of wage w.

We have to impose, therefore, restrictions on the form of utility function to make the demand for labor inelastic with respect to wage. Suppose c_1 and c_2 are intrinsically or perfectly complementary, so that indifference curves are L shaped with kinks on the 45 degree line in c_1–c_2 plane. Then, condition (3) is replaced by condition that $c_1 = c_2$, since the optimal consumption plan is always at the kink, i.e., on the 45 degree line, for any intertemporal price ratio, i.e., $(1+r)$. From (1) and (2), then, we have

$$(w + \underline{a})(Y - \underline{a}L) = 0 \tag{4}$$

in view of our supposition that $L' = Y/\underline{a}$. The demand for labor L is $Y/\underline{a}$, and independent of w.

A rise in wage merely reduce the capitalist's consumption and the wages fund increases proportionally to rate of wage, so that demand for labor is completely inelastic with respect to wage. This can be explained by the endogenous decision process of the capitalist, though Ekelund argued that "Mill treated this decision process as exogenous."

University of Tokyo

REFERENCES

1. EKELUND, R. B., "A Short-Run Classical Model of Capital and Wages: Mill's Recantation of the Wages Fund," Oxford Economic Papers, 28(1976), pp. 66–85.
2. HOLLANDER, S., The Economics of David Recardo, University of Toronto Press, 1979.
3. SCHUMPETER, J. A., History of Economic Analysis, Oxford University Press, 1954.

[6]

History of Political Economy 18:4
© 1986 by Duke University Press
CCC 0018-2702/86/$1.50

Thornton's criticism of equilibrium theory and Mill

Takashi Negishi

I

The name of W. T. Thornton is well known in the history of economic thought with respect to J. S. Mill's recantation of the wages fund doctrine, but the significance of his criticism of the equilibrium theory of demand and supply has not been fully recognized in the literature,[1] partly because Mill in 1869 (Mill 1967, 631–68) misunderstood the nature of the examples Thornton constructed to show the irrelevancy of the equilibrium theory. Although Mill's model of the labor market to recant the wages fund doctrine is itself interesting from the point of view of equilibrium theory,[2] it is more important to realize that Thornton's attempt was a pioneering one in developing a disequilibrium model of markets—a model which has recently been extensively studied, for example, so as to give microeconomic foundations to macroeconomics.

In Section II we start with Thornton 1869's example of fish auctions and Mill 1967's interpretation of it, on which the recantation of the wages fund doctrine was based. Section III is devoted to Thornton 1870's rejoinder to Mill, while it is argued in Section IV that the common feature of all the examples Thornton constructed is the possibility of trades carried out in disequilibria. Finally, our conjecture on Mill's final position towards Thornton is given in Section V.

II

Thornton's *On labour, its wrongful claims and rightful dues, its actual present and possible future* (1869) caused Mill to recant the wages fund doctrine. It contains, however, not only an attack on a specific equilibrium theory of the wages fund doctrine but also a criticism of the equilibrium theory in general. Thornton presented several counterexamples to the 'equation theory' that the equation of supply and demand determines price.

Correspondence may be addressed to the author, Faculty of Economics, The University of Tokyo, Bunkyo-Ku, Tokyo 113 JAPAN.

1. The representative literature on Thornton and Mill is Breit 1967, which is critical of Thornton 1869.

2. While Breit 1967 and Ekelund 1976 are critical of Mill 1869, in that Mill confused monetary and real wages funds, Negishi 1985b, 67–71, tried to construct a consistent model for Mill's recantation.

The first example given by Thornton is the so-called Dutch auction for fish resorted to by certain fishermen, and its contrast with the usual English auction:

> When a herring or mackerel boat has discharged on the beach, at Hastings or Dover, last night's take of fish, the boatmen, in order to dispose of thier cargo, commonly resort to a process called Dutch auction. The fish are divided into lots, each of which is set up at a higher price than the salesman expects to get for it, and he then gradually lower his terms, until he comes to a price which some bystander is willing to pay rather than not have the lot, and to which he accordingly agrees. Suppose on one occasion the lot to have been a hundredweight, and the price agreed to twenty shillings. If, on the same occasion, instead of the Dutch form of auction, the ordinary English mode had been adopted, the result might have been different. The operation would then have commenced by some bystander making a bid, which others might have successively exceeded, until a price was arrived at beyond which no one but the actual bidder could afford or was disposed to go. That sum would not necessarily be twenty shillings; very possibly it might be only eighteen shillings. The person who was prepared to pay the former price might very possibly be the only person present prepared to pay even so much as the latter price; and if so, he might get by English auction for eighteen shillings the fish for which at Dutch auction he would have paid twenty shillings. In the same market, with the same quantity of fish for sale, and with customers in number and every other respect the same, the same lot of fish might fetch two very different prices.[3]

Mill in 1869 interpreted this example wrongly—that "the demand and supply are equal at twenty shillings, and equal also at eighteen shillings" (1967, 637)—and argued that the equilibrium theory is incomplete but not incorrect and that this case may be conceived, but in practice is hardly ever realized, since it is an exception to the rule that demand increases with cheapness. Breit 1967 also interpreted and criticized Thornton in the same way. Mill, however, in his recantation of the wages fund doctrine considered this particular case of indeterminacy to be due to demand that was inelastic with respect to price. Supply being given constant, this is the case where schedules of supply and demand are coincidental, at least within certain limits:[4]

> When equation of demand and supply leaves the price in part indeterminate, because there is more than one price which would fulfil the

3. Thornton 1869, 47–48. See also Thornton 1870, 56–57.
4. See Negishi 1985b, 67–71, for a model which generates demand for labor inelastic with respect to wage.

law [of the equation of demand and supply] . . . the price, in this case, becomes simply a question whether sellers or buyers hold out longest; and depends on their comparative patience, or on the degree of inconvenience they are respectively put to by delay.

If it should turn out that the price of labour falls within one of the excepted cases—the case which the law of equality between demand and supply does not provide for, because several prices all agree in satisfying that law; we are already able to see that the question between one of those prices and another will be determined by causes which operate strongly against the labourer, and in favour of the employer.

The doctrine hitherto taught by all or most economists (including myself), which denied it to be possible that trade combinations can raise wages, or which limited their operation in that respect to the somewhat earlier attainment of a rise which the competition of the market would have produced without them,—this doctrine is deprived of its scientific foundation, and must be thrown aside.[5]

Figure 1 shows both Mill's interpretation of Thornton's example of fish and Mill's model of the labor market in his recantation of the wages fund doctrine. In the former, price of fish is measured vertically and quantity of fish horizontally. The given supply is indicated by OS, and the demand curve is DCC'D', which violates the rule that demand increases with cheapness between C and C'. Equilibrium price is not uniquely determined, since any price between AO and BO equates demand and supply. The price established by Dutch auction is OA and that arrived at by English auction is OB. Similarly, wage is measured vertically and number of laborers horizontally, in the model of the labor market. There is no predetermined wages fund, since, clearly, aggregate wages paid is larger at C than at C'. Though the wages fund doctrine is recanted by Mill, the equilibrium theory is confirmed, since demand and supply are equalized at any point between C and C'.[6]

III

Mill in 1869 interpreted Thornton's example of auctions for fish wrongly. In the second edition of *On labour* (1870) Thornton reproduced the same example, with prices changed from twenty and eighteen shillings to eight and six shillings, and made a rejoinder to Mill:

5. Mill 1967, 642–43, 646. See also Thornton 1870, 87: "Whenever, as in the case of labour, demand does not increase with cheapness, demand, as Mr. Mill has further pointed out, may be perfectly equalized with supply at many different prices."

6. Mill himself did not draw a figure like Figure 1; it was Jenkin who first produced such a figure. See Jenkin 1931, 84.

570   *History of Political Economy 18:4 (1986)*

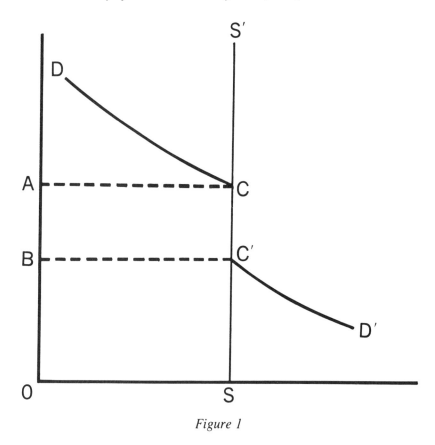

Figure 1

In this particular case it would not be possible for supply and demand to be equal at two different prices. For the case is one in which demand would increase with cheapness. A hawker who was ready to pay 8 *s.* for a hundred herrings, would want more than a hundred if he could get a hundred for 6 *s.* There being then but a given quantity in the market, if that quantity were just sufficient to satisfy all the customers ready to buy at 8 *s.*, it follows that it would not have sufficed to satisfy them if the price had been 6. If supply and demand were equal at the former price, they would be unequal at the latter.[7]

In Figure 2, the price of fish is measured vertically and the quantity of fish horizontally. The given supply of fish, a hundred herrings, is indicated by OS, and DD′ is the demand curve which satisfies the rule that demand increases with cheapness. We may suppose that the person who wants fish

7. Thornton 1870, 57–58. See also p. 60.

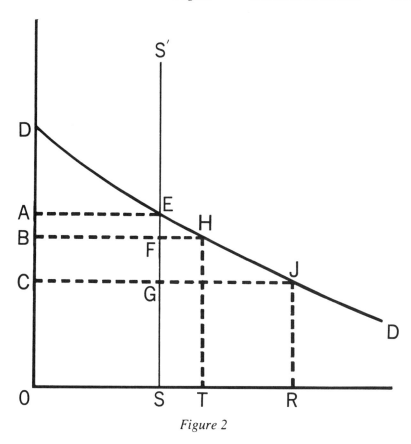

Figure 2

most strongly demands up to T, the one who wants next most strongly demands, at most, TR, and so on.[8] The price established by Dutch auction is AO and that arrived at by English auction is BO.

In Thornton's example of fish correctly interpreted, therefore, there is only an equilibrium price which equalizes demand and supply, i.e., the price AO established by Dutch auction. If English auction is adopted, however, trade takes place at lower price BO with demand larger than supply and unsatisfied demand ST remains after trade is over. The reason why this is possible is, firstly, that there is no competition to bid up the price, since no one except the actual purchaser, the one who most strongly wants fish, is willing to buy any at that price. Secondly, the actual purchaser would not himself bid up the price even though he wants to buy

8. In other words, DH is the demand curve of the most urgent buyer and EJ is that of the second most urgent buyer.

more than the quantity supplied, since he knows that the supply will not be increased.[9]

The price BO is not determined by the equality of demand and supply, but, according to Thornton, by the competition:[10]

> It is competition, wherever competition exists, that determines price. Competition remains the same, price cannot possibly vary. For, it is competition that determines the lowest price at which goods are offered for sale.—In a free and open market, and among dealers and customers actuated by the self-interest which political economy always takes for granted, competition is the only thing which determines price; the only thing indeed that directly influences it [1870, 77].

In Figure 2, competition with the person who next most strongly wants fish makes the price not lower than BO.

Figure 2 can also be used to describe a model of the labor market without a predetermined wages fund, a model different from and much more general than the one considered by Mill. Measuring wage vertically and the number of laborers horizontally, let us assume that a group of employers who need laborers most strongly demand up to T, the group of employers who need laborers next most strongly demand at most TR, and so on. Suppose the wage is determined at BO, with excess demand of labor ST. Why is not the wage bid up by excess demand? According to Thornton, "in practice it is not the mutual competition, but the mutual combination of customers, which, in general, really determines the price of isolated labour":

> But even though that should not be the case [i.e., employers cannot get as much labour as they are disposed to pay for at the current rate], every employer would probably make shift as well as he could with the labour which he could procure at the current rate, and anyone who should endeavour to tempt away another's servants by offers of increased pay, would be treated by his fellow-masters as a traitor to the common cause. Such is the habitual policy of customers for labour. Instead of suffering the rate of wages to be settled naturally by competition, they endeavour by combination to settle it arbitrarily [1870, 100, 103–4].

Wage BO is therefore determined not by the equality of demand and supply, but by the combination of actual employers and competition with

9. While in an English auction the most urgent buyer knows he is the only buyer at the price BO, at the price AO in a Dutch auction he does not know he will be the only buyer at the price BO. This is the reason why the price is determined at AO in a Dutch auction.

10. Thornton's point is not so much that different institutions (bid forms) generate different prices as that under some institutional condition the price is not determined by the equality of demand and supply.

potential employers. The wage may be determined, however, not at BO but CO, and is similarly not bid up by the excess demand SR. Thus, the wage rate is largely indeterminate, depending on the size of the group of actual employers who are in mutual combination. Even if there is a pre-determined wage fund, the aggregate wages paid at E is larger than at F. Thornton denied not only the wages fund doctrine but also the equilibrium theory of demand and supply, which insists that the excess demand changes the price.

IV

One may argue that Thornton's example of fish and the corresponding model of the labor market is the case of imperfect competition with free entry in the sense that the actual purchaser is a single person or the actual employers are in combination.[11] What Thornton emphasized, however, was not so much the imperfectness of competition as the possibility of trade carried out at disequilibrium prices, since he produced two additional examples of the failure of supply and demand as the law of prices—horses and gloves:

Suppose two persons at different times, or in different places, to have each a horse to sell, valued by the owner at £50; and that in the one case there are two, and in the other three persons, of whom every one is ready to pay £50 for the horse, though no one of them can afford to pay more. In both cases supply is the same, viz., one horse at £50; but demand is different, being in one case two, and in the other three, horses at £50. Yet the price at which the horses will be sold will be the same in both cases, viz., £50.

When a tradesman has placed upon his goods the highest price which any one will pay for them, the price cannot, of course, rise higher, yet the supply may be below the demand. A glover in a coun-try town, on the eve of an assize ball, having only a dozen pair of white gloves in store, might possibly be able to get ten shillings a pair for them. He would be able to get this if twelve persons were willing to pay that price rather than not go to the ball, or than go ungloved. But he could not get more than this, even though, while he was still higgling with his first batch of customers, a second batch, equally numerous and neither more nor less eager, should enter his shop, and offer to pay the same but not a higher price. The demand for gloves, which at first has been just equal to the supply, would now be exactly doubled, yet the price would not rise above ten shil-lings a pair. Such abundance of proof is surely decisive against the

---

11. Breit 1967 argued that demand and supply are not equalized in the case of monopoly. For relations between imperfectness of competition and excess supply, see Sraffa 1926, Arrow 1959, Hart 1982, and Negishi 1985a.

574   *History of Political Economy 18:4 (1986)*

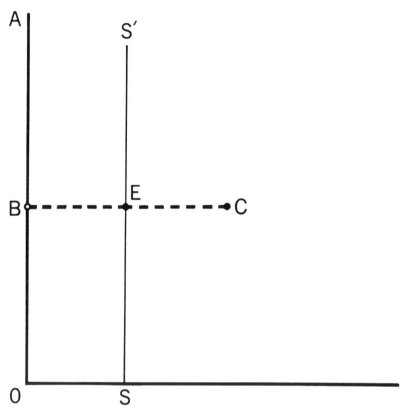

Figure 3

supposition that price must rise when demand exceeds supply [1869, 49, 51–52, also 1870, 59].

Figure 3 shows examples of horses and of gloves. Price of horse or of gloves is measured vertically and quantities horizontally. The given supply is OS, a horse or twelve pairs of gloves, and BO indicates £50 or ten shillings.[12] The demand curve consists of a half-line, AB (but point B is not included) and a point C. As Mill correctly recognized and Thornton agreed, there exists no equilibrium of demand and supply in this case, and trade has to be carried out at a disequilibrium price BO. There is no imperfectness of competition since, for example, actual purchasers are twelve persons who are not in mutual combination in the example of gloves.

12. Strictly speaking, the supply curve is discontinuous and consists of OB (but not including B) and ES' in the example of horses.

One might object, like Mill, that these examples are too specific:

At £50 there is a demand for twice or three times the supply; at 50.£ O *s*. 0¼*d*. there is no demand at all. When the scale of demand for a commodity is broken by so extraordinary a jump, the law fails of its application; not, I venture to say, from any fault in the law, but because the conditions on which its applicability depends do not exist.

Though Thornton recognized that the examples of horses and gloves show the non-existence of equilibrium due to a discontinuous demand curve, his original aim was not so much to show the non-existence of equilibrium as to deny the equilibrium theory that prices are determined by the equality of supply and demand by showing the cases where goods are traded at disequilibrium prices (Mill 1967, 638; Thornton 1870, 68).

Even though demand curves are continuous and there exists an equilibrium toward which prices are adjusted by excess demand or supply, goods are traded at disequilibrium prices, unless adjustments are instantaneous.

Even if it were true that the price ultimately resulting from competition is always one at which supply and demand are equalized, still only a small proportion of the goods offered for sale would actually be sold at any such price, since a dealer will dispose of as much of his stock as he can at a higher price, before he will lower the price in order to get rid of the remainder [Thornton 1869, 53; 1870, 65].

In other words, Thornton had in mind, not Walrasian *tâtonnement* in which trade does not take place and contracts can be cancelled unless demand and supply are equalized, but the so-called non-Walrasian, non-*tâtonnement* process without recontract in which goods are exchanged at prices which do not equate demand and supply.[13] The significance of such disequilibrium trades is much greater than admitted by Mill and Breit, since the position of equilibrium eventually established is shifted by the conditions and volumes of such trades. In the case of the labor market, the equilibrium wage would be different (even if the wages fund is predetermined), depending on how many laborers are employed at each different level of wages while demand and supply are not equal and wages are changing.

V

In the preface of the 7th edition of his *Principles of political economy* (1871), Mill stated (1965, xciv):

. . . there has been some instructive discussion on the theory of Demand and Supply, and on the influence of Strikes and Trades

13. See Arrow and Hahn, 324–46, and Negishi 1972, 207–27.

Unions on wages, by which additional light has been thrown on these subjects; but the results, in the author's opinion, are not yet ripe for incorporation in a general treatise on Political Economy.

He footnoted:

The present state of the discussion may be learnt from a review (by the author) of Mr. Thornton's work "On Labour," [Thornton 1869], in the "Fortnightly Review" of May and June, 1869, [Mill 1869], and from Mr. Thornton's reply to that review in the second edition of his very instructive book [Thornton 1870].

It is significant that not Thornton 1869 but Thornton 1870 is referred to, and that both the theory of demand and supply and the wages fund doctrine (i.e., the influence of strikes and trades unions on wages) are mentioned equally here.[14] This is in clear contrast with Mill's position in 1869: "My object in the Fortnightly was to shew that the cases supposed by Thornton do not contradict and invalidate, as he thinks they do, the equation of supply and demand. But in its application to labour, it does not merely add to our speculative knowledge; it destroys a prevailing and somewhat mischievous error [i.e., the wages fund doctrine]."[15]

In other words, in view of Thornton 1870, Mill recognized in 1871 that his interpretation of Thornton's example of fish auctions, on which his recantation of the wages fund doctrine was based, was clearly wrong and that all of Thornton's examples consistently assert the possibility of trades carried out in disequilibria. While Mill was ready to deny the validity of the wages fund doctrine in equilibrium theory, Thornton insisted in denying it from the point of view of disequilibrium theory. To accept Thornton's suggestion, however, is impossible for Mill, for whom the law of equality of supply and demand is the basic law which is antecedent to the law of cost of production and the labor theory of value.[16] Mill could not help but argue that "results are not yet ripe."

The author is greatly indebted to anonymous editorial readers whose comments were highly useful for the preparation of the final manuscript. This study is supported by Grant-in-Aid for Scientific Research of the Japanese Ministry of Education, Science and Culture.

References

Arrow, K. J. 1959. 'Towards a theory of price adjustment.' In M. Abramovitz et al., *The allocation of economic resources* (Stanford, Calif.), 41–51.
———— and F. H. Hahn 1971. *General competitive analysis.* New York.

14. This point is not noticed by Breit 1967.
15. See Mill's letter to John Elliot Cairnes, on June 23, 1869, Mill 1972, 1616, and Mill 1967, 646.
16. See Mill's theory of reciprocal demand, Mill 1965, 596.

Breit, W. 1967. 'The wages fund controversy revisited.' *Canadian Journal of Economics and Political Science* 33:523–28.

Ekelund, R. B. 1976. 'A short-run classical model of capital and wages: Mill's recantation of the wages fund.' *Oxford Economic Papers* 28:66–85.

Hart, O. D. 1982. 'A model of imperfect competition with Keynesian features.' *Quarterly Journal of Economics* 97:109–38.

Jenkin, F. 1931. 'The graphical representation of the laws of supply and demand, and their application to labour' (1870). In idem, *The graphical representation of the laws of supply and demand, and other essays on political economy* (London), 76–106.

Mill, J. S. 1965. *Principles of political economy.* Toronto.

———— 1967. 'Thornton on labour and its claims,' (1869). In idem, *Essays on economics and society* (Toronto), 631–68.

———— 1972 *The later letters of John Stuart Mill, 1849–1873.* Toronto.

Negishi T. 1972. *General equilibrium theory and international trade.* Amsterdam.

———— 1985a. 'Non-Walrasian foundations of macroeconomics.' In G. R. Feiwel, ed., *Issues in contemporary macroeconomics and distribution* (London), 169–83.

———— 1985b. *Economic theories in a non-Walrasian tradition.* Cambridge.

Sraffa, P. 1926. 'The law of returns under competitive conditions.' *Economic Journal* 36:535–50.

Thornton, W. H. 1869. *On labour,* London.

———— 1870. *On labour,* London.

[7]

History of Political Economy 21:4
© 1989 by Duke University Press
CCC 0018–2702/89/$1.50

On equilibrium and disequilibrium: a reply to Ekelund and Thommesen

Takashi Negishi

I

First of all, I am grateful to Professors Ekelund and Thommesen for taking the trouble to give me no fewer than twenty comments (*HOPE*, this issue), though some of them are repetitious while some others are interrelated. I am pleased particularly because it was Ekelund and Hébert's book (1983) that made me interested in the history of economics. Naturally I cannot accept some of the comments; others I accept with many thanks, as will be shown below. After a brief summary in this section of what I emphasized in Negishi 1986, I shall discuss the difference between equilibrium theory and disequilibrium theory in section II. Sections III and IV are devoted to scrutinizing Ekelund and Thommesen's criticism of Thornton's examples. In the final section I reply to a comment of Ekelund and Thommesen on a chapter in Negishi 1985.

What I first emphasized in Negishi 1986 was as follows. Three examples given by Thornton (1869) against equilibrium theory were interpreted by Mill (1869) as examples of the nonuniqueness (indeterminateness) and the nonexistence of demand and supply equilibrium. In the second edition of his book Thornton (1870) replied to Mill, however, that what he meant by his fish auction example is not that equilibrium is multiple when demand does not increase with cheapness, but that goods are sold in an English auction at the price where demand exceeds supply when demand does increase with cheapness. Unfortunately, not much attention has been paid so far to this second edition.[1] If we consider that Thornton sharpened and clarified his views in the second edition, however, the example of the fish auction should be interpreted, in spite of Mill, as that of disequilibrium trade rather than that of multiple equilibria. Then the examples of horses and gloves should also be interpreted not so much to show the nonexistence of equilibrium as to show the possibility that goods are traded at disequilibrium prices.

Correspondence may be addressed to the author, Faculty of Economics, The University of Tokyo, Bunkyo-Ku, Tokyo 113, Japan.

1. See, for example, Breit 1967, Ekelund 1976, and Ekelund and Hébert 1983, 172, where only the first edition is referred to. Ekelund and Thommesen take the second edition into consideration (their note 3) but follow Mill's interpretation (their sections II, IV).

593

This interpretation is confirmed by Thornton's argument following his three examples: "Even if it were true that price ultimately resulting from competition is always one at which supply and demand are equalized, still only a small proportion of the goods offered for sale would actually be sold at any such price, since a dealer will dispose of as much of his stock as he can at a higher price, before he will lower the price in order to get rid of the remainder" (1869, 53; 1870, 65). If so, argues Thornton, the equilibrium theory would be a truth of small significance, since it does not explain the prices at which the bulk of the goods offered for sale would actually be sold.

I concluded, therefore, that Thornton's criticism of equilibrium theory is not on the multiplicity and nonexistence of equilibrium but on the problem of disequilibrium trade, and that his attempt was a pioneering one to develop a disequilibrium model of markets. This, of course, does not mean that he developed such a model successfully. As a matter of fact one may say that we as yet have no model which would satisfactorily explain the behavior of disequilibrium trade in markets. Nor does it mean that Thornton had a good knowledge of demand and supply equilibrium theory. Even a naive question from a rather mediocre student can, however, sometimes disclose the existence of a problem in the theory as lectured by a professor and suggest a new direction of research.

If the problem is one of multiplicity or nonexistence of equilibrium, equilibrium theorists can generously admit it, as Mill (1869) did, even if it implies that additional assumptions are required or that some of their theorems are to be discarded. If it is a proposal of disequilibrium theory, however, they cannot admit it, since that is a theory which belongs to an entirely different and unmatured paradigm, as will be discussed below.[2]

II

In their section III Ekelund and Thommesen say that I have greatly exaggerated the differences between Thornton and Mill on the matter of disequilibrium (see Negishi 1986). On the contrary, however, it is Ekelund and Thommesen who have greatly underrated the differences. In his argument just quoted above, Thornton (1869, 53; 1870, 65) emphasized the possibility that *only a small proportion* of the goods would be sold at equilibrium price and therefore *the bulk* of them would be sold at disequilibrium prices. Certainly it is true that Mill also admitted the existence of trade at disequilibrium prices. Mill (1869) replied to this argument of Thornton's (1) that even though a dealer may keep up his price until buyers actually fall off, still if there is *a larger supply* in market than can be sold on these terms, his price will go down until it reaches the point which will

---

2. In my opinion, such was Mill's reaction as shown in the preface to the seventh edition of his *Principles* (1871). See Mill 1965, xciv.

call forth buyers for his *entire stock,* and (2) that the equilibrium theory cannot be called an insignificant truth merely because *a customer* who is ignorant or in a hurry may pay a disequilibrium price. It is clear that, unlike Thornton, Mill considered that *only a small proportion* of goods may be sold at disequilibrium prices and that *the bulk* of them can be sold at equilibrium prices.

I think this is the crucial difference between equilibrium and disequilibrium theories. Since Ekelund and Thommesen have asked me whether I mean that Thornton had an "equilibrium never" theory or an "equilibrium sometimes" theory and whether I mean to imply that Mill had an "equilibrium always" theory, let me explain what I have in mind when I discuss equilibrium and disequilibrium theories. The equilibrium is merely an abstract, theoretical concept, as Ekelund and Thommesen have also emphasized in their section IV; hence we cannot consider that an actual economy or market is always in an equilibrium state. The basic presumption of the equilibrium theory, classical or neoclassical, is, however, that we can safely ignore the effects of what happens in disequilibrium and that the behavior of the economy or market can be approximately described by, say, comparative statics analysis of equilibria. This presumption is based on the assumption that disequilibrium is to be cleared easily and smoothly by changes in prices caused by the law of supply and demand. An equilibrium may not be reached, but it is always approached. Disequilibrium theory is, on the other hand, a theory of an alternative, different paradigm, which does not share this basic presumption of equilibrium theory.

Disequilibrium theory need not deny the existence of equilibrium, despite Ekelund and Thommesen's reservations. Nor does it necessarily insist that no equilibrium can be approached even in the long run. But since excess demand or supply is considered to be not cleared (at least temporarily or in the short run), disequilibrium theorists believe, as did Thornton, that the bulk of goods cannot be traded at equilibrium price and therefore that the behavior of the economy or market cannot be described even approximately by equilibrium theory. Many different versions of disequilibrium theory can be proposed, depending on different reasons why excess demand or supply cannot be easily cleared. A common feature throughout them, however, is that the behavior of disequilibrium price is not governed by the law of supply and demand. Hicks (1965, 78) called it the "fix-price" method.

Although it may belong to a different version from that of Thornton, a modern example of disequilibrium theory is the microeconomic theory of Keynesian economics (see Benassy 1982; Malinvaud 1985; and others).

The term *involuntary* unemployment makes it obvious from the start that the labour market is one in which supply exceeds demand. Suppliers are therefore rationed in the sense that some of them do not find jobs. . . . Given the short-run price rigidities that actually exist, the theory under consideration here is . . . going to be a "fix-price" theory according to the denomination proposed by J. R. Hicks. . . . We do not mean that the prices will remain the same . . . we simply mean that their movement is . . . not significantly influenced for our purpose by the formation of demands and supplies on which attention will concentrate. (Malinvaud 1985, 1, 11)

The first important step toward disequilibrium theory is thus to recognize the existence of demand and supply disequilibrium which cannot be cleared, at least in the short run, by changes in prices. In this respect I called Thornton a pioneer of disequilibrium theory. It is true that recent disequilibrium theory generally uses a general equilibrium model. Despite Ekelund and Thommesen's objections, however, I did not, of course, consider that Mill or Thornton had general equilibrium in mind. Nor did I see the problem from the point of view of general equilibrium theory in Negishi 1986. Perhaps, to avoid misunderstanding, I should not have used the terms *tâtonnement* and non-*tâtonnement*, which are certainly Walrasian and post-Walrasian. But neither *tâtonnement* nor non-*tâtonnement* is itself a general equilibrium concept. They can be applied to the problem of a particular market as well.[3]

III

In their section IV Ekelund and Thommesen criticize Thornton's examples from the point of view of modern economic analysis. Before considering the details of their criticism, let me first emphasize the nature of Thornton's examples in his criticism of equilibrium theory. Although Thornton referred, in the course of his discussion defending the singularity of his examples, to the role of a single exception to a scientific law, each of his examples should not be regarded as something like a counter-example in mathematical sciences. Thornton's examples are rather means to express his criticism of equilibrium theory. This is why he raised three examples, not just a single one, and argued further that the bulk of goods may be traded at disequilibrium prices, even if his examples may not be applicable and the equilibrium can be reached in the long run. Thus what is important is to understand what Thornton really meant by his examples, rather than to criticize the consistency and generality of examples as such from the point of view of modern analysis.

In his fish auction example, Thornton was of course not interested in developing the general theory of auctions but in considering a *particular*

---

3. The fact that one worked in general equilibrium theory when he was a graduate student does not necessarily mean that in his fifties he is still, or always, looking at everything from that perspective. I am grateful, however, to Ekelund and Thommesen for referring to my old papers and raising my Blaug index (?).

case in which the price is higher in a Dutch auction than in an English auction. This is contrasted by Ekelund and Thommesen with the result of modern analysis of auctions, wherein English and Dutch auctions produce the same *average* price. In the latter analysis it is assumed that bidders are risk-neutral with a linear utility function and that their valuations are randomly drawn from the probability distributions. On that basis it is impossible to deny the possibility of Thornton's *particular* case with the given valuation of bidders, when bidders, having diminishing marginal utility, are risk-averters. In a Dutch auction the most eager buyer would pay a high price rather than take the risk of loosing the opportunity to buy, if he is a risk-averter. Although modern analysis, complicated with probability, integrals, and the like, seems to be very general, actually it is based on some restrictive assumptions which do not necessarily cover the simple case of Thornton's example.[4]

Furthermore, since Thornton's examples are devices to give concrete forms to his basic thought that trade takes place mostly at disequilibrium, the essential point of his fish auction example is not so much to compare Dutch and English auctions as to show an implicit excess demand left in the case of an English auction. In other words, Thornton recognized that the price the most eager buyer pays in an English auction is just above the demand price of the second most eager buyer, and therefore that the former buyer wishes to buy more, if he can, than the quantity supplied. I have to admit, of course, that this is a very clumsy example of disequilibrium trade, since the excess demand here is merely a subjective one and not explicit in the market.[5] Still we should try to find what Thornton tried to convey to us by this example, unless the equilibrium of demand and supply is to be interpreted (as Ekelund and Thommesen have) merely to mean "What is bought is what is sold." His point is, at least, not the nonuniqueness of equilibrium, nor that price is different under different institutional conditions. "It shall be proved . . . not to be the fact that if demand exceeds supply, price must rise; not to be the fact that the prices at which sales are effected are those at which supply and demand are equal" (Thornton 1870, 58–59).

IV

Despite Ekelund and Thommesen's contention, I did not argue in Negishi 1986 that imperfection of competition is irrelevant to the outcome in the fish auction example. On the contrary, I pointed out that the actual

4. The result of the simulation study cited by Ekelund and Thommesen is very interesting, though by its nature it cannot deny the possibility of a particular case Thornton considered. It can refute a general theory, which, however, was not attempted by Thornton.
5. I owe this point to Professor M. Morishima. I am also grateful to Professors Morishima, Ekelund, and Thommesen, for detecting a misprint in note 8 in Negishi 1986. EJ should read HJ.

purchaser is a single person in the fish auction, and that actual employers are in combination in Thornton's model of the labor market which corresponds to that of fish, and I referred to Breit 1967 and some recent literature on disequilibrium for the relation between imperfectness of competition and excess supply. Indeed, it is imperfection of competition on the demand side that makes the actual trade occur off the demand curve in the usual sense in Thornton's arguments of fish and labor markets, while suppliers do not reserve prices and are "in such desparate straits as to have no alternative but to sell" (Thornton 1870, 58). I argued, however, that for Thornton it is more important to emphasize disequilibrium trade with excess demand than imperfectness of competition, in view of his other examples which follow that of the fish auction, i.e., those of horses and gloves.

Referring to Edgeworth's *Mathematical psychics* (1881), Ekelund and Thommesen emphasize that small numbers bargaining under imperfect competition produce settlements off the demand curve but on the contract curve. As post-Edgeworthian economists, however, we should be extremely careful in criticizing naive and clumsy examples used by pre-Edgeworthian economists from the point of view of Edgeworth's theory. We should not indulge ourselves in an easy victory like a modern army, slipped through time, that overcomes a band of medieval knights in science fiction. We should rather try to find implicit assumptions so that classical examples make sense, as Edgeworth himself did for Jevons's theory of exchange.

> The Jevonian "Law of Indifference" has place only where there is competition, and, indeed, *perfect* competition. Why, indeed, should an isolated couple exchange every portion of their respective commodities at the same rate of exchange? Or what meaning can be attached to such a law in their case? . . . This consideration has not been brought so prominently forward in Professor Jevons's theory of exchange, but it does not seem to be lost sight of. His couple of dealers are, I take it, a sort of typical couple, clothed with the property of "indifference," whose origin in an "open market" is so lucidly described; not naked abstractions like the isolated couples imagined by a De Quincey or Courcelle-Seneuil in some solitary region. Each is in Berkleian phrase a "representative particular"; an individual dealer only is presented, but there is presupposed a class of competitors in the background. (Edgeworth 1881, 109)

Ekelund and Thommesen (note 20) claim that in Negishi 1986 I overlooked the fact that there is only one seller and stated that there is no imperfectness of competition in Thornton's example of gloves, in which actual purchasers are not in mutual combination. Even without appealing to an Edgeworth-like generous interpretation, however, I can reply to this criticism by pointing out that Thornton here assumed "one of those few situations in which goods are sold without reserve; in the shop, for instance, of a bankrupt tradesman, whose remaining stock consisting, say, of a thousand pair of gloves, must be cleared away before night" (1870, 64). Even though there is only one seller, therefore, competition prevails in the market, since buyers are in competition with each other, as Ekelund and Thommesen admit. Perhaps I should have said that there is no problem of imperfectness of competition involved.

Finally, Ekelund and Thommesen consider Thornton's horse and glove examples, where prices are not raised in the face of excess demands, from the point of view of the full price. Mill (1869) frankly replied to these examples that in them the law of supply and demand fails because the conditions on which its applicability depends do not exist. I agree, however, with Ekelund and Thommesen that these examples can be explained by equilibrium theory if we take search costs, transaction costs, etc., into account. Equilibrium theory can explain unemployment as voluntary by introducing costs of job search or money illusion. This does not, however, exclude the possibility of a disequilibrium theory of involuntary unemployment. We can always defend equilibrium theory by introducing ad hoc new variables and modifying the concept of equilibrium subtly. But this does not mean the impossibility of an alternative approach with a simple definition of equilibrium, which starts with the recognition of a more persistent existence for disequilibrium than is admitted by equilibrium theory.

V

Ekelund and Thommesen (section V) also criticized chapter 6 of Negishi 1985, where I constructed a model of Mill's (1869) recantation of the wages fund doctrine with zero elasticity of demand for labor.[6] Ekelund (1976) constructed a compact *general equilibrium* model and skillfully demonstrated Mill's analytical error due to confusion between real and nominal wages, under what I called a wage-good assumption that laborers consume different goods from capitalists. However, "Mill had quite habitually worked in monetary terms in discussing the offer of employment, and had never insisted on a rigid distinction between wage goods and luxuries" (Hollander 1985, 414). If this wage-good assumption is discarded, I argued, Mill is not in error, since labor's real earnings would then increase in consequence of increased demand for labor in money terms. To support the wage-good assumption Ekelund also referred to Pasinetti's (1960) model of Ricardian economics; but again, according to

6. Ekelund and Thommesen cite some reviews of Negishi 1985. They are, however, not exhaustive, nor impartial. Let me add Boland 1987, Hare 1986, Levine 1987, and Newman 1989.

Hollander (1979, 332), "it is precisely this assumption which we have seen cannot be attributed to Ricardo."

References

Benassy, J. P. 1982. *The economics of market disequilibrium*. New York.

Boland, L. A. 1987. On the relevance of neo-Walrasian economic theory: a review. *HOPE* 19:659–66.

Breit, W. L. 1967. The wages fund controversy revisited. *Canadian Journal of Economics and Political Science* 33:509–28.

Edgeworth, F. Y. 1881. *Mathematical psychics*. London.

Ekelund, R. B., Jr. 1976. A short-run classical model of capital and wages: Mill's recantation of the wages fund. *Oxford Economic Papers* 28:66–85.

———, and R. F. Hébert. 1983. *A history of economic theory and method*. New York.

———, and S. Thommesen. 1989. Disequilibrium theory and Thornton's assault on the laws of supply and demand. *HOPE,* this issue (21.4).

Hare, P. G. 1986. Review of Negishi's *Economic theories in a non-Walrasian tradition*. *History of Economic Thought Newsletter* 36:11–12.

Hicks, J. R. 1965. *Capital and growth*. Oxford.

Hollander, S. 1979. *The economics of David Ricardo*. Toronto.

———. 1985. *The economics of John Stuart Mill*. 2 vols. Oxford.

Levine, A. L. 1987. Review of Negishi's *Economic theories in a non-Walrasian tradition*. *Canadian Journal of Economics* 20:903–7.

Malinvaud, E. 1985. *The theory of unemployment reconsidered*. Oxford.

Mill, J. S. [1869] 1967. Thornton on labour and its claims. In *Collected works,* 5:631–68. Toronto.

———. [1871] 1965. *Principles of political economy*. New York.

Negishi, T. 1985. *Economic theories in a non-Walrasian tradition*. Cambridge.

———. 1986. Thornton's criticism of equilibrium theory and Mill. *HOPE* 18:567–77.

Newman, P. 1989. Review of Negishi's *Economic theories in a non-Walrasian tradition*. *Economic Studies Quarterly* 40:90–91.

Pasinetti, L. 1960. A mathematical formulation of the Ricardian system. *Review of Economic Studies* 27:78–98.

Thornton, W. T. 1869. *On labour: its wrongful claims and rightful dues, its actual present and possible future*. London.

———. 1870. *On labour: its wrongful claims and rightful dues, its actual present and possible future*. 2nd ed. London.

Takashi Negishi
Professeur à l'Université de Tokyo

F. D. Longe and Refutation of Classical Theory of Capital

F. D. Longe et la réfutation de la théorie classique du capital

F. D. Longe - Wages Fund Theory - Classical Theory of Capital

F. D. Longe - Théorie du fonds des salaires - Théorie classique du capital

Rev. écon. pol. 102 (6) nov.-déc. 1992

Summary. — Following our study on Mill and Thornton on the recantation of wages fund theory (*History of Political Economy* [1986]), this note aims to study *A Refutation of the Wages-Fund Theory* [1866] of F. D. Longe, who was the first to refute the theory, though he was ignored by both Thornton and Mill. It is found that all of his three reasons to refute wages fund theory are important and interesting from the point of view of the subsequent development of economic theory. But what is most significant is the fact that Longe refuted not only wages fund theory, a mere protective belt of classical research programme, but also the essence of the classical theory of capital that wages must be advanced by the capitalists, a part of the hard core of the programme which both Thornton and Mill did not refute.

Résumé. — *A la suite de notre étude de la* rétractation *de la théorie du fonds déterminé des salaires de Mill et Thornton (History of Political Economy* [1986]*), nous étudions ici* A Refutation of the Wages-Fund Theory *[1866] de F. D. Longe, qui fut le premier à rétracter la théorie du fonds des salaires, mais non reconnu par Mill et Thornton. Ce qui est important c'est que Longe réfute non seulement la théorie classique du fonds déterminé des salaires, qui n'est qu'une « protective belt » du « research programme » de l'école classique, mais aussi la théorie classique du capital (l'avance du fonds des salaires), qui est certainement le « hard core » du « research programme » classique et n'est pas réfuté par Mill et Thornton.*

1. The aim of this note is to do justice to Francis D. Longe [1831-1910], since we have elsewhere discussed W. T. Thornton's refutation of wages fund theory and J. S. Mill's recantation of it, but Longe was the first to refute the theory, though he was ignored by both Thornton and Mill (1). From our study of Longe's *A Refutation of the Wages-Fund Theory* [1866], we found that all of his three reasons to refute wages fund theory are important and interesting from the point of view of the subsequent development of economic theory. But what is most significant is the fact that Longe refuted not only wages fund theory, a mere protective belt of classical research programme, but also the essence of the classical theory of capital that wages must be advanced by capitalists, which forms a part of the hard core of the programme.

We explain in section (2) the problem of wages fund theory and its recantation in general. Section (3) and (4) are devoted to quotations from Longe. The significance of Longe's contribution is discussed in sections (5) and (6).

2. The wages fund theory, with which this note is concerned, is defined concisely by J. S. Mill. « Wages, like other things then, depend mainly upon the demand and supply of labour ; or, as it is often expressed, on the proportion between population and capital. By population is here meant the number only of the labouring class, or rather of those who work for hire ; and by capital only circulating capital, and not even the whole of that, but the part which is expended in the direct purchase of labour » (Mill [1909], p. 341).

_____

(1) See NEGISHI [1986] and [1989a], pp. 181-190.

It is important to see behind this simple statement a fundamental assumption of the classical economics that wages must be advanced by capitalists. According to Marshall, « the ordinary bargain between employers and employed is that the latter receives things ready for immediate use and the former receives help towards making things that will be of use hereafter. When anyone works for hire, his wages are, as a rule, advanced to him out of his employer's capital — advanced, that is, without waiting till the things which he is engaged in making are ready for use. These simple statements have been a good deal criticized, but they have never been denied by anyone who has taken them in the sense in which they were meant » (Marshall [1961], p. 823).

Marshall continues that « [t]he older economists, however, went on to say — that the total amount of wages that could be paid in a country in the course of, say a year, was a fixed sum. Those who have said this have perhaps thought of agricultural produce, which has but one harvest in the year. But this does not justify the statement that the amount of wages payable in a country is fixed by the capital in it, a doctrine which has been called « the vulgar form of the Wages fund theory » (Marshall [1961], p. 823).

In his famous recantation of the wages fund doctrine, Mill in 1869 clearly admitted that the wages fund is not a fixed amount. This was done in his review of Thornton [1869] by mistakingly interpreting the nature of an example which Thornton presented as the one of the trading at disequilibrium prices. Mill interpreted it, however, as an example of the case in which a fall of the price does not increase the demand and the demand is equalized to the given supply at infinitely many prices. Mill admitted that the labor market falls within one of such excepted cases, so that the wages fund cannot be a constant amount (2).

« [Mr. Thornton] supposed the case to be an exception to the rule, that demand increases with cheapness : and since this rule, though general, is not absolutely universal, he is scientifically right. If there is a part of the scale through which the price may vary without increasing or diminishing the demand, the whole of that portion of the scale may fulfill the condition of equality between and demand » (Mill [1967], p. 637).

« [The] employer does not buy labour for the pleasure of consuming it ; he buys it that he may profit by its productive powers, and he buys as much labour and no more as suffices to produce the quantity of his goods which he thinks he can sell to advantage. A fall of wages does not necessarily make him expect a larger sale for this commodity, nor, therefore, does it necessarily increase his demand for labour. Exist there any fixed amount which, and neither more nor less than which, is destined to be expended in wages ? Of course there is

---

(2) See NEGISHI [1986] and THORNTON [1870], pp. 57, 87.

an impassable limit to the amount which can be so expended ; it cannot exceed the aggregate means of the employing classes. It cannot come up to those means ; for the employers have also to maintain themselves and their families. But, short of this limit, it is not, in any sense of the word, a fixed amount » (Mill [1967], p. 644).

Three things are clear. Firstly, Mill did not deny the existence of the wages fund which is to be advanced by capitalists. He simply denied the assumption that it is fixed. Secondly, in spite of Thornton's criticism of equilibrium theory from the point of his disequilibrium theory, Mill maintained his equilibrium theory that all the laborers are employed at an equilibrium wage which, though not unique, clears the labor market. Finally, neither Thornton, nor Mill, did not mention the name of Longe.

3. Longe argued in 1866 against the wages fund theory for the following three reasons (Longe [1903], p. 27). (1) Because the capital applicable to the payment of the wages of labor does not consist of a definite fund destined for the purchase of labor. (2) Because the laboring population foes not constitute a supply of labor. (3) Because the supposition that wages fund would be all distributed among the laborers involved an erroneous notion of the demand and supply principle.

The first reason seems to be not so much that the wages fund is not fixed as that wages are, at least partly, independent of such a fund advanced by employers.

« The fallacy in the notion that the wages of productive labourers are limited by the amount of wealth or funds which are or can be employed as capital, consists in a confusion of these two founds : (1) the wealth or capital available for the *maintenance of labourers while employed in producing new goods or wealth ;* which wealth or capital may come either from their own resources of those of their employers, or be borrowed from bankers or elsewhere ; and (2) the amount of wealth available for *the purchase of their work,* which may consist of funds belonging to the consumers, or of funds belonging to the employer, or both, or may even be taken out of the very goods which the labourers produce, or their money value. It is by the amount of his latter fund that the wages of the labourer are limited, and not by the former, whether they are paid out of the employers' pre-existing capital or not » (Longe [1903], p. 47).

« The history of productive trade would not probably, afford a single instance where the order of nature was so reversed, that employers were in the habit of paying the wages of the labourers they hired before the labourers had completed the work, the price of which their wages represented. The funds out of which the laborer and his family are maintained from week to week are his own capital and not that of his employers, whether those funds consist of wages which have been paid to him by his employer on every preceding Saturday, or of money inherited from an ancestor » (Longe [1903], p. 47-48).

After quoted from Adam Smith that « [i]n all arts and manufactures the greater part of the workmen stand in need of a master to advance them the materials of their work, and their wages and maintenance till it be completed » (Smith [1976], p. 83), Longe argued as follows.

« As in Adam Smith's days, so now, the means by which the majority of workmen and their families are maintained consist of wages derived principally from the capital their employers have at their disposal prior to the sale of the work on which the workmen are engaged. But if we take a glance at the different industrial trade of this country, we shall see that the notion that the wages of such labourers are limited to the amount of their employers' capital, to which fund, according to the definition of capital given by Mr. Mill and Mr. Fawcett, the wage-fund accessible to such labouers is confined, is but little supported by the system on which these trade are conducted » (Longe [1903], p. 50).

4. As for the second reason to refute the wages fund theory, the following argument of Longe may be interesting.

« [B]oth Mr. Mill and Mr. Fawcett use the different expressions « supply of labour », « laboring class », « population » (meaning thereby labouring population), « those whose are anxious to labour », almost indiscriminantly, as if they were equivalents. An increase or diminution in the dependent population, or labouring classes of a country, is not necessarily accompanied by a corresponding increase or diminution in the labour or wealth-producing power of a country. There cannot be any greater error in a theory of political economy, than to confuse labour and population. A supply of labour is a supply of potential work, and every practical man knows that the quantity of work to be got from labourers is no more determined by their numbers, than the quantity of apples to be got from an orchard by the number of trees in it » (Longe [1903], p. 55-56).

« [A] true Political Economy would require the employer to study well the difference between cheap labour and low wages, a distinction which the false theory we have been considering entirely ignores. A true Political Economy would teach the employers of labour that the reduction of the wages of any class of labourers below a certain point, although it would enable them to employ more labourers for the same money, would be naturally accompanied by a decrease instead of an increase in the quantity of good work which they would get done for their money » (Longe [1903], p. 65).

Longe started the consideration of his third reason by the quotation of a passage from J. S. Mill on the analogy between the operation of competition on the price of goods and of labor (Mill [1909], p. 362). Mill argued that « wages can only be lowered by competition until room is made to admit all the labourers to a share in the distribution of the wages-fund. If they fell below this point, a portion of capital would remain unemployed for want of laborers ; a counter-competition would commence on the side of capitalists, and wages would rise ». Longe warned that this rise in wage does not assure the identical amount of total wages to be paid in comparison with the case in which the original equilibrium wages are paid to all the laborers.

« The fallacy in the above passage consists, not in treating a « demand » for labour and for goods as a definite sum, but in treating that sum, in the case of the « demand » for labour, as a sum which would all be spent in labour, notwithstanding the purchase of a part of the supply with a smaller portion of it than would represent the proper price of the part bought, as determined by the proportion between the whole supply and the money-measure of the original demand. Suppose the consumers of a commodity would give 10001. for a given supply, such sum would only represent the amount of money which they would give rather than go without it ; but if they or any of them could get any part of it at a price less than the assumed proportionate price, the money so saved, instead of going to increase the value of the residue, would be absolutely lost to the sellers. Mr. Mill's theory would require the lucky purchasers who got their goods too cheap to give the money thus saved to the other consumers, and that then their demand for or want of the remaining supply would be such as to induce them to pay the whole of the increased funds thus at their disposal in the purchase of that remaining part ; — a supposition which is simply absurd » (Longe [1903], p. 30).

« Although employers could, *ex hypothesi,* give the amount of wage-fund, there would be no cause whatever, according to the true theory of the demand and supply principle, to induce, much less compel, them to give one farthing more than the smallest quantity of wealth or money for which they could get the labourers to do the work they wanted. That is, the amount of the aggregate wage-fund, which would exist at any given time or during any given period, would have no bearing on the amount of wages to be obtained either by the whole body or by individual labourers » (Longe [1903], p. 37-38) (3).

5. Let us begin with the discussion of the third reason raised by Longe against wages fund theory. The argument of Longe quoted in the previous section clearly points out the difference between the equilibrium obtained by the intersection of the static demand and supply curves and the equilibrium to be reached by the law of supply and demand with exchanges at disequilibrium prices taking place. In the modern terminology, we may call the former tâtonnement equilibrium and the latter non-tâtonnement equilibrium. The difference is due to the shift of supply and demand curves caused by exchanges at

---

(3) Longe tried to make other comments on Mill's application of the theory of supply and demand, most of which are, unfortunately, making not much sense, at least to the present author.

disequilibrium prices (4). This point was further developed by Thornton ([1869], p. 47-53) who emphasized the importance of trade at disequilibrium prices. Since the wages fund theory clearly presupposes the tatonnement equilibrium, its relevancy should be doubted if one believes that the bulk of goods cannot be traded at equilibrium prices. In this respect, we have to admit that Longe in 1866 was a predecessor to Thornton in 1969. As we pointed out in Negishi [1986], however, Mill in 1871 recognized the problem, by citing Thornton [1870], but confined himself to the traditional equilibrium analysis and refrained himself from considering the new problems of disequilibrium economics (5).

Longe's argument concerning to his second reason to refute wages fund theory is also quoted in the previous section. It is very interesting, since it reminds us of the recent theory of efficiency wages (6). It is concerned, however, with the supply of labor and does not directly related to the concept of the wages fund which represents the demand for labor. Furthermore, Longe himself admitted that the short-run market wage is to be explained by the demand for labor, while his theory of wages suggested by his second reason against wages fund theory is concerned with wages as long-run cost prices of labor (Longe [1903], p. 69).

Finally, Longe's first reason to refute wages fund theory is concerned with the classical theory of capital that wages must be advanced by capitalists. In the classical theory of capital, wages fund constitutes, even though not exclusively, an important part of the capital of an economy. According to Say, for example, « [t]he human agent of industry must, besides, be provided with pre-existing products ; — 1. The tools and implements — 2. The products necessary for the subsistence of the industrious agent — 3. The raw materials — » (Say [1832], p. 11-12). « When the land-owner is himself the cultivator, he must posses a capital over and above the value of his land ; — Ploughs, and other farming implements and utensils, together with the animals employed in tillage — Finally, he must have stores of various kinds ; seeds for his grounds, provisions, fodder for his cattle, and food as well as money for his labourers' wages, — » (Say [1832], p. 48-49).

Although both fixed capital (like tools and implements) and wages fund are mentioned in such a descriptive explanation of capital, it is the wages fund which plays the leading role in a more theoretical model of classical economics. For example, in Pasinetti [1960]'s model of Ricardian economics, the production function of the wage good (corn) is, given the quality and quantity of land, $X_1 = f(N_1)$,

_____

(4) In spite of FORGET [1991], this problem of the path-dependence exists even if one is dealing with a particular market. See MARSHALL [1961], pp. 331-336.
(5) See MILL [1909], p. xxxi, DE MARCH [1988], EKELUND-THOMMESEN [1989], and NEGISHI [1989].
(6) See, for example, BLANCHARD-FISCHER [1989], p. 455.

where X_1 is the output and N_1 is the labor input, the production function of a luxury good is $X_2 = aN_2$, where X_2 and N_2 are the output and the labor input, and a is a given constant, and the labor population $N = N_1 + N_2$ must be supported by the given wages fund W (stock of corn) so that $wN = W$, where w is the rate of wage. The existence of fixed capital is completely ignored and only the wages fund is considered as the capital (7).

In his discussion of the first reason, Longe insisted that the existence of such wages fund is not necessary to pay wages to laborers. It is, then, to refuse not merely wages fund theory but also the classical theory of capital itself (8).

6. Classical economics and neo-classical economics after the marginal revolution share many common features, like the emphasis of the deductive method and equilibrium analysis, so that they may be considered as a single research programme in economics. There are, however, some important differences between them. For example, it is interesting to compare the definition of capital given by Say in the previous section with that of capital goods proper given by Walras.

« *[L]anded capital, personal capital* and *capital goods proper* yielding productive services, that is to say, items of income transformable into products through agriculture, industry or trade. Example of such landed capital are farm land, sites for office buildings, factories, workshop and warehouses ; examples of personal capital of this type are wage-earners, professional men, etc. ; and example of such capital goods proper are office buildings, factories, workshops, warehouses, fruit-bearing trees and crop plants, work animals, instruments and tools » (Walras [1954], p. 218).

Land (landed capital), labor (personal capital) and capital (capital goods proper) are symmetrically considered in the production and only the fixed capital is exemplified as capital proper. Wages fund emphasized in classical economics simply disappeared from the description of capital of an economy. Thus, in Solow [1956]'s miniature Walrasian model, the aggregate production function is $Y = F (L, K)$, where, Y, L and K signify output, labor and capital, with the existence of land ignored, and the rate of wage w is determined by $w = \partial F/\partial L$. Wages are not paid from wages fund advanced by capitalists. Labor shares output with capital by the marginal productivity principle. According to Longe as cited in section (3), « the amount of wealth available for *the purchase of their work* — may even be taken out of the very goods which the labourers produce, or their money value ».

_____

(7) In Marxian economics too, the variable capital (wages fund) is more important than the constant capital (depreciation of fixed capitals), since the only the former can produce surplus value to be exploited by capitalists. See NEGISHI [1989a], pp. 206-210.

(8) See TAUSSING [1896], pp. 241-244, and FUKAGAI [1992].

F. D. Longe and Refutation of Classical Theory of Capital _____ 923

We agree, therefore, with Eagly that « [f]or Walras, capital consisted narrowly of fixed capital ; *i.e.,* goods which enter production but are not used up in a single time period. Prior accumulation of the commodities which constituted variable capital was thus no longer required by economic theory. Accordingly, the responsibility formerlly assigned the capitalist class dropped from sight and received no further attention beyond the Austrian school. It was, in the other words, Walras's new definition of capital, not any recantation by John Stuart Mill, that killed the wages fund component of classical theory » (Eagle [1974], p. 7-8) (9).

As far as the first reason to refute wages fund theory is concerned, it is no wonder that the name of Longe was not mentioned by Thornton and J. S. Mill. They never dreamed to deny the existence of the wages fund itself. Whether it is a fixed amount or not was their concern. In this respect, Longe is the predecessor not to Thornton, but to Walras.

Bibliographie

BLANCHARD O. J. and FISCHER S. [1989], *Lecture on Macroeconomic,* MIT Press.

DE MARCH N. [1988], John Stuart Mill Interpretation Since Schumpeter, in *Classical Political Economy,* ed., by W. O. THWEATT, Kluwer.

EAGLE R. V. [1974], *The Structure of Classical Economic Theory,* Oxford University Press.

EKELUND R. B., Jr. and THOMMESEN S. [1989], Disequilibrium Theory and Thornton's Assault on the Laws of Supply and Demand, *History of Political Economy,* 21, p. 567-592.

FORGET E. L. [1991], MILL J. S., LONGE F. D. and THORNTON W. T., on Demand and Supply, *Journal of the History of Economic Thought,* 13, p. 205-221.

FUKAGAI Y. [1992], MILL J. S. no Keizaishakairon (Economic and Social Theory of J. S. Mill), in *J. S. Mill Kenkyu* (Studies on J. S. Mill), eds., by S. Sugihara, S. Yamasita and A. Koizumi, Ochanomizu-Shobo.

LONGE F. D. [1903], *A Refutation of the Wage-Fund Theory,* The Johns Hopkins Press.

MARSHALL A. [1909], *Principles of Economics,* I, Macmillan, 1961.

MILL J. S., *Principles of Political Economy,* Longmans, Green and Co.

MILL J. S. [1967], Thornton on Labour and Its Claim, in *Essays on Economics and Society,* Toronto University Press.

NEGISHI T. [1986], Thornton's Criticism od Equilibrium Theory and Mill *History of Political Economy,* 18, p. 567-577.

---

(9) Even in the case of Austrian school, their capital theory can be reconstructed in terms of fixed capital. See NEGISHI [1989a], pp. 297-307.

NEGISHI T. [1989], On Equilibrium and Disequilibrium, *History of Political economy,* 21, p. 593-600.
NEGISHI T. [1989a], *History of Economic Theory,* North-Holland.
PASINETTI L. L. [1960], A Mathematical Formulation of the Ricardian System, *Review of Economic Studies,* 27, pp. 78-98.
SAY J. B. [1932], *A Treatise on Political Economy,* tr. by C. R. PRINCEP, GRIGG and ELLIOT.
SOLOW R. M. [1956], A Contribution to the Theory of Economic Growth, *Quarterly Journal of Economics,* 70, pp. 65-94.
TAUSSIG F. W. [1896], *Wages and capital,* Appleton.
THORNTON W. T. [1869], *On Labour,* Macmillan.
THORNTON W. T. [1870], *On Labour,* Macmillan.
WALRAS L. [1954], *Elements of Pure Economics,* tr. by W. JAFFE, IRWIN.

9

Marx and Böhm-Bawerk in the Theory of Interest

T. Negishi

I. — INTRODUCTION

Böhm-Bawerk's *Karl Marx and the Close of his System* (1896) has been regarded as a criticism of Marxian theory of value so representative that "the arguments advanced by the others are either directly borrowed from Böhm-Bawerk or are variations on the same tune deserving no particular attention"[1]. As is well known, Böhm-Bawerk is mainly concerned here with two problems, i.e., whether labor or value in use should be a common factor of the same amount existing in the things exchanged and whether volume I and volume III *of Das Kapital* are contradictory. The first problem is rather a philosophical than a scientific one. We can accept, at least, as a working hypothesis that being products of abstract human labor is the common factor. The second problem is smartly cleared by Hilferding. There is no contradiction, since the theory of price in volume III aims to elucidate the actual exchange relations of commodities while the theory of value in volume I aims to show that the surplus value or the profit originates from production and not from circulation. Marxian price theory, properly modified, is not necessarily wrong under the assumed condition, though it may not be a most convenient theory to elucidate a given phenomenon. There are many phenomena which can be explained by Ptolemaic theory as well as by Copernican theory, though the former is very inconvenient.

---

[1] BOUDIN [4], 85.

The crux of Marxian labor theory of value is, therefore, to explain how and why the surplus value is created and exploited in the process of production. We can find the best argument against this part of Marxian theory, not in Böhm-Bawerk's *Close*, nor in his section on Marx in *Capital and Interest* (1884), but in his section on Rodbertus. Even though surplus value is produced by labor alone, it accrues only after the passage of time. Criticizing Rodbertus Böhm-Bawerk insists that there is no exploitation if workers do receive the entire present value of their future output which is smaller than the future value since the physically same goods located at different time points are not identical in view of the existence of time preference. The most important criticism of Marx given by Böhm-Bawerk is, therefore, concerned not so much with Marxian theory of price as with Marxian theory of interest, i.e., a refutation of exploitation theory of interest from the point of view of time preference theory of interest. Following Böhm-Bawerk, we shall argue that Marxian exploitation theory does not work even if there is no time preference and that the distinction of paid and unpaid labors and therefore the exploitation are nothing more than wishful definitions, have no real meaning, though they can be formal apparatus to explain the relative prices, and are not necessary to explain the origine of interest in the process of production.

II. — REAL AND MONETARY RATES OF INTEREST

The most important criticism of Marx given by Böhm-Bawerk is concerned with a problem of the theory of interest, i.e., the refutation of Marx's exploitation theory of interest from the point of view that interest is a premium attached to the present consumers' good when it is exchanged against the future consumers' good. Before to explain the details of this criticism, however, it is appropriate to consider first whether these rates of interest are real or monetary rates of interest.

In a neo-classical general equilibrium, real and monetary rates of interest are identical in the sense that money has no influence on the determination of the rate of interest. As a matter of fact, Walras introduced money in his system only at the final stage of the argument. The real rate of interest is already determined in his theory of credit and capital formation where money has not yet been introduced. Money is finally introduced in his theory of money and circulation only to determine the level of absolute prices. Under fairly plausible conditions, it can be seen that relative prices including the real rate of interest, determined in the theory of credit and capital formation, remain unchanged when money is introduced in the theory of money and circulation. This is the neutrality of money [2].

If real and monetary rates of interest differ, there is a general rise or fall of prices according as the real rate is higher or lower than the monetary one, as was argued by Wicksell (in terms of natural and market rates), Marshall and Fisher (in terms of effective and nominal rates), provided that prices are flexible. If prices including wage are downwardly rigid as in the Keynesian situation [3], the effective demand and therefore the employment fall short of the full employement level, if the real rate in the sense of the marginal efficiency of capital at the full employment is lower than the monetary rate of interest determined by the liquidity preference. In such disequilibrium situations in the sense of neo-classical equilibrium theory, certainly money does matter and real and monetary rates of interest differ. In a neo-classical equilibrium, however, it is not necessary to make a distinction between real and monetary rates of interest.

Böhm-Bawerk, being a typical and representative neo-classical economist, naturally believed that money does not play in the determination of the rate interest "any other role than that of a technical device that occasionally get out of order" [4]. He held a sort of quantity theory of money

---

[2] See NEGISHI [14], and MORISHIMA [11], 130, [13], chap. 11.
[3] For the explanation of Keynesian rigidity of prices, see NEGISHI [15], chap. 7-9.
[4] SCHUMPETER [17], 928.

which implies the neo-classical neutrality of money and his theory of interest runs all in terms of goods. For Böhm-Bawerk, there is no monetary rate of interest which is different from the real rate of interest, i.e., Kapitalzins.

The case with Marx is somewhat different. He considered the rate of interest as an essentially monetary phenomenon which is only weakly connected with the rate of profit in the sense that interest is a derived income from profit. The rate of profit determined by the rate of surplus value is considered to be independent of such monetary rate of interest[5]. This may reflect the fact that the relation between business activity and the loan market is, unlike in the case of neo-classical theory, not fully developed in the system of Marxian economics, which leads to the neglect of time element in the theory of capitalist production. Another difficulty Marxian economists have when they deal with the relation between real rate (rate of profit) and monetary rate (rate of interest) is their lack of the marginal or differential concepts with the result that there is no profit left if real and monetary rates are identical[6].

Even though the rate of profit and the monetary rate of interest are different in Marxian system, it is evident that the former is the essential concept in the Marxian theory of income distribution, i.e., the theory of capitalistic exploitation while the latter plays merely an auxiliary role having no influence to the former. It is, therefore, the Marxian theory of the rate of profit, ore more essentially that of the rate of surplus value, and not the Marxian theory of credit and menotary rate of interest which has been criticized by such neo-classical economists as Böhm-Bawerk and Schumpeter as the exploitation theory of interest.

---

[5] MARX [8], vol. III, chap. 21-23. See also BLAUG [1], 265. His quotation from MARX [8], vol. III, chap. 13 is, however, irrelevant, since it is concerned with the case of precapitalistic economy.

[6] It was impressive that Professor M. Takahashi, a noted Marxian economist and an economic adviser to Dr. Minobe, the former Governor of Tokyo, once criticized Keynes to the effect that there is no profit left for capitalists if the marginal efficiency of capital and the rate of interest are equal.

III. — THE ROLE OF VALUE THEORY

The rate of surplus value is, however, the crux of the theory of value in Marxian economics. The role of the theory of value in Marxian economics is, furthermore, different from the one expected by neo-classical economists. It is the confusion of these two roles of the value theory which explains why the critiques of Marx in the past were mostly unproductive.

The neo-classical economists expect the theory of value, whether it is the labor theory of value or not, to explain the ratio of exchange or relative prices in the exchange of goods against goods. In spite of the criticism of Marx given by neo-classical economists, it seems that Marxian labor theory of value scores fairly high for this role, if not merely the volume I of *Das Kapital*, but the volumes I and III are considered jointly and systematically. One should not consider, however, the volumes I and III separately, as did Böhm-Bawerk. The labor theory of value in the volume I to the effect that relative prices are porportional to the labor quantities embodied is to be considered as a theoretical hypothesis of the first approximation, which should be modified into the theory of prices of production in the volume III in view of the equalization of the rate of profit among sectors with different organic compositions of capital.

One cannot blame, firstly, the labor theory of value merely because it can only be applied to the case of products of labor. It is true, certainly, that not all the goods are labor products, though most of them are. A more general theory might be better, but not necessarily. A theory can be interesting and useful, even if the range of its application is somewhat restricted, provided it has interesting implications for and can give us a rich insight into the working of the economy. A special but interesting theory is better than a general but vacuous one. It is worthwhile, for example, to consider a special situation where relative prices are independent of demand. If the share of direct and indirect wage costs in the cost of production is 93 per cent[7], furthermore, it is quite natural to assume, for the starting theoretical hypothesis, that relative prices are proportional to the quantities of labor embodied.

The so-called Great Contradiction of Marx pointed out by Böhm-Bawerk is, secondly, derived from the interpretation of Marxian system to the effect that the first volume of *Das Kapital* as such is a complete theory of relative price which is different from another theory of relative prices given in the third volume. This interpretation is wrong, since Marx was well aware, as was insisted by Schumpeter[8], from an early stage of his thought that exchange ratios do not confirm to Ricardo's equilibrium theorem on value, i.e., they are proportional to the ratios of labor embodied. We cannot blame, however, Böhm-Bawerk since, as was admitted by Schumpeter, he could not see the *Theorien über den Mehrwert* in which the material indicating this recognition of Marx was published[9]. Volumes I and III should be considered as a single theory of relative prices, in which volume I is a first step to the final stage in volume III.

The bridge which connects these two volumes is the so-called transformation problem. It is the bridge between the system of embodied labor values and the rate of surplus value and the system of prices of production and the rate of profit. One cannot blame Marx, thirdly, on the ground that his own solution of the transformation problem was, as Marx admitted, not perfect. The problem was completely solved by later mathematical economists[10]. The case is somewhat similar to the case with Walrasian solution of the existence proof of a general equilibrium.

One might insist, finally, that to solve directly for the prices of production and the rate of profit is simpler and that Marxian way via labor values and the rate of surplus value is indirect and round-about. A simpler theory is, however, not necessarilly better than a more roundabout

[7] STIGLER [18], 326-342.
[8] SCHUMPETER [17], 597.
[9] See, however, BLAUG [1], 252.
[10] See, for example, MORISHIMA [12].

one, if the latter is with interesting implications. An example of such implications of transformation problem is that the rate of profit equals the rate of surplus value if the economy is on the von-Neumann equilibrium growth path or more generally that the rate of profit can be positive if and only if the rate of surplus value is positive [11].

Marxian theory of value including theory of prices of production is in this way not entirely a failure to explain the relative prices, though it may not be a convenient theory to elucidate the actual exchange relations of commodities. Marxian economists insist, however, that the role of value theory is not so much to elucidate such relations as to show how and why the surplus value or the profit is created and exploited, not in the process of circulation, but in the process of production. In other words, they insist that Marxian value theory should be considered not as the value theory in the sense of neo-classical economists but as a Kapitalzinstheorie, i.e., what neo-classical economists call the exploitation theory of interest. It is very ironical, however, that Marxian value theory fails completely as a theory of interest.

IV. — EXPLOITATION THEORY OF INTEREST

The exploitation theory of interest is based on the fundamental assumption of the capital theory of the classical economics to which Marx identified himself as the sole orthodox successor. The assumption is that the variable capital (food and necessaries, i.e., the wage goods) is advanced by capitalists to workers, which is quite in contrast to post-Walrasian neo-classical assumption that wage is paid out of current, not past, output. We may consider, as was pointed out by Eagly, that this is originally due to the time structure of production in the Quesnaysian model [12]. Capital must be advanced because there is a time lag between

---

[11] It is not worthwhile, on the other hand, to consider the case where relative values and prices are equalized.

[12] EAGLY [5].

4

input of labor and output of commodities and workers are stripped of any means of subsistence. By making a distinction between productive labor employed by capital advanced and unproductive labor employed by revenue, A. Smith clearly saw that commandable and embodied labors are identical and there is no surplus in the case of the output of the unproductive labor, since there is no time delay between labor input and service output.

In view of the reproduction schema developed in the second volume of *Das Kapital*, it is evident that Marx assumed the advancement of the variable capital by capitalists so as to support the reproduction of labor power in the household of workers. There is, however, a confusing statement in chapter 4, section 3 of the first volume to the effect that workers advance the use-value of labor power to capitalists. It is true, certainly, that weekly wages are paid at the end of the week and that workers sometimes lose their wage when the capitalist is bankrupt. Even so, it is the capitalists who advence on the average, in the sense that wages must be paid before the realization of the sale of output, though they are often paid after the consumption of the labor power. Otherwise the variable capital cannot claim to be taken into consideration along side with constant capital in the calculation of the average rate of profit in the third volume. There is also a same kind of statement in chapter 6, section 3 of the *Theorien über den Mehrwert*, in which Marx denied the advancement by capitalists to workers in the sense that wages are paid before the use of labor power. This does not deny, of course, the advancement in the sence that wages are paid before the realization of value of output, i.e., the labor embodied in the output [13].

To see the essence of the exploitation theory of interest, let us consider a simple case of an economy composed of labor power and wheat. Homogeneous land is assumed to exist infinitely, and the existence of constant capital is ignored, as was done by Marx in chapter 7, section 1 of the

---

[13] Marx also emphasized there that there can be no profit if capitalists advance merely constant capital. See also Marx [9], appendix 12.

first volume of *Das Kapital,* so as to make the story as
simple as possible. The only capital to be advanced is the
variable capital, to be paid in exchange for the labor power
to laborers who are stripped of any means of subsistence,
which takes the form of wheat, the sole output of the
economy. Exchanges are carried according to embodied labor
values and therefore the amount of the variable capital to be
advanced is given by the amount of wheat necessary to reproduce the labor power used up in the production. The period
of production is naturally one year and the harvest of new
wheat is one year later than the first payment of wheat
wage from the capitalists' stock of wheat accumulated from
past harvests. Now because of the peculiar property of
labor power to be the source of surplus value, the amount
of output of new wheat is larger than the amount of wheat
advanced as the variable capital. This difference is called
surplus product and the ratio of the surplus product to the
variable capital is defined as the rate of surplus value or the
rate of exploitation. Since exchanges are made according
to values, this surplus and exploitation originates, not from
circulation, but from production. The whole product is a
labor product, but only a part of its embodied labor value
corresponding to the advanced variable capital is paid, while
the rest corresponding to surplus product is unpaid and
exploited by the capitalists.

If the new wheat harvested at the end of the production
period and the old wheat advanced by capitalists to laborers
are identical, not only physically, but also socially and
economically, the exploitation theory makes a sense and
there is no objection to it. The new wheat and old wheat
are, however, dated differently and there is no assurance
that they are identical in their relations to capitalists and
laborers. When the old wheat is advanced, it might be
very scarce while new wheat is not yet available until it is
redundunt. Unless they are identical, there is no guarantee
to be able to compare the physical amount of new and old
wheats and to talk about the surplus and exploitation. It
is of no use in this respect merely to translate physical
amount of wheat into expressions in terms of money, abs-

tract human labor or anything else. Since there can be no
labor movement between different time periods, embodied
labors cannot be used to compare the value of commodities
differently dated. Embodied labor cannot be a measure of
value, unless labor can freely move between different sectors
of production. Since Marx did not offer any plausible argument that present and future goods physically identical are
also identical, socially and economically, the exploitation
theory remains incomplete as a theory of interest.

V. — BÖHM-BAWERK AND HILFERDING

Böhm-Bawerk [2] attacked the exploitation theory of
interest of Rodbertus on the ground that the future and
present goods are wrongly considered identical and stated
that the same argument can be applied to the theory of
Marx [14]. He considered the following example.

Suppose a single worker spend five years to complete
independently a steam engine from the beggining, which
commands, when completed, a price of $ 5,500. There is
no objection to give him the whole steam engine or $ 5,500
as the wage for five years' continuous labor. But when?
Obviously it must be at the expiration of five years. It is
impossible for him to have the steam engine before it is in
existence. He cannot receive the steam engine valued at
$ 5,500 and created by him alone, before he has created it.
His compensation is the whole future value at a future time.

But the worker having no means of subsistence cannot
and will not wait until his product has been fully completed.
Suppose our worker wishes, after the expiration of the first
year, to receive a corresponding partial compensation. The
worker should get all that he has labored to produce up to
this point, say, a pile of unfinished ore, or of iron, or of
steel material, or the full exchange value which this pile of
material has now. The question is how large will that
value be in relation to the price of the finished engine, $ 5,500.

[14] BÖHM-BAWERK [2], 263-65.

Can it be $ 1,100, since the worker has up to this time performed one-fifth of the work?

Böhm-Bawerk said "No". One thousand one hundred dollars is one-fifth of the price of a completed, present steam engine, which is different from what the worker has produced in the first year, i.e., one-fifth of an engine which will not be finished for another four years. The former fifth has a value different from that of the latter fifth, in so far as a complete present machine has a different value from that of an engine that will not be available for another four years. Our worker at the end of a year's work on the steam engine that will be finished in another four years has not yet earned the entire value of one-fifth of a completed engine, but something smaller than it. Assuming a prevailing interest rate of 5%, Böhm-Bawerk concluded that our worker should get the product of the first year's labor which is worth about $ 1,000 at the end of the first year.

By using this example, Böhm-Bawerk criticized Rodbertus and Marx who insisted, ignoring wrongly the difference between present and future goods, that there is exploitation unless worker do receive the entire future (not the present) value of his product now (not in the future) though it is available only in the future. Unfortunately, Böhm-Bawerk developed this criticism mainly in his section on Rodbertus in [2], and did not repeat it sufficiently in his section on Marx in [2], nor in [3]. This might be the reason why there seems to be no rejoinder from Marxian economists to this most important critical comment on the value theory of Marx. It is natural that Hilferding's famous rejoinder [6] to Böhm-Bawerk [3] merely emphasized the significance of value theory as the exploitation theory and did not touch the problem of the difference of present and future goods.

In [3] Böhm-Bawerk referred to this problem only when he discussed the theory of value in the pre-capitalistic conditions. According to Marx, prices were in accordance with the embodied labor values under simple commodity production in which each worker has his own means of production and subsistence. Böhm-Bawerk criticized that, in exchanges in accordance with value, workers whose products require longer years to be completed are unfavorable in comparison with other workers whose products need not much time and that prices diverge from values as a result of the movement of workers between occupations. Hilferding considered that the crux of this comment lies not so much in the problem of the time required in production as in the problem of simple commodity production. Therefore, he even argued that workers are not so free to move between occupations under simple commodity production. Hilferding misunderstood, furthermore, the point of Böhm-Bawerk's comment and argued that also the workers whose products require not much time have to wait, after the completion of their works, the completion of products of other party, which require longer years. This is, of course, not the case with Böhm-Bawerk. Böhm-Bawerk considered the exchange of two products which are completed at the same time but required different length of period to be completed. It is very unfortunate that by such a funny misunderstanding Hilferding was robbed of the opportunity to make his rejoinder, if any, to Böhm-Bawerk's most important and serious comment [15].

It seems that Böhm-Bawerk assume the existence of the interest due to time preference to argue the difference of physically identical goods located at different time points. This might sound, at least to Marxists, a circular reasoning, since the exploitation theory of interest is denied by the assumption of the theory of interest which is, unlike the exploitation theory, not based on the process of production but on the irrational psychology of consumers. Even so, it is Marxian economists who are responsible to show that there is no difference between the identical goods located at different time points to vindicate the exploitation theory of interest.

---

[15] Böhm-Bawerk [3], 42-45, and Hilferding [6], 166-168.

VI. — STATIONARY STATE OR SIMPLE REPRODUCTION AND INTEREST

Marxian exploitation theory of interest does not work, if present and future goods are not identical. They are, of course, not identical in general, but there is a special situation where they are identical. If Marxian exploitation theory can work in such a special situation, we have to admit that Marxian theory is not entirely a failure as an interest theory. Such a special situation conceivable is a stationary state or what Marxian calls simple reproduction. In every period, exactly identical activitities are repeated, individually and aggregately, in production, distribution and consumption. In such a state, then, physically identical goods, even though dated differently, have exactly identical relations to all other goods as well as to all the agents, i.e., workers, capitalists, consumers, etc. in the economy. Physically identical goods are economically and socially identical, whether they are currently available or available in the future. We can compare the physical amount of a good currently produced and that of the same good advanced in the past and talk about surplus, exploitation and so on. In other words, what Schumpeter called synchronization is possible in a stationary state. We can consider as if output and input are simultaneous even if output is delayed from input. Marxian concepts of exploitation are effective now.

Very unfortunately, however, the rate of interest is zero in a stationary state, as was emphasized by Schumpeter [16] [16]. Rate of surplus and that of exploitation are all zero, though they are perfectly effective concepts. Marxian theory is right only in trivial sense.

Let us explain the zero rate of interest in a stationary economy in terms of Marxian simple reproduction schema. The economy is divided into two departments, department 1 being capital goods industry and department 2, consumers' goods industry. Gross output y_i of department i is decomposed into the constant capital c_i (corresponding to the replacement of depreciated capital goods), the variable capital v_i

[16] See also KUENNE [7], 275-79.

(corresponding to the replacement of advanced wage funds) and the surplus m_i, i.e.,

(1) $y_1 = c_1 + v_1 + m_1$

(2) $y_2 = c_2 + v_2 + m_2$

The condition for the simple reproduction is

(3) $c_2 = v_1 + m_1$

where all items are measured in terms of either value or money. From (1) and (3), we have

(4) $y_1 = c_1 + c_2,$

i.e., the production of new capital goods is just sufficient to replace the depreciation of stocks, while surplus values are assumed to be consumed and not saved at all. There are no net additions to constant and variable capitals. Every economic variable repeats, therefore, the same values in each period. In the numerical example given by Marx, m_i's are not zero and therefore the rate of surplus value (m_i/v_i) and that of profit $(m_i/(c_i + v_i))$ are not zero [17].

If capitalists are rational, however, Mar'x numerical example is wrong. We can safely assume that the level of consumption of capitalists is well above the level sufficient to reproduce their functions including overseeing labor, the reproduction of which should be financed by a sort of wage, and that they can save if they wish to do so. Since the level of consumption as well as the social milieu around themselves are unchanged, the marginal rate of substitution between consumptions in different periods is one for capitalists in a stationary state. They are indifferent, roughly speaking, if the current consumption is reduced by one small unit (in terms of either value or money) and the consumption is increased by the same amount in a future period. The positive rate of profit permits, however, that one can increase his consumption in future more than he reduces his consumption currently. If the rate of profit is positive in the simple

[17] MARX [8], vol. II, chap. 20.

reproduction, therefore, rational capitalists do save to increase their satisfaction in the long run and the simple reproduction cannot be maintained as a result of capital accumulation.

Capitalists might not save and there can be a positive interest in the simple reproduction if capitalists are irrational with a myopia to underevaluate the future, which Böhm-Bawerk held as a general characteristic of normal man. Such a psychological explanation of the positive rate of interest is, however, the last thing on which Marx would like to depend. The simple reproduction schema with positive rate of surplus value is, therefore, not a logically consistent system to be used as a model, however abstract, of a capitalistic economy, though it can be considered merely as a provisional step toward the expanded reproduction schema. In the latter schema, however, the concepts of exploitation do not work, since there is no assurance that present and future goods are identical.

Incidentally, it is interesting to note that there is a rent but no profit in a stationary state of Quesnay's *Tableau economique*, which Marx considered as a pioneer to his reproduction schema. Whatever reason Quesnay had in mind to explain zero rate of profit, it seems that Quesnay can stand, at least formerly, neo-classical examination more easily than Marx.

VII. — Economic Growth, Scarcity and Interest

While Quesnay denied the existence of profit in *Tableau economique*, A. Smith introduced the positive profit into his theoretical system in the *Wealth of Nations*. It is important to note that Smith did it only in the case of a growing economy. In a growing economy we can develop a theory of interest which elucidates how the profit originates not from circulation but from production, without having recourse neither to the exploitation nor to the time preference. A compensation given to any factor of production over its reproduction cost is due to its scarcity in the process of production. While the rent is due to the absolute scarcity of land as a primary factor of production, the profit is due to a temporary scarcity of capital as a produced means of production in a growing economy. In a growing economy, present goods are always relatively scarce in comparison with future goods. The rate of interest is a premium attached to present goods whose supply is limited in comparison to its availability in the future. The profit is a compensation to the advancement of such scarce goods in exchange for the less scarce goods which are physically identical but dated later.

The relation between growth and interest can best be seen in von-Neumann balanced growth path [18]. In the case of two department model of reproduction given in the above, the price determining equations are

(4) $p_1 = (1 + r) (p_1 A_1 + w L_1)$

and

(5) $p_2 = (1 + r) (p_1 A_2 + w L_2)$

where p_1, p_2, w, A_1, A_2, L_1 and L_2 are respectively the price of the capital goods, the price of the consumers' goods, the rate of wage, the input coefficients of the capital goods and the input coefficients of the labor. Real wage w/p_2 is given from the reproduction cost of labor power. In view of Frobenius theorem on a positive matrix

$$N = \begin{bmatrix} A_1 & A_2 \\ w L_1/p_2 & w L_2/p_2 \end{bmatrix},$$

$p = (p_1, p_2) > 0$ is an eigen vector which corresponds to the Frobenius root $(1 + r) > 0$ of N'. A dual system to (4) and (5) is

(6) $y_1/(1 + g) = A_1 y_1 + A_2 y_2$

(7) $y_2/(1 + g) = w L_1 y_1/p_2 + w L_2 y_2/p_2$

[18] See, e.g., MORISHIMA [10], chap. 5.

where y_1, y_2 and g can be interpreted as the current output of capital goods, that of consumers' goods and the maximum potential rate of growth, since the left-hand side signifies the last year's output (supply) while the right-hand side, current demand when capitalists do not consume. It is easy to see $(1 + g) > 0$ is the Frobenius root of N and therefore $g = r$.

If g is higher, present goods are more scarce relative to future goods and therefore r is higher. The real rate of growth attained when capitalists do consume is lower than g. We showed, however, that real growth rate cannot be zero if $g = r > 0$. The real rate of growth may depends on the time preference of the capitalists, but the rate of interest and the rate of potential growth are determined solely by the technical input coefficients (and the reproduction cost of labor power) in the process of production.

From the point of view of our interest theory, Marxian exploitation theory is most extraordinary and implausible with concepts defined in quite unusual ways. We attributed value productivity in the sense of surplus over reproduction cost to factors of production which are scarce, while Marx refuted to attribute value productivity (not physical productivity) to capital and land and attributed it entirely to labor power. In view of the existence of the reserved army of industry, i.e., unemployed workers, however, labor power is by no means scarce and can be obtained as much as one like at the subsistence wage in Marxian economic system[19]. One can define, of course, theoretical concepts in unusual ways, which are against common sense, for the purpose of theoretical hypothesis and no one can blame him for doing so, as far as the derived results are interesting, as in the case of Marxian value theory to explain relative prices. What one should not do is, however, to interpret such unusually defined concepts, or let them interpreted, in usual ways, unless his purpose is not science but propaganda. Exploitation, paid labor, unpaid labor, etc. defined in Marxian

[19] In this respect, Quesnay who attributed surplus entirely to land makes more sense than Marx. See SCHUMPETER [17], 238.

ways are useful concepts for Marxian theory of relative price, but they are quite confusing if one wishes to use them to elucidate how the profit originates in the process of production.

REFERENCES

[1] BLAUG (M.), *Economic Theory in Retrospect*, Irwin, 1962.

[2] BÖHM-BAWERK (E.V.), *Capital and Interest*, The History and Critique of Interest Theories, Huncke and Semholz tr., Libertarian, 1959.

[3] BÖHM-BAWERK (E.V.), *Karl Marx and the Close of his System*, Sweezy ed., Kelly, 1966.

[4] BOUDIN (L.B.), *The Theoretical System of Karl Marx*, 1907.

[5] EAGLY (R.V.), *The Structure of Classical Economic Theory*, Oxford, 1974.

[6] HILFERDING (R.), "Böhm-Bawerk's Marx-Kritik", in [3].

[7] KUENNE (R.E.), *The Theory of General Economic Equilibrium*, Princeton, 1963.

[8] MARX (K), *Das Kapital*.

[9] MARX (K), G. *Theorien über den Mehrwert*, 1 Teil, Dietz Verlag, 1956.

[10] MORISHIMA (M.), *Equilibrium Stability and Growth*, Oxford, 1964.

[11] MORISHIMA (M.), *Theory of Demand*, Oxford, 1973.

[12] MORISHIMA (M.), *Marx'x Economics*, Cambridge, 1973.

[13] MORISHIMA (M.), *Walras' Economics*, Cambridge, 1977.

[14] NEGISHI (T.), "Money in Walrasian General Equilibrium Theory", *Economie Appliquee*, XXX (1977), 599-615.

[15] NEGISHI (T.), *Microeconomic Foundations of Keynesian Macroeconomics*, North Holland, 1979.

[16] SCHUMPETER (J.A.), *Theorie der Wirtschaftlichen Entwicklung*, 1926.

[17] SCHUMPETER (J.A.), *History of Economic Analysis*, Oxford, 1954.

[18] STIGLER (G.J.), *Essays in the History of Economics*, Chicago, 1965.

10

The Economic Studies Quarterly

Vol. 37   March 1986   No. 1

MARX AND BÖHM-BAWERK

By TAKASHI NEGISHI*

1.

In his *Marx's Economics* (1973), Morishima introduced our Association to the economists in the world as the one of non-Marxists in opposition to Keizai Riron Gakkai (Japan Society of Political Economy) formed by Marxian economists. It is not correct, however, if you think that our Association has nothing to do with Marxian economics. Having longer history than the latter association, we had once many Marxian economists as members and still have some very eminent ones, particularly those mathematically minded ones, let alone those of us who are critically interested in Marxian economics. If you call our Association non-Marxist because many of those interested in Marx are critical, you should also call us non-neo-classical, since nowadays many of us are critical to neo-classical economics. We are non-Marxists only in the same sense that we are non-neo-classical economists. Furthermore, according to Bronfenbrenner, every Japanese economists knows elementary Marxism while many anti-Marxists in America refuse to learn anything about it. These facts may justify my attempt to start with Marx's theory of exploitation.[1]

2.

In *Capital* (1867–94) and *Theories of Surplus Value* (1905–10) Marx insisted two different types of exploitation. The first one is, of course, the exploitation of labor by capital in the case of equal labor quantity exchange, while the second is the exploitation of poor countries by rich ones through unequal labor quantity exchanges.

In Chapter 1, Volume 1 of *Capital*, Marx argued that commodities, say, a coat and 10 yards of

---

* The manuscript for the presidential address of Japan Association of Economics and Econometrics (Riron-Keiryo Keizai Gakkai), delivered in Japanese at Tohoku University (Sendai, Japan) on September 22, 1985. This is supported by a Grant-in-Aid for Scientific Research of the Ministry of Education, Science and Culture.

1) Morishima [11], p. 1, and Bronfenbrenner [5].

T. Negishi: Marx and Böhm-Bawerk

linnen, are exchanged according to the values, *i.e.,* the embodied quantities of labor, by reducing tailoring and weaving labors into the abstract human labor.[2]   This is possible if and only if the labor is perfectly mobile between tailoring and weaving.   Otherwise, we cannot compare tailoring labor with weaving labor easily, and in general it is not true that commodities are exchanged according to the embodied quantities of respective labors.

Suppose laborers are stripped of any means of subsistence and capitalists have to advance wages which correspond to the value of labor power, *i.e.,* "the value of the means of subsistence necessary for the maintenance of the labourer."[3]   Can we say that capitalists exploit laborers on the ground that the value of labor products produced by the hired laborers is larger than the value of labor power which is paid by capitalists?   Such a statement can be made if and only if the labor embodied in the labor products in question and the labor embodied in the means of subsistence bought by laborers with wages are reduced into the homogeneous abstract human labor.

These two labors are, however, differently dated, since the latter labor is the past labor already expended when the former is going to be expended.   Except for the world of science fictions, labor is not perfectly mobile through time, since we cannot use the future labor in the present. Differently dated labors cannot be reduced into the abstract humen labor.   Unless all the productions are instantaneous or wages need not be advanced by capitalists, therefore, we cannot accept Marxian statement of the first type of exploitation easily.

This is essentially the point raised by Böhm-Bawerk against Marx, not in his famous *Karl Marx and the Close of His System* (1896) but in his criticism of the exploitation theory of interest in *Capital and Interest, The History and Critique of Interest Theories* (1884).   Böhm-Bawerk attacked the exploitation theory of interest of Rodbertus on the ground that future and present goods are wrongly considered identical and stated that the same argument can be applied to the theory of Marx.   Even though surplus value is produced by labor alone, it accrues only after the passage of time.   There is no exploitation if workers do receive at present the entire present value of their future output which is smaller than the future value since the physically same goods located at different time points are not identical in view of the existence of the rate of interest.[4]

One may rightly argue that the physically same but differently dated goods can be regarded identical in a stationary state which Marxians call a simple reproduction, since exactly identical activities are repeated in every period and inputs and outputs can be synchronized in spite of the period of production.   Since Marx assumes the subsistence wage just sufficient to reproduce labor power so that laborers remain laborers and cannot become capitalists, capitalists have to be assumed to remain capitalists forever.   Stationary state is possible, then, if and only if capitalists consume whole profit and keep their capital unchanged.   Since the level of consumption as well as the social milieu around themselves are unchanged, the marginal rate of substitution between

---

2) Marx [9], pp. 50–51.

3) Marx [9], p. 167.   It is interesting to see that Smith's definition of the natural rate of wage is different from the natural price of labor of Ricardo and from Marx's value of labor power.   Smith recognized positive relations among growth, wages and profit, and had the concept of human capital.   Smith [18], pp. 72, 91, 118, 282, Ricardo [15], p. 93, Spengler [19] and Negishi [14], Chapter 1.

4) Böhm-Bawerk [2], pp. 263–265.   See for the details, Negishi [13], Chapter 7.   We owe invaluable suggestions to Professor Masayuki Iwata of Chiba University.

consumptions in different periods is equal to 1 for rational capitalists who do not underevaluate the future wants. If the rate of profit is positive, however, they can increase their consumption in future more than what they reduce in their consumption today by saving and investing their profit. Stationary state cannot be maintained, unless the rate of profit is zero and there is no exploitation.

Some Marxian economists may wrongly hope that the physically same but differently dated goods can be regarded identical in a von-Neumann-like balanced growth path where relative prices and relative quantities remain unchanged. Consider a simple Ricardo-like model of an economy composed of labor and wheat only. Homogeneous land is assumed to exist infinitely, and the existence of constant capital is ignored. The only capital to be advanced is the variable capital in the form of wheat, to be paid to laborers who produce wheat. Suppose the rate of profit is 100 per cent and all the profit is reinvested so that the rate of growth is also 100 per cent. A bushel of wheat in 1983 grows into 4 bushels in 1985 while a bushel in 1984 grows only to 2 bushels in 1985. To regard 1983 wheat and 1984 wheat identical means to make 4 bushels of wheat identical to 2 bushels of wheat in 1985.

Comparing output of wheat in 1985 and wheat wages paid in 1984, Marx would not discount the former and insist that the rate of exploitation is 100 per cent, while Böhm-Bawerk would discount the former by the rate of profit (100 per cent) and conclude that there is no exploitation at all. There seems to be no reason that Marx is right and Böhm-Bawerk is wrong.[5]

3.

As for the second type of exploitation, Marx argued that the richer country with higher productivity and higher money (not real) wages exploits the poorer one with lower productivity and lower money wages in the sense that three days of labor of the latter country are exchanged against one of the former country.[6] How can Marx make such a statement? Here Marx is implicitly assuming that labor of different countries are identical. Since labor is not mobile between countries, this assumption cannot, in general, be justified. Unlike in the case of the immobility through time that the future goods cannot be consumed in the present, however, at least traded goods are internationally mobile between countries. We may argue, therefore, that physically identical labor, *i.e.,* labor with the same intensity, equally trained, of different countries are socially and economically identical, if the quantities of internationally traded goods directly and indirectly necessary to reproduce the labor power are identical between countries.

Let us construct a simple model of a two country three goods economy. The first good is a

---

5) This simple model generates, furthermore, two additional difficulties with Marx. Since wheat and labor are symmetric in the model, we can define embodied wheat values, in terms of which there is no surplus value in the wheat production but there appears a surplus value in the production of labor power. This suggests that exploitation of the first type in the sense of Marx is merely a problem of definition. If there is no industrial reserve army, secondly, there is no balanced growth if wages are at subsistence level corresponding to reproduction of labor power expended in the production of wheat (Negishi [14], Chapter 1). Introduction of reserve army generates, however, the difficulty that relative quantities do not remain unchanged, let alone the problem that excess labor supply is inconsistent with exchanges according to values (see Negishi [13], Chapter 7).

6) Marx [9], p. 525 and [10], pp. 105–106.

T. Negishi: Marx and Böhm-Bawerk

non-wage good and the last two goods are wage goods while the first two goods are internationally tradable and the last good is a local or non-traded good. By taking units properly, we can assume that the unit of the labor power can be reproduced by the consumption of a unit of the second good and of a unit of the third good. By choosing the first good as numeraire, we denote the price of the second good, that of the third good in the first country, and that of the third good in the second country by p, w, and v, respectively. Finally, let us denote by a_{ij} the quantity of labor necessary to produce a unit of the j-th good in the i-th country and assume that the first country has the comparative advantage in the first good, i.e., $a_{11}/a_{12} < a_{21}/a_{22}$.

The price-cost equations are

(1) $1 = (1 + r)a_{11}(w + p)$

(2) $p = (1 + s)a_{22}(v + p)$

(3) $w = (1 + r)a_{13}(w + p)$

(4) $v = (1 + s)a_{23}(v + p)$

where r and s are rate of profit in the first and second countries, respectively. The first and the third goods are produced in the first country where the rate of wage is $w + p$ while the second and the third goods are produced in the second country where the rate of wage is $v + p$.

Let us denote by x_i the quantity of the second good directly and indirectly necessary to reproduce one unit of labor power in the i-th country and by y_i the quantity of the second good directly and indirectly necessary to produce one unit of the third good in the i-th country. Since one unit of labor power can be reproduced by the consumption of one unit of the second and the third goods,

(5) $x_i = 1 + y_i$, $i = 1, 2$.

Since the input of a_{i3} labor is necessary to produce one unit of the third good in the i-th country,

(6) $y_i = a_{i3} + a_{i3}y_i$, $i = 1, 2$.

Since we must have $x_1 = x_2$, to make the labor in different countries identical, we see $a_{13} = a_{23}$ by solving x_i from (5) and (6).

Without losing the generality, let us suppose that the second country is the richer one, with higher productivity, i.e., $a_{11} > a_{21}$ and $a_{12} > a_{22}$. Then we have

(7) $p \geq a_{22}/a_{21} > a_{22}/a_{11}$

since

(8) $a_{22}/a_{21} \leq p \leq a_{12}/a_{11}$

from the principle of comparative costs.

Between two countries, p units of the first good, which contains pa_{11} units of labor of the first country are exchanged against one unit of the second good, which contains a_{22} units of labor of the second country. Therefore, $p > a_{22}/a_{11}$ implies that the second, the richer country exploits the first, the poorer country. Since real wages are identical between countries, it is the rate of profit that is higher in the richer country. In other words, capitalists exploit capitalists.

Since $a_{13} = a_{23}$, we have from (1)~(4)

(9) $p = a_{22}v/a_{11}w$.

In view of (7), therefore, this implies that $v > w$. The money wage is, as Marx argued, higher in the richer country, since we can assume that the gold is (a part of) the first good. In other words, the value of money (gold) is lower in the richer country than in the poorer country, since it is

The Economic Studies Quarterly

a_{22}/p in the former, depending on the value (not physical) productivity of its export industry, while it is a_{11} in the latter, and $p > a_{22}/a_{11}$.[7]

We can accept, therefore, Marx's theory of international value, which unfortunately Marx could not develop fully, though we agree Böhm-Bawerk that Marx's exploitation theory of interest does not make sense.

4.

Böhm-Bawerk, who rejected the exploitation theory of interest, adduced three causes of the existence of interest, Kapitalzins, in *Capital and Interest, Positive Theory of Capital* (1889). They are (1) better provision for wants expected in the future than in the present, (2) undervaluation of future wants, and (3) the superiority of more roundabout or more protracted method of production.[8] It is interesting to see why a positive rate of interest is possible in a stationary state, since modern theories of economic growth suggest positive relations between the rate of growth and the rate of interest.

In view of his detailed exposition by the use of numerical examples,[9] it is clear that Böhm-Bawerk put the utmost emphasis on the third cause, *i.e.*, the superiority of roundabout production. It merely explains, however, that the capital or saving is demanded even if the rate of interest is positive. To assure that the equilibrium rate of interest is positive, it has also to be explained that the supply of capital or saving requires a positive rate of interest. This can be explained independently either by the first cause, *i.e.*, the better provision of future wants or by the second cause, *i.e.*, the undervaluation of future wants. While the recent theories of capital and interest rely too heavily on the second cause,[10] it should be noted that the third cause, which Böhm-Bawerk emphasized, can explain a positive rate of interest without the help of the second cause, since the third cause itself generates and works through the first cause, as Böhm-Bawerk admitted in the controversy with Fisher and Bortkiewicz.[11]

As was already pointed out by Arvidsson, of course, the consideration of the first cause in a stationary state requires a life-cycle model in which an individual lives for a finite period, has rising consumption through time, and consumes his life-income in his lifetime.[12] Elsewhere, therefore, I tried to explain a positive rate of interest on the basis of the first and third causes by constructing a stationary two period life-cycle model in which younger savers can have larger consumption when they are old.[13] This is possible, since, unlike Marx, we do not assume the subsistence wage. The result was, however, quite unsatisfactory, partly because it is difficult to

---

7) See for the details, Negishi [14], Chapter 7. We owe invaluable suggestions to Professors Etsuji Kinoshita of Kyushu University and Shigehiro Naruse of Kanagawa University. For Japanese studies on international value, see Naruse [12].

8) Böhm-Bawerk [3], pp. 259-289, especially p. 283.

9) Böhm-Bawerk [3], pp. 356-358.

10) See Hirshleifer [7]. We are grateful to Mr. Toshihide Mizuno of Kobe Commercial College for useful discussions.

11) Böhm-Bawerk [4], pp. 192-193.

12) See Arvidsson [1]. We are indebted to Professors G. O. Orosel of University of Vienna and M. Faber of University of Heidelberg for useful suggestions.

13) Negishi [13], Chapter 9.

T. Negishi: Marx and Böhm-Bawerk

combine a life-cycle model of the first cause with the circulating capital model à la Wicksell of the third cause in terms of the period of production, without introducing the second cause.

Actually Böhm-Bawerk had two models of the third cause, *i.e.*, the model of the circulating capital which he explained by his numerical examples and was later formulated into a mathematical model by Wicksell,[14] and the model of the fixed capital for which Böhm-Bawerk gave some examples like a boat and net in fishing and a sewing machine in tailoring.[15]

In the circulating capital model, the third cause of interest, *i.e.*, the superiority of the roundabout method of production implies that the labor productivity is an increasing function of the period of production, *i.e.*,

(10) $Y = f(t)L, \qquad f'(t) > 0,$

where Y is the volume of output of a consumers' good, L is labor input and t is the time interval between Y and L, *i.e.*, the period of production. Wages have to be advanced at the time of labor input since laborers are stripped of any means of subsistence, though wages can be higher than the subsistence level so that capital can be accumulated. Capital in this model is heterogeneous, composed of past labor inputs of different dates or of semi-finished goods of different stages, and its value is

(11) $K = \sum_{s=0}^{s=t-1} w\bar{L}(1 + r)^s$

where w, r and $\bar{L}$ denote respectively the rate of wage, the rate of interest, and the given total supply of labor.

Since the maximization of r with respect to t gives

(12) $f(t)/f(t - 1) \geq 1 + r \geq f(t + 1)/f(t),$

$r > 0$ in a stationary state, provided that $t \geq 1$. The latter condition is assured in our life-cycle model. If t is not shorter than the life-span of individuals, however, the value of existing capital is larger than the value of the saving made in the past by the retired generation in the present. In a stationary state an individual cannot dissave all his capital at the end of his life but must leave the capital to the next generation, the value of which is equal to that of what he inherited at the beginning of his life. The problem of the bequest and inheritance makes it difficult to avoid the existence of the second cause of the interest.[16]

In the case of the fixed capital model, the more roundabout method of production implies higher capital-labor-ratio, as in the examples of the use of a boat and net in fishing and of a sewing machine in tailoring.[17] If we assume away the durability aspect of fixed capital and suppose that the life-span of capital goods is given and shorter than the life-span of individuals, we can get rid of the problem of inheritance of capital, and therefore, that of the second cause so as to show the positive rate of interest on the ground of the first and the third causes only. The superiority of more roundabout method of production is defined that the production with higher capital-labor-

---

14)   Böhm-Bawerk [3], pp. 356–358, and Wicksell [20], pp. 173–184.

15)   See for an example of a boat and net, which is originally due to Roscher, Böhm-Bawerk [3], pp. 280–281. An example of a sewing machine is discussed in Böhm-Bawerk [3], p. 83.

16)   Discussion with Professor Makoto Yano of Cornell University was very useful in this respect.

17)   See Böhm-Bawerk [3], pp. 83, 280–281, [4], pp. 57, 59. See also Kaldor [8], and Hawtrey [6], p. 31, the reference to the latter we owe to Professor Ryuichiro Tachi of Aoyamagakuin University.

ratio requires smaller amount of labor directly and indirectly necessary to produce a given amount of consumers' goods.

It may seem that the second cause of Böhm-Bawerk is inherent in a life-cycle model in which an individual lives for a finite period.[18] It is certainly true if the problem of bequest and inheritance of capital is assumed away even though the life-span of capital goods is longer than that of individuals. By considering its own utility only, each generation of individuals underevaluates the wants of future generations completely, which implies the existence of a variety of the second cause. In our case, however, such a second cause does not exist, since the possibility of bequest and inheritance is ruled out by the assumption that the life-span of capital goods is shorter than that of individuals. The latter assumption is, of course, highly unrealistic. But, our purpose is not so much to construct a realistic model as to make conceptual experiments by separating causes of the positive rate of interest.

5.

Let us consider a small pilot model.

Consumers' goods may be assumed to be produced instantaneously, since "the sewing by machine is only a portion—and indeed the smallest portion—of the circuitous capital path."[19] Its production function is

(13) $X = F(L, K)$

where X, L, K are respectively the output, labor input, and capital input, and F is homogeneous of degree one with respect to L and K. By defining capital-labor-ratio a as

(14) $a = K/L$,

we can reduce (13) into

(15) $X = Lf(a)$

where $f(a) = F(1, a)$.

Capital goods are assumed to take a unit period to be produced, to have a life-span of a unit period, and to be putty-clay, in the sense that a can be variable when capital goods are newly to be produced, but remains unchanged once capital goods are installed. If we assume that the amount of labor necessary to produce a unit of capital good with given a is $N(a)$ such that $N'(a) > 0$, total amount of labor directly and indirectly necessary to produce X is given as

(16) $W(X, a) = L + KN(a) = X(1 + N(a)a)/f(a)$.

The superiority of more roundabout method of production, *i.e.*, the third cause of interest is defined that for given X, W is a decreasing function of a.

The rate of return or the rate of interest r is implicitly defined by

(17) $f(a) - w = wN(a)a(1 + r)$

where w is the rate of wage in terms of consumers' goods. Competitive firms producing capital goods choose a so as to maximize r, when w is given. By differentiating (17) with respect to a and r to obtain $dr/da = 0$, we have

---

18) See Samuelson [16] where Turgot's fructification theory of interest is considered by a life-cycle model.

19) Böhm-Bawerk [3], p. 83. Böhm-Bawerk continued further that "the principal length of that path is covered by the making of the sewing machine."

T. Negishi: Marx and Böhm-Bawerk

(18) $f'(a) - wN(a)(1 + r) - wN'(a)a(1 + r) = 0$.

Let us suppose that the population is stationary, each individual lives for two periods so that the size of young and working population and that of old and retired population are equal in each period. In the first period each individual works for given hours but consumes less than he earns and lends his saved capital to firms, while he not only consumes yield from his capital but also dis-saves all his capital in the second period. The life-time budget equation for an individual is

(19) $c_1 + c_2/(1 + r) = w\bar{L}$

where c_1, c_2 and $\bar{L}$ are respectively the amount of consumers' good he consumes in the first and second period, and the given supply of labor.

If the life-time utility $U(c_1, c_2)$ is maximized being subject to (19),

(20) $U_1(c_1, c_2)/U_2(c_1, c_2) = 1 + r$

should be satisfied, where U_1 and U_2 are marginal utilities of the first and the second period consumption. Since the second cause of interest is assumed away, the left-hand side of (20) is 1, if $c_1 = c_2$. When r is positive, therefore, c_2 should be larger than c_1 from the usual assumption of quasi-concavity of U, which implies that the future want is better provided than the present one, *i.e.*, the first cause of interest.

The model is closed by

(21) $b(c_1 + c_2) = Lf(a)$

(22) $b\bar{L} = L + LN(a)a$

where b denotes the given identical size of young and old populations. Demand and supply of consumers' goods are equalized in (21) while those of labor are equalized in (22) since $aL = K$. We can determine six variables w, r, a, L, c_1 and c_2 from six equations, (17)~(22).[20]

By eliminating w from (17) and (18), r can be expressed as a function of a. It is easily seen, then, $r > 0$ from the condition that W is a decreasing function of a when X is given in (16). In words, the rate of interest is positive in a stationary state if the third cause exists and the first cause is generated by it. The existence of the third cause requires, of course, some stringent conditions on production functions. By specifying the form of utility function, for example, we can see that the elasticity of consumers' goods output with respect to capital is fairly large.[21] Otherwise, the rate of interest is not positive. Even then, however, individuals wish to maintain capital so as to transfer their income from the work days to the retired life.

Schumpeter also argued that there is no positive rate of interest in a stationary state, though his reason is different from ours. He seems to insist that capital continues to be increased so far as its marginal productivity is positive.[22] At least theoretically, therefore, he denied the possibility of a positive rate of interest completely. In our model, however, the amount of capital which individuals wish to maintain at the zero rate of interest may be different from the amount which makes the marginal productivity of capital zero, and a positive rate of interest is possible, provided

---

20) The assumption that capital goods are produced by labor alone may be typically Austrian but is certainly unrealistic. The model can be, however, easily generalized so that capital goods are necessary to produce capital goods. See Negishi [14], Chapter 9.

21) If capital goods are necessary to produce capital goods, it is further required that the capital input coefficient in the production of capital goods is fairly small. See for the details, Negishi [14], Chapter 9.

22) Schumpeter [17], pp. 45–46. See for the details, Negishi [14], Chapter 10.

The Economic Studies Quarterly

that certain conditions on utility and production functions are satisfied.

6.

In the Chino-Japanese system of zodiacal symbols to count years, each year is given the name of an animal, for example, a tiger for 1818, a boar for 1851, and a rooster for 1933. This address is, therefore, to express a prowling rooster's view of how a big tiger roared and how a wild boar dashed, since it is believed that one took on the character of the animal of one's birth year.

REFERENCES

[1]   Arvidsson, G., "On the Reasons for a Rate of Interest," *International Economic Papers*, 6 (1956), pp. 23–33.

[2]   Böhm-Bawerk, E. V., *Capital and Interest, The History and Critique of Interest Theories*, G.D. Huncke and H. F. Sennholz, tr., Libertarian Press, 1959.

[3]   Böhm-Bawerk, E. V., *Capital and Interest, The Positive Theory of Capital*, G. D. Funcke and H. F. Sennholz, tr., Libertarian Press, 1959.

[4]   Böhm-Bawerk, E. V., *Capital and Interest, Further Essays on Capital and Interest*, H. F. Sennholz, tr., Libertarian Press, 1959.

[5]   Bronfenbrenner, M., "Western Economics Transplanted to Japan," *The History of Economics Society Bullentin*, V-2 (1984), pp. 5–18.

[6]   Hawtrey, R. G., *Capital and Employment*, Longmans, Green and Co., 1952.

[7]   Hirshleifer, J., "A Note on the Böhm-Bawerk/Wicksell Theory of Interest," *Review of Economic Studies*, 34 (1967), pp. 191–199.

[8]   Kaldor, N., "Annual Survey of Economic Theory: The Recent Controversy on the Theory of Capital," *Econometrica*, 5 (1937), pp. 201–233.

[9]   Marx, K., *Capital*, I, Progress Publishers, 1954.

[10]   Marx K., *Theories of Surplus-Value*, 3, Progress Publishers, 1971.

[11]   Morishima, M., *Marx's Economics*, Cambridge University Press, 1973.

[12]   Naruse, S., "Kokusai Kachiron (Theory of International Value)," *Shokei-Ronso* (Kanagawa University Journal of Economics and Commerce), 19–4 (1984), pp. 111-154.

[13]   Negishi, T., *Economic Theories in a Non-Walrasian Tradition*, Cambridge University Press, 1985.

[14]   Negishi, T., *Keizaigaku niokeru Koten to Gendairiron* (Classics and Modern Theories in Economics), Yuhikaku, 1985.

[15]   Ricardo, D., *On the Principles of Political Economy and Taxation*, Cambridge University Press, 1951.

[16]   Samuelson, P. A., "Land and the Rate of Interest," H. I. Greenfield and Others, eds., *Theory for Economic Efficiency*, MIT Press, 1979.

[17]   Schumpeter, J. A., *The Theory of Economic Development*, R. Opie, tr., Harvard University Press, 1934.

[18]   Smith, A., *An Inquiry into the Nature and Causes of the Wealth of Nations*, Oxford University Press, 1976.

[19]   Spengler, J. J., "Adam Smith on Human Capital," *American Economic Review*, 67 (1977), pp. 32–36.

[20]   Wicksell, K., *Lectures on Political Economy*, I. E. Classen, tr., Kelley, 1977.

11

21

SAMUELSON, SAIGAL AND EMMANUEL'S THEORY OF INTERNATIONAL UNEQUAL EXCHANGE*

TAKASHI NEGISHI

RICARDO-MILL theory of comparative advantage has been one of the few theory that economists of all schools understand and agree with.[1] A. Emmanuel in *L'échange inégal* (1969), however, criticised the basic assumptions of the theory and tried to replace it with a new theory that a country with given low wage level is exploited by a country with given high wage level when they trade with each other and the capital is imported from the latter to the former. Being alerted by this Marxian attack on the neo-classical orthodoxy, Samuelson stood up quickly and tried to show the illogicality of neo-Marxian doctrine of unequal exchange.[2]

Samuelson seems, unfortunately, misunderstand the main point of Emmanuel's arguments. His demonstration of gains from international trade and investment is irrelevant to Emmanuel, since the latter does not necessarily deny it. What Emmanuel insisted mainly is the deterioration of the terms of trade of the lower wage country in comparison with the situation where there is no wage-differentials. He compares two situations (with and without wage-differentials) where international trade and investment actually take place. He does not, unlike Samuelson, compare

---

* The author is grateful to Professor H.D. Evans for correct interpretation of Emmanuel's theory, and many other useful comments.

autarky or pre-trade situation and actual situation with international trade and investment. As such, therefore, there is no illogicality in Emmanuel's theory.

Emmanuel's theory has been followed and developed further by many including Oscar Braun, Samir Amin and Jagdish C. Saigal.[3] According to the most recent and the quantitatively most detailed study among them, i.e., that of Saigal,

> Pour des niveaux de salaire réel donnés dans les economies A et B, nous calculerons le taux de profit et le prix de transformation de l'équipement en terms de biens de consommation. La comparison des deux situations (i.e., before and after international trade and investment) nous permettra de savoir s'il existe ou non un échange inégal.[4]

The definition of échange inégal is different between Emmanuel and Saigal, since Saigal, unlike Emmanuel, compares the autarky with the situation with international trade and investment. In other words, Saigal is not only criticising basic assumptions of neo-classical theory of international trade but also denying the gains from international trade and investment. Saigal's theory is, fortunately or unfortunately, illogical and cannot be supported, since in his model capitalists are not really trying to maximise profit, even though the rate of profit is equalised.[5]

Though we do not agree with Saigal's arguments as it stands, we have to admit that the model with rates of profit equalised and local difference in wages gives does fit present-day reality much more than the orthodox neo-classical model, i.e., the so-called Heckscher-Ohlin model with international factor price equalisation. We can clear, however, present inconsistencies in Saigal' model by introducing risk premium in international investment, which Ricardo and Emmanuel emphasised. By so doing, ironically, we can show that two countries with different wages but identical technology can gain, in terms of Saigal' criterions, from international trade and investment. In a new-classical model where wage is endogenously determined by marginal productivity of labour, the rate of profit falls in a capital importing country. In Saigal's model, however, wages are given exogenously by socio-economic or bio-economic factors, and the rate of profit rises even in capital importing country as a result of international trade and investment between countries with identical technology.

Emmanuel considered two cases of unequal exchange, i.e., a primary form of nonequivalence (equal rate of surplus value with unequal organic compositions) and nonequivalence in the strict sense (unequal rates of surplus value).

Let us begin with the first case.[6] Consider two countries, each having three branches with different organic composition of capital. Transformation of values into prices of production in Marxian way is given in the left-hand part of Table 21.1 when two countries are completely separated. Within each country a transfer of surplus value takes place from Branch III to Branch II. If two countries come into contact with each other and the three articles of country B, taken together, are exchanged at the rate of 360 for 240, against the three articles of country A, taken together, then, B exchanges 120 units of its national living labour for 120 units of A's labour, the difference between 360 and 240 arising from the fact that the three articles of country A, taken together, contain 240 units of past labour as compared with 120 in country B.

If capital is freely transferred between two countries, and as a result, equalisation of profit rates takes place, we have the right-hand part of Table 21.1. Commodities produced in country B and no longer exchanged for those produced in A at the rate of 360 for 240, but at 375 for 225. Whereas one hour of B's living labour was exchanged on the average for one hour of A's living labour before, it is now exchanged on the average for 21/27 [= (225 - 120)/(375 - 240)] hours of this labour. Though the terms of trade of country B is deteriorated and a transfer of surplus value of 15 units (375 - 360 or 240 - 225) takes place from country B to country A, Emmanuel does not regard this type of exchange as truly unequal.

The reason is that the first case is the one with the same general rate of wages (the same rate of surplus value) in two countries, which resulted from a bioeconomic law, common to the two countries. In Ricardian system, according to Emmanuel, wages are incapable either of exceeding the physiological minimum or of being reduced below the level, through the working of a kind of biological law, the same for every country, while in Marx's system, according to Emmanuel, the social and historical factor can bring about considerable differences in wage levels and make impossible the equalisation of wages on a world scale.[7] In the world of today the notion of the subsistence minimum is sufficiently elastic for no tendency to automatic equalisation to be possible. The second case of unequal exchange is, therefore, truly important, as is emphasised by Emmanuel.

TABLE 21.1

Branches	c	v	m	V	T	p	L	T	p	L
IA	80	20	20	120		20	120		25	125
IIA	90	10	10	110		20	120		25	125
IIIA	70	30	30	130		20	120		25	125
A	240	60	60	360	20%	60	360	25%	75	375
IB	40	20	20	80		20	80		15	75
IIB	50	10	10	70		20	80		15	75
IIIB	30	30	30	90		20	80		15	75
B	120	60	60	240	33(1/3)%	60	240	25%	45	225
	360	120	120	600		120			120	600

Notes:

c   Constant capital
v   Variable capital
m   Surplus value

V Value $c + v + m$
T Rate of profit $(\Sigma m)/(\Sigma c + \Sigma v)$
p Profit $T(c + v)$
L Price of production $c + v + p$

TABLE 21.2

Country	K	c	v	m	V	R	T	P	L
A	240	50	60	60	170	110	33(1/3)%	80	*190*
B	120	50	60	60	170	110		40	*150*
	360	100	120	120	340	220		120	*340*
A	240	50	100	20	170	150	33(1/3)%	80	*230*
B	120	50	20	100	170	70		40	*110*
	360	100	120	120	340	220		120	*340*

Notes:

K   Total capital invested
c   Constant capital consumed
v   Variable capital
m   Surplus value
V   Value c + v + m
R   Cost of production c + v
T   Rate of profit $(\Sigma m)/(\Sigma k)$
p   Profit TK
L   Price of production

Table 21.2 shows an effect of international wage difference when international trade and investment take place between two countries A and B. The upper part shows a case where there is no international difference in wage while the lower part, where different wage levels are exogenously given. In comparison with the case of no wage differential, the terms of trade of country B is reduced from 150/190 to 110/230, when her wage is lower than the wage in country A. Emmanuel's definition of unequal exchange is this reduction of the terms of trade.[8] It should be emphasised that Emmanuel does not compare autarky and trade situations and therefore does not deny the gains from international trade. His criticism is on the assumption that wage is endogenous and capital is immobile internationally, which, in the case of Heckscher-Ohlin theory, leads to international factor price equalisation. He assumed, on the other hand, that internationally different wages are exogenously given and capital is freely mobile between countries.

Samuelson considered only the first case of Emmanuel, which Emmanuel himself did not consider important. He interpreted wrongly that the left-hand part of Table 21.1 shows the before trade situations of two countries and the right-hand part of Table 21.1 shows the after trade situation at a common rate of profit in two countries. In this case, as Samuelson argued, it is certainly a nonsense calculation that B's terms of trade is deteriorated from 240 of B for 360 of A to 225 of B for 375 of A, since in autarky terms of trade is meaningless and indeterminate. Samuelson also wondered why trade is ever possible in Emmanuel's Tables 21.3 and 21.4 where domestic price ratios are identical between countries both before and after trade. Samuelson is right if two countries are producing the same three goods. It is no wonder, however, if two countries are producing completely different three goods, i.e., six goods in all.[9] Finally, Samuelson constructed a counter-example to Emmanuel, i.e., a Ricardo-like model with profit rate equalisation appended where labour employment is fixed in each country, unchanged before and after trade, to show that trade and investment does benefit both countries in exactly the same way that Recardo claimed. This is, however, irrelevant to Emmanuel, since labour employment should be variable in Ricardo-Marxian model where wages are fixed. When capital is imported from country A to country B, labour employment has to decease in A and increase in B.[10]

TABLE 21.3

	Economie A			Economie B		
	Equipe-ment	Heures de travail	Produit	Equipe-ment	Heures de travail	Produit
Secteur I	10e	40h	30e	10e	40h	30e
Secteur II	10e	80h	60c	1e	8h	6c

TABLE 21.4

	Equipement	Heures de travail	Produit
Economie A Secteur I	10e	40h	30e
Economie B Secteur II	4e	32h	24c

Although Emmanuel does not deny the gains from trade,[11] some of his followers seem to do so, by employing a different definition of unequal exchange. For example, to Saigal (1973), unequal exchange means that terms of trade are unfavourable to lower wage country in comparison with its domestic price ratio in autarky and that the rate of profit is decreased (increased) in lower (higher) wage country when international trade (with complete specialisation) and investment (with rate of profit equalised) take place. This is a direct refutation of classical and neo-classical theory of gains from trade, given in terms of prices and rate of profit.

Let us examine the Exercises N. 1 and N. 2 proposed by Saigal, where two countries i.e., A (l'économie du centre) and B (l'économie dépendante ou périphérique) and two sectors or two goods, i.e., I (biens d'équipement ou matériel) and II (biens de consommation), are considered. Input-output data are given in Table 21.3, where identical technology for two countries are assumed and e, c, and h signify equipment, consumption goods, and labour hour. Let us suppose that ratio of wage rates in A and in B is 4 : 1 and that $W^A = (1/2) c$ and $W^B = (1/8)$ cc, where W^A and W^B signify wage rates for one labour hour in each country.

In autarky, then, from price-cost equations,[12]

$$10P_e^A (1 + R^A) + 40 W^A = 30P_e^A \tag{21.1a}$$

$$10P_e^A (1 + R^A) + 80 W^A = 60c \tag{21.2a}$$

$$10P_e^B (1 + R^B) + 40 W^B = 30P_e^B \tag{21.1b}$$

$$P_e^B (1 + R^B) + 8 W^B = 6c, \tag{21.2b}$$

we can solve for

$$1 + R^A = 1.5$$
$$1 + R^B = 2.73$$
$$P^A_e = (4/3)\,c = 1.33\,c$$
$$P^B_e = (11/6)\,c = 1.83\,c,$$

where R^A and R^B are rates of profit in two countries, P^A_e and P^B_e are price of the good I (equipment) in terms of the good II (consumption goods) in two countries.

When international trade and investment are free and country A (B) is specialzed in good I (II), input-output data are given in Table 21.4, and from price-cost equations, taking into consideration that $W^A = (1/2)\,c$ and $W^B = (1/8)\,c$,

1. $10\,P_e\,(1 + R) + 20\,c = 30\,P_e$
2. $4\,P_e\,(1 + R) + 4\,c = 24\,c,$

we can solve for

$$1 + R = 15/7 = 2.14$$
$$P_e = 7c/3 = 2.33\,c$$

where R and P_e are rate of profit equalised and the price of the good I in terms of II.

Saigal observed from the above that the condition for the unequal exchange, i.e, $P_e > P^B_e > P^A_e$ and $R^B > R > R^A$, are realised, which implies that (1) country B has to export 2.33 units of consumption goods to import 1 unit of equipment while it could obtain 1 unit of the latter by sacrificing only 1.83 units of the former in the autarky, and (2) the maximum rate of accumulation falls from 1.73 to 1.14 in B. Similar results are obtained also in the case where country A (B) is specialised in good II (I).[13]

Fortunately or unfortunately, we cannot accept Saigal's argument in the previous section. Why country B has to be specialised in good II? In the free capitalist world, given technology and wage differences as in Saigal's example, Evans (1981a:129), (1981b:125) pointed out that capital moved from country A to B can profitably be invested in the sector I in B, since price cost relation is

$$10P_e\,(1+R)+40W^B \quad < \quad 30P_e \tag{21.1}$$

when $P_0 = 2.33\ c$, $R = 1.14$ and $W^B = (1/8)\ c$, i.e., $40W^B = 5\ c$. In other words, higher wage country A cannot compete with lower wage country B in any good, when technology is identical and rate of profit equalised.[14] The result is that all the capital moves from A to B.[15]

Of course, such an extreme solution is highly unrealistic. What we should do to save Saigal's model with wage differential and mobile capital is to admit that the rate of profit is not equalised even though capital is mobile freely between countries. According to Ricardo,

Experience, however, shows that the fancied or real insecurity of capital, when not under the immediate control of its owner, together with the natural disinclination which every man has to quit the country of his birth and connections, and intrust himself, with all his habits fixed, to a strange government and new laws, check the emigration of capital. These feelings, which I should be sorry to see weakened, induce most men of property to be satisfied with a low rate of profits in their own country, rather than seek a more advantageous employment for their wealth in foreign nations.[16]

And even Emmanuel (1972:71) himself admitted that

If the risk premium in Brazil is + 1/2, compared with the United States, and the general rate of profit in the latter country is 10 per cent, then parity occurs when the rate of profit in Brazil reaches 15 per cent. At 16 per cent capital should move from the United States to Brazil, and at 14 per cent from Brazil to the United States.

Let us, then, reconstruct Saigal's model properly, giving the conditions for the complete specialisation fully and admitting that mobility of capital does not equalise rate of profit completely. The result will be completely contrary to that insisted by Saigal, that lower wage country can gain both in the comparison of domestic price ratio and the terms of trade as well as in terms of the rate of profit by international trade and investment.

When country A (B) is specialised in good I (II), not only the cost price equations

$$P_e = (1+R)aP_e + bW^A \tag{21.3}$$

$$1 = (1+Rq)cP_e + dW^B \tag{21.4}$$

but also the cost price relations

$$P_e < (1+Rq)aP_e + bW^B \qquad (21.5)$$

$$1 < (1+R)cP_e + dW^A \qquad (21.6)$$

have to be satisfied, where a, b and c, d are input coefficients of good I and labour in the production of two goods, respectively, and $q > 1$ implies that capital emigration from A to B is checked by factors mentioned in quotations from Ricardo and Emmanuel in the above.[17]

In autarky, on the other hand, price cost equations in country B are

$$P_e^B = (1+R^B)aP_e^B + bW^B \qquad (21.7)$$

$$1 = (1+R^B)cP_e^B + dW^B. \qquad (21.8)$$

From (21.4) and (21.8), we have

$$(1+Rq)cP_e = (1+R^B)cP_e^B \qquad (21.9)$$

while from (21.5) and (21.7) we have

$$P_e[1-(1+Rq)a] < P_e^B[1-(1+R^B)a] \qquad (21.10)$$

Now we are ready to show that, contrary to Saigal's result, (21.3) - (21.8) imply the gains from trade and investment, i.e., $P_e < P_e^B$ and $(1+Rq) > (1+R^B)$. Suppose that $P_e > P_e^B$. Then, from (21.9) we have $R_e < R^B$. This is, however, a contradiction, since we have, then, $P_e < P_e^B$ from (10). Therefore, it has to be $P_e < P_e^B$. Then, from (21.9) we have $(1+R_e) > (1+R^B)$.

Similarly, in autarky, price cost equations in A are

$$P_e^A = (1+R^A)aP_e^A + bW^A \qquad (21.11)$$

$$1 = (1+R^A)cP_e^A + dW^A \qquad (21.12)$$

and we have

$$P_e^A[1-(1+R^A)a] = P_e[1-(1+R)a] \qquad (21.13)$$

$$(1+R)cP_e > (1+R^A)cP_e^A \qquad (21.14)$$

from (21.3), (21.6), (21.11) and (21.12). If we suppose that $P_e < P_e^A$, then we have a contradiction, i.e., $P_e > P_e^A$ from (21.13) and (21.14). Therefore, we have $P_e > P_e^A$ which implies $R > R^A$ from (21.13).

Both of Saigal's conditions for unequal exchange are not realised, since we have $P_e^B > P_e > P_e^A$ and $Rq > R^B, R > R^A$. While the former is rather a common sense from the point of view of classical and neo-classical theory of trade, it may be interesting to see the latter, which is due to the assumption of given wage rates.[18] A rise in the rate of profit in capital importing country is an unexpected result from a neo-classical model where wage is endogenously determined by marginal productivity of labour. Of course, Saigal's argument can also be refuted similarly if we assume that country A (B) is specialised in good II (I).[19]

According to Saigal (1973:133),

On peut envisager la possibilité d'un échange équitable de produits entre les pays moins développés et les pays dévelopés − lorsque les rapports de production et de commerce dans l'économie mondiale ne sont pas régis par les lois du mode de production capitalists, mais socialiste.

It is quite ironical that unequal exchange in the sense of Saigal is impossible, as we showed, in a free capitalist world, while it may be possible in a socialists world when an advanced country imposed a wrong pattern of specialisation to other countries.

NOTES

1. Ricardo's own theory can, however, be interpreted as the different one from the so-called Ricardo-Mill theory. See Negishi (1982).
2. "Illogic of Neo-Marxian Doctrine of Unequal Exchange," in (1977), pp. 649-660.
3. See Amin (1976), p. 150, (1973), pp. 27-29, 62-63, Braun (1972), and Saigal (1973). For further details on Emmanuel and his followers, see Bacha (1978), Evans (1980), (1981a), (1981b), (1981c), Mainwaring (1980), and Smith (1980).
4. Saigal (1973), p. 122. Insertion in English is mine.
5. Evans (1981a), pp. 129-130, (1981b), p. 125, already pointed out that Saigal's equilibrium is not sustainable under free trade and perfect competition unless it is sustained by a set of extra market forces.
6. Emmanuel (1972), pp. 52-60. This is the case discussed by Samuelson, though Emmanuel himself does not regard as important. From the point of view of Marxian labour theory of value, however, this is a classical case. See Sweezy (1942), pp. 290-291.
7. Emmanuel (1972), pp. xxxiii - xxxiv. However, see Ricardo (1976), pp. 54-55. "It is not to be understood that the natural price of labour, estimated even in food and necessaries, is a absolutely fixed and constant. It varies at different times in the same country, and very materially differs in different countries. It essentially depends on the habits and customs of the people".

8. Emmanuel (1972), pp. 59, 61, 62.
9. This implies that wage goods consist of local goods only in each country, which explains why rate of surplus value is not changed before and after trade and why rate of profit is reduced in lower wage country after trade and investment. If we correct Marxian way of transformation of value into price and evaluate input in terms of price, however, lower wage country's rate of profit has to be increased unless the importables are non-basic goods. (See note 18) below.
10. Inadequacy of Samuelson's interpretation of Ricardo can also be seen in his calling Portugal rich and England poor. See Negishi (1982). In this respect, however, Amin made the same mistake. See Amin (1976), p. 134.
11. It is self-evident in Emmanuel's six good model given in the previous section that there exist gains from trade in terms of quantity of goods, since the importables cannot be produced domestically even in autarky. For neo-Ricardian reexamination of trade theory, which is not unrelated to but different from unequal exchange theory, see Evans (1980), (1981b), (1981c) and Steedman (1979).
12. Trivial corrections are made. See Japanese translation of Amin (1973), p. 133.
13. See Saigal (1973), pp. 121-128.
14. Similar arguments can be made to the case where country A (B) is specialised in good II (I). See Saigal's Exercise N. 3, where condition for unequal exchange is $P_e < P_e^g < P_e^A$.
15. Emmanuel (1972), p. xiii, argued with respect to Ricardian example of comparative advantage as follows. "It is clear that this specialisation constitutes only a relative optimum. The absolute optimum would be, not for Portugal to specialise in wine and England in cloth, but for the English to move to Portugal with their capital in order to produce both wine and cloth. − But such as absolute condition would be neither possible nor desirable. − man is the hardest to transport". Whether desirable or not, however, English capital alone, without the English, will move to Portugal to make larger profit.
16. Ricardo (1976), p. 83. See also Negishi (1982).
17. If q is given, we can solve (3) and (4) for P_e and R, without taking reciprocal demand into consideration. See Negishi (1982).
18. Evans (1981b; 125) showed this result for the case of complete equalisation of rate of profit and different technologies. See note 9 above.
19. This can be seen simply by exchanging the role of two countries, since the proof of the non-existence of unequal exchange in the above is independent of the conditions $W^A > W^B$ and $q > 1$.

REFERENCES

Amin, S., (1976). *Unequal Development*, Pearce tr., Monthly Review Press, (Le *Développement inégal*, Les Editions de Minuit, 1973).

Amin, S., (1973), *Léchange inegal et la loi de la valeur*, Editions Anthropos, (Futokakokan to Kachihosoku, Hanasaki tr. Aki Shobo, 1979).

Bacha, E.L., (1978), "An Interpretation of Unequal Exchange from Prebisch-Singer to Emmanuel," *Journal of Development Economics*, Vol. 5 pp. 319-330.

Braun, O., (1972), *Comercio internacional e imperialismo*, Siglo XXI, Buenos Aires.

Emmanuel, A., (1972), *Unequal Exchange*, Pearce tr., Monthly Review Press, (L'*échange inégal*, Librairie Francois Maspero, 1969).

Evans, H.D., (1980), "Emmanuel's Theory of Unequal Exchange: Critique, Counter Critique and Theoretical Contribution," Discussion Paper, 149, Institute of Development Studies, University of Sussex.

Evans, H.D., (1981a), "Trade, Production and Self-Reliance," in D. Seers (ed.), *Dependency Theory : A Critical Assessment*, Frances Pinter, London, pp. 119-134.

Evans, H.D., (1981b), "Unequal Exchange and Economic Policies: Some Implications of the Neo-Ricardian Critique of the Theory of Comparative Advantage," in I. Livingston (ed.), *Development Economics and Policy : Readings*, George Allen and Unwin, London, pp. 117-128.

Evans, H.D., (1981c), "A Critical Assesment of Neo-Marxian Trade Theories," Discussion Paper, 12/81, La Trobe University.

Mainwaring, L., (1980), "International Trade and the Transfer of Labour Value," *Journal of Development Studies*, Vol. 17 pp. 22-31.

Negishi, T., (1982), "The Ricardian Labour Theory of Value in the Theory of International Trade," *History of Political Economy*, 14 (1982), pp. 199-210. (*Kotenha Keizaigaku to Kindai Keizaigaku*, Iwanami, 1981, Chp. 6).

Ricardo, (1976), *The Principles of Political Economy and Taxation*, Everyman's Library.

Saigal, J.C., (1973), "Réflexions sur la théorie de 'l'échange inégal'," in, Amin (1973).

Samuelson, P.A., (1977), *The Collected Scientific Papers*, IV, MIT Press.

Smith, S., (1980), "The Ideas of Samir Amin: Theory or Tautology?" *Journal of Development Studies*, Vol. 17, pp. 5-21.

Steedman, I., (1979), *Fundamental Issues in Trade Theory*, Macmillan.

Sweezy, P.M., (1942), *The Theory of Capitalist Development*, Oxford University Press.

PART II

MARGINAL REVOLUTION AND AFTER

[12]

Japan and the World Economy 2 (1990) 199–209
North-Holland

STUDIES OF VON THÜNEN IN JAPAN

Takashi NEGISHI *

University of Tokyo, Bunkyoku, Tokyo, Japan

Received November 1989, final version received February 1990

Studies of von Thünen in Japan have a long history and suggest an interpretation of von Thünen's theory, which is different from those of recent studies of von Thünen in the English speaking world. A simple model of a stationary economy is constructed on the basis of such an interpretation, in which workers are assumed to be free to save in their life-cycles though the level of consumption of working families is kept at the subsistence level. Von Thünen's famous formula of the natural wage is derived from the model, which is free from the criticisms given to von Thünen's original model.

Keywords: Von Thünen, natural wage, history of economic thought.

1. No one can deny the important contributions made by Johann Heinrich von Thünen (1783–1850) as an independent discoverer of the marginal productivity theory and as the father of the economics of space. Commemorating the two hundredth anniversary of his birth, Samuelson (1983) analyzed these contributions beautifully and skillfully. Von Thünen is also known by the formula of natural wage inscribed on his grave stone. Interest on this formula was revived by the recent discussions between Samuelson (1983, 1986) and Dorfman (1986). Both Samuelson and Dorfman, along with some others, seem to consider that von Thünen's natural wage is the socially optimal wage from the point of view of welfare economics. [1]

Studies of von Thünen in Japan have a very long history, longer than in the English speaking world. [2] Important pioneering contributions were made by Kondo (1928) and Yamada (1934), and Kondo interpreted von Thünen's natural wage as the competitive equilibrium wage in a long-run stationary economy. Both Kondo and Yamada criticized von Thünen and offered sugges-

---

* The author is grateful to a referee and Professors Martin J. Beckmann, Horst Herberg, Yuzo Yamada and Ryuzo Sato for encouragements and useful comments.

[1] See also Blaug (1986) and Niehans (1987).

[2] Von Thünen's *Der isolierte Staat*, part I, which was first published in 1826, was partly translated by Ruisuke Tanii into Japanese in 1916 and Kondo's translation which includes Part I and Part II, section 1 (originally published in 1850) was published in 1929. See Dickinson (1969) for an English translation.

tions on what von Thünen should have done to derive his formula correctly. Unfortunately, however, these suggestions have been left undeveloped and no formal models have been constructed to vindicate von Thünen.

In sections 2 and 3, we briefly review Samuelson (1983, 1986), Dorfman (1986), Kondo (1928) and Yamada (1934). Section 4 is devoted to some quotations from von Thünen's *Der isolierte Staat* (the isolated state), which may indicate the possibility of an interpretation of von Thünen's theory of the natural wage, suggested by Kondo and Yamada, but different from that of Samuelson, Dorfman and Yamada. A simple model based on this interpretation is given, then, in sections 5, 6 and 7 to derive von Thünen's formula of the natural wage.

2. Von Thünen derived his formula of the natural wage from the maximization of zy, where z is the rate of interest and y is the annual surplus of each working family, which is converted into capital. If a denotes the subsistence amount of consumer goods (which we take as the numeraire), the annual wage of a family is $a + y$. Assuming that one unit of labor (supplied annually by a working family) is necessary to produce one unit of capital which does not depreciate, z can be written as

$$z = [p - (a + y)] / q(a + y), \tag{1}$$

where p denotes the annual product of the consumer goods for a working family assisted by q units of capital. If p, q and a are considered as constants, then the maximization of zy with respect to y requires the condition that $(a + y)^2 = ap$. In words, the natural wage is the geometric mean of the necessary subsistence a and the average product of a working family. [3]

Samuelson (1983) strongly argued against the assumption of the constant q. If the wage rate is higher, q and therefore p should be larger. [4] Assuming that the production function of consumer goods is homogeneous of degree one with respect to labor and capital inputs, and denoting that $p = f(q)$, $f' > 0$, $f'' < 0$, we have

$$a + y = f(q) - qf'(q), \tag{2}$$

where f' denotes the marginal productivity of capital and annual rent for a unit of capital. From (1) and (2),

$$z = f'(q) / (a + y), \tag{3}$$

and

$$zy = f'(q) - af'(q) / (f(q) - qf'(q)). \tag{4}$$

---

[3] See von Thünen (1910, pp. 542–550, particularly, p. 549). See also Dempsey (1960, pp. 288–294, particularly, p. 293).

[4] See, however, von Thünen's verbal discussions and numerical examples in von Thünen (1910, pp. 501–508), Dempsey (1960, pp. 260–264).

Both Samuelson (1983) and Dorfman (1986) insisted that von Thünen should have maximized (4) with respect to q, and Dorfman (1986) found that it also requires the condition that $(y + a)^2 = ap$.

Dorfman (1986) found, however, that the social welfare function zy that von Thünen invoked to derive his formula was uncongenial. Dorfman called it a peculiar welfare function which he could not defend. The maximization of zy is called by Samuelson (1983) a crime against both normative and positivistic economics. In Samuelson (1986) it is suggested that von Thünen had to consider, for example, an alternative welfare economics exercise in which all workers' surplus of wages over their consumption, a, is one time saved and that we should seek the society's q that maximizes society's increment of perpetual flow of consumer goods that results. Even then, however, the question remains that there is no reason why all the surplus of wage over the subsistence level should be saved, as was rightly pointed out by Samuelson (1986) and Niehans (1987). Samuelson (1986) concluded the discussion with Dorfman that von Thünen added to this important positivistic theory (spatial equilibrium and marginal productivity) a rather strange normative discussion.

We may conclude, therefore, that both Samuelson and Dorfman considered von Thünen's zy as a social welfare function and von Thünen's natural wage as the optimal wage. [5] It is evident that zy is very peculiar as a social welfare function and that the socially optimal wage cannot be the geometric mean of p and a if it is replaced by an alternative, more plausible social welfare function, as was done by Samuelson (1986). The question that remain, however, are whether the natural wage that von Thünen was groping for is such an optimal wage and whether there can be room for an alternative interpretation in this respect.

3.   Studies of von Thünen in Japan were pioneered by Kondo (in 1928) and Yamada (in 1934). Both Kondo and Yamada did their studies of von Thünen in their youth. Kondo, who became a professor of agricultural economics at the University of Tokyo, made important contributions to agricultural economics, and had a great influence on the development of agricultural policies in Japan. As a professor of economics at Hitotsubashi University, Yamada contributed widely to economic theory, economic planning and the history of economics, made a pioneering contribution to the estimation of national income in Japan, and also had a great influence on the development of welfare policies in Japan. It is interesting to see that both Kondo and Yamada started their academic careers by careful studies of von Thünen's marginal productivity theory.

---

[5] See also Blaug (1986) and Niehans (1987). Leigh (1946) considered, however, in his classical study of von Thünen in the English speaking world, that the natural wage was supposed by von Thünen to prevail in the real world.

Kondo interpreted von Thünen's natural wage as the competitive equilibrium wage in a stationary state, which is achieved through competition after forces of demand and supply have worked out. According to Kondo, von Thünen's theory is a theory of the rational behavior of private farms in a competitive situation. In part 1 of von Thünen's *Isolated State*, entrepreneurs-landowners organize farms optimally, with respect to the choice of crops and the intensity of cultivation, so as to maximize land rent or net revenue, when prices of products are given. Similarly, argued Kondo, in part 2 of the *Isolated State*, entrepreneurs (capital-producing workers) organize farms optimally (with respect to the capital–labor ratio q) so as to maximize rent for capital, when prices and the wage rate of hired workers are given and there is no land-rent. Kondo criticized von Thünen that the latter should not try to explain the wage rate in his theory of rational behavior of entrepreneurs-farmers, since under competitive conditions they have to take the wage rate as given. [6]

Samuelson (1983) felt odd at von Thünen's assumption that the prime source of saving is workers' wages. Yamada emphasized, however, that von Thünen considered such a hypothetical unrealistic case to see the effects of workers' saving on wages and interest, since he recognized that in reality saving is monopolized by capitalists so that interest is high and wages are low. Criticizing the conclusion of Kondo, Yamada argued that the (natural) wage and the interest rate should be determined by the macroscopic equilibrium condition of saving (supply of the surplus) and investment (consumption of the surplus). According to Yamada, the marginal productivity theory explains merely the demand for labor. To determine the optimal wage, therefore, we must also explain the supply side, taking into consideration the relations between subsistence consumption and the surplus, and between saving and investment of a whole economy. Though von Thünen tried it, Yamada concluded, the results was quite unsatisfactory, since his assumptions were wrong. [7]

4.   Von Thünen's famous explanation of the natural wage (der naturgemässe Arbeitslohn) runs as follows:

> 'This wage, not originating in the relation of supply and demand (nicht aus dem Verhältnis zwischen Angebot und Nachfrage entspringenden), not measured by the needs of the worker, but proceeding from the free self-determination of the worker, this $\sqrt{ap}$, I call the natural level wage, or even the natural wage'. [8]

---

[6] See Kondo (1928, pp. 57–59 and 246–250).
[7] See Yamada (1934, pp. 131–132, 159–160, 171–172, and 208–209).

Here, 'not originating in the relation of supply and demand' should not be taken as independent of supply and demand (Angebot und Nachfrage). This is rather a classical way of saying that demand and supply are equalized. It merely implies that the natural wage is different from the market wage. The latter wage changes according to the temporary relation between supply and demand, when the supply adjustment of rational workers has not fully worked out yet. The natural wage is the equilibrium wage determined by the equality of supply and demand, when workers have already adjusted their supply fully. In the period of the classical economics, however, the role of supply and demand was not so much emphasized for the determination of the equilibrium wage as for the changes in the market wage.

This interpretation can be confirmed by the following statement of von Thünen, in which we can clearly see that von Thünen is interested in a stationary economy and that the natural wage is considered as the wage to equate supply and demand of labor. 'Competition, or the interrelation of supply along with the demand for labor, according to Adam Smith, determines the level of wages. But the level of the demand for workers is also dependent upon whether the national wealth is rising, stationary (stillstehend) or declining. We have now set ourselves the task to investigate the level of wages for the stationary state (den beharrenden Zustand) of civil society. In such a state the demand and supply are in equilibrium (sind Nachfrage and Angebot im Gleichgewicht). They offset each other to a certain extent, or appear as resting.' [9] Clearly, von Thünen is not denying the effect of demand and supply on the natural wage, he is merely saying that demand and supply *appear* as resting (erscheinen als ruhend) when they are equalized.

Von Thünen repeatedly mentioned that he is concerned with a stationary state (der beharrende Zustand or Zustand des Stillstandes). 'Our inquiry is based on the assumption that the Isolated State is in a stationary state; therefore its magnitude and extent must be unchanged'. 'In the Isolated State, on the other hand, we have had in mind only the final goal. With the reaching of the final goal there is then no further change and disturbance. There appears a stationary state'. [10] In a stationary economy, the labor population has to remain constant. 'As it is our aim to find the laws which determine wages and the rate of interest for the stationary state of society, we must assume that the number of workers remains unchanged and that the working families, on the whole, have as many children as are necessary to substitute for

---

[8] See von Thünen (1910, p. 549). See also Dempsey (1960, p. 293). The natural wage is an equilibrium wage in a hypothetical world constructed on unrealistic assumption on saving, as pointed out by Yamada (1934, p. 131), and Blaug (1986). It does not, however, necessarily imply that it is an optimal wage obtained by the maximization of a social welfare function.

[9] See von Thünen (1910, p. 449). See also Dempsey (1960, pp. 226–227).

[10] See von Thünen (1910, pp. 538 and 431). See also Dempsey (1960, pp. 284 and 213).

those withdrawn by age and death. The labor force then appears as an unchanging magnitude which is not used up. The sum of means of subsistence which a working family, under this restricting assumption, must necessarily have *for the maintenance of its capacity for work*, I will set for every family as being equal to *a* bushels of rye'. [11]

To keep the labor population constant, the consumption (not the wage level) of each working family has to be at this subsistence level *a*. Therefore, the surplus *y* of wage over the subsistence level *a* is assumed by von Thünen to be saved and invested. 'The surplus which labor yields can have a twofold aspect, for it can happen (1) that it can be accumulated, saved, and stored with a view to living on it later without work; and (2) that it can be applied to productive investment in agriculture or industry'. [12] This suggests a life-cycle model of working families, in which each generation of workers lives for two periods. In the first period, each worker works for wage, keeps the consumption of his family at the subsistence level *a*, and saves the surplus *y* of wage over *a*. In the second period, he consumes the saving (possibly with interest on it) which he saved in the previous period, so that without working (ohne zu arbeiten) he can keep the family consumption at the subsistence level.

5.   Let us consider a simple two-commodity model of a stationary economy in which each individual worker lives for two periods, works only in the first period, and is replaced by his successor. Consumer goods are assumed to be produced by labor and capital while capital goods are assumed to be produced by labor alone, as was done by von Thünen. To make the story simple, we assume that the life-span of capital goods is a unit period.

Since the labor population remains unchanged in a stationary state, we have to assume from the classical law of population that the level of consumption is at the subsistence level *a* for each worker's household. The life-time budget constraint for each worker is then

$$w = a + a/(1 + r), \tag{5}$$

where *r* is the rate of interest and *w* is the wage for the first period. Both *a* and *w* are given in terms of consumer goods. This can be decomposed into single period budget constraints:

$$w = a + S \tag{6}$$

and

$$(1 + r)S = a, \tag{7}$$

where *S* is the saving in the first period, which is consumed, with interest

---

[11]   See von Thünen (1910, p. 476). See also Dempsey (1960, pp. 244–245).
[12]   See von Thünen (1910, p. 590). See also Dempsey (1960, p. 320).

earnings, in the second period. From (6) and (7) we have

$$(1 + r) = a/(w - a). \tag{8}$$

Let us assume that a unit of labor can produce a unit of capital goods and that the production function of consumer goods is homogeneous of degree one with respect to labor and capital. If x denotes the number of workers used to produce consumer goods, then the output of consumer goods can be given by $x f(q)$, where f is the average product of labor (von Thünen's p) and q is the capital–labor ratio in the production of consumer goods. As emphasized by Kondo, entrepreneurs under competitive conditions maximize the surplus over wage and interest payments,

$$(f(q) - w)x - (1 + r)wqx, \tag{9}$$

when w and r are given. From the condition for the maximization of (9) with respect to q, i.e.,

$$f'(q) = (1 + r)w, \tag{10}$$

the optimal q is determined. [13] Since such a surplus disappeared in a long-run equilibrium of a stationary economy, however, we also have

$$f(q) - w = (1 + r)wq. \tag{11}$$

Suppose there are L workers in their first period and L workers in their second period in a stationary state. The equilibrium condition of demand and supply of consumer goods is

$$xf(q) = 2aL, \tag{12}$$

since each worker demands consumer goods a in each period. From (12), the ratio of workers in consumer goods industry x to the total active labor force L is

$$x/L = 2a/f(q). \tag{13}$$

Now we can determine the natural wage w from the equality of saving and investment, as was suggested by Yamada. The condition is from (6):

$$L(w - a) = wxq, \tag{14}$$

since xq of capital goods has to be produced in each period. From (14),

$$x/L = a/(f(q) - w), \tag{15}$$

since we have from (5) and (11):

$$(w - a)/wq = a/(f(q) - w). \tag{16}$$

---

[13] Alternatively, the optimal q is obtained by the maximization of r (considered as the internal rate of return) in (11), as was suggested by Dorfman (1986). The condition is again (10).

Now, by eliminating x/La in (15) through the substitution from (13), we arrive at the relation between w and $f(q)$:

$$w = f(q)/2. \tag{17}$$

The natural wage as the competitive wage in a stationary state is exactly one half of the average product of labor.

6. As for the rate of interest, the problem is whether it can be positive in a stationary state. As is well known, von Böhm-Bawerk adduced three causes of the existence of a positive rate of interest in a stationary state. [14] They are (1) expectation of a better provision for wants in the future than in the present, (2) undervaluation of future wants, and (3) the superiority of a more roundabout method of production. The first cause implies that the marginal utility of the future consumption is lower than that of the present consumption, since one is given more goods in the future than in the present, while the second cause insists that the marginal utility of the future consumption is lower than that of the present consumption, even if one is provided equally in the future and in the present. These two causes are concerned with the supply of capital or saving in the sense that there will be no supply if the rate of interest is zero. The third cause implies that the capital or saving is demanded even if the rate of interest is positive, since the more roundabout and more capital-using method of production is technically superior to the less roundabout and less capital-using one.

As Samuelson (1983) rightly argued that 'Thünen – ought to understand the – analysis of the Wicksell–Jevons model', it cannot be said that there is no third cause in von Thünen. Since it takes a unit period to produce the capital goods to be used in the production of consumer goods and the capital–labor ratio q in the production of the consumer goods can be variable, the production with the higher q implies the more roundabout method of production. To derive, however, the economic superiority of more roundabout production (value productivity of capital) from this technical superiority of more roundabout production (physical production of capital), it is necessary to have either the first or the second cause of interest. The first cause is irrelevant for von Thünen, since it is assumed that the classical law of population keeps the level of consumption at the subsistence level in a stationary state. There might be, furthermore, no strong evidence of the second cause assumed by von Thünen, for whom von Böhm-Bawerk asserted that he did not know the law of marginal utility. [15]

---

[14] See von Böhm-Bawerk (1959b, pp. 259–289, especially 283). See also Negishi (1989, pp. 297–300).

[15] See von Böhm-Bawerk (1959b, p. 458). See von Böhm-Bawerk (1959a, pp. 111–116) for von Böhm-Bawerk's criticism on von Thünen's interest theory.

We must admit, therefore, that the net rate of interest r might be zero in our von Thünen-like model of a stationary state. This conclusion might also be supported by the fact that von Thünen evaluated Adam Smith very high. [16] According to Smith, the natural wage rate is at the subsistence level and the natural interest rate is very low in a stationary economy, while both wage rate and interest rate can be much higher in a growing economy. [17] Von Thünen argued against Smith that the wage rate (not the consumption) can be higher than the subsistence level in a stationary state. He made, however, no such clear argument against Smith in the case of the interest rate.

If $r = 0$ in our model of a stationary economy, from (8) we can conclude that

$$w = 2a. \tag{18}$$

The natural wage in a stationary economy is twice as high as the subsistence level of the consumption of workers' households. Now we have two expressions for the natural wage rate, (17) and (18). Combining them together, we can arrive at von Thünen's formula for the natural wage,

$$w^2 = af(q), \tag{19}$$

or, in von Thünen's own notations,

$$(a + y) = \sqrt{ap}. \tag{20}$$

7.   Let us consider how robust is our conclusion (20), if we drop some of our simplifying assumptions. Suppose, first, that the life span of capital goods is n (> 1) periods and they depreciate linearly, i.e., in each period $1/n$ of the stock of capital goods is retired and must be replaced in a stationary state. Now we have only to replace (11) and (14), respectively, by

$$f(q) - w = rwq + wq/n \tag{11'}$$

and

$$L(w - a) = wxq/n. \tag{14'}$$

It can be easily seen that (17) remains unchanged if $r = 0$, since (15) remains unchanged from (5) and (11'). Therefore, the formula of the natural wage (20) is unchanged, even if the life span of capital goods is longer.

Next, let us suppose that workers live for n (> 2) periods but work only in the first period. If $r = 0$, then, (18) must be replaced by

$$w = na. \tag{18'}$$

---

[16] See von Thünen (1910, pp. 461 and 462). See also Dempsey (1960, pp. 234–235).
[17] See Smith (1976, pp. 72, 91, and 109). See also Negishi (1989, pp. 83–89).

Now we have

$$xf(q) = naL \tag{12'}$$

and

$$x/L = na/f(q) \tag{13'}$$

instead of (12) and (13). From (11), (14), and (18'), on the other hand, (15) should be replaced by

$$x/L = (n-1)a/(f(q) - w), \tag{15'}$$

when $r = 0$. Then, from (13') and (15'), we have

$$w = f(q)/n \tag{17'}$$

instead of (17). From (17') and (18'), however, we have again (20) unchanged.

Now suppose that workers live for n periods but have to work in the first m ($< n$) periods. Instead of (18'), we then have

$$mw = na. \tag{18''}$$

While (12') and (13') remain unchanged, now (14) should be replaced by

$$mL(w - a) = wxq. \tag{14'}$$

From (11), (14') and (18''), on the other hand, (15') should be replaced by

$$x/L = (n-m)a/(f(q) - w), \tag{15''}$$

when $r = 0$. Then, from (13') and (15''), we have

$$w = mf(q)/n \tag{17''}$$

instead of (17'). From (17'') and (18''), however, we arrive at (20) again.

Finally, let us return to our original model given in section 5 and assume that goods are malleable and there is no distinction between consumer goods and capital goods. The stationary state equilibrium of supply and demand requires

$$f(q) = 2a + q, \tag{21}$$

where q and f denote the capital–labor ratio and the average productivity of labor in the production of goods which can be used both in consumption and in production as capital goods. Since the equality of saving and investment requires $q = S$, we have

$$(1 + r)q = a \tag{22}$$

from (7). Using (8), we then arrive at

$$w = f(q) - a \tag{23}$$

from (21) and (22). In view of (18), however, this implies that

$$f(q) = 3a \tag{24}$$

and

$$w = (f(q) + a)/2, \tag{25}$$

which coincides with Samuelson's (1986) natural wage. [18]

References

Beckmann, M.J., 1987, Managers as principals and agents, in: G. Bamberg and K. Spremann, eds., Agency theory, information, and incentives (Springer Verlag, Berlin) 379–388.
Blaug, M., 1986, The economics of Johann von Thünen, in: W.J. Samuels, ed., Research in the history of economic thought and methodology, Vol. 3 (JAI Press, Greenwich, CT) 1–25.
Dempsey, B.W., 1960, The frontier wage (Loyola University Press, Chicago, IL).
Dickinson, H.D., 1969, Von Thünen's economics, Economic Journal 79, 894–902.
Dorfman, R., 1986, Comment: P.A. Samuelson, 'Thünen at two hundred', Journal of Economic Literature 24, 1773–1776.
Kondo, Y., 1928, Thünen Koritsukoku no Kenkyu (Studies of Thünen's Isolated State) (Nishigahara-Kankoukai, Tokyo).
Leigh, A.H., 1946, Von Thünen's theory of distribution and the advent of marginal analysis, Journal of Political Economy 64, 481–502.
Negishi, T., 1989, History of economic theory (North-Holland, Amsterdam).
Niehans, J., 1987, Thünen, Johann Heinrich von, The new Palgrave, Vol. 4 (Macmillan, London).
Samuelson, P.A., 1983, Thünen at two hundred, Journal of Economic Literature 21, 1468–1488.
Samuelson, P.A., 1986, Yes to Robert Dorfman's vindication of Thünen's natural-wage derivation, Journal of Economic Literature 24, 1777–1785.
Smith, A., 1976, An inquiry into the nature and causes of the wealth of nations (Oxford University Press, Oxford) (Original version 1776).
von Böhm-Bawerk, E., 1959a, History and critique of interest theories (G.D. Huncke and H.F. Sennholz tr.) (Libertarian Press, South Holland, IL).
von Böhm-Bawerk, E., 1959b, Positive theory of capital (G.D. Huncke tr.) (Libertarian Press, South Holland, IL).
von Thünen, Johann Heinrich, 1910, Der isolierte Staat in Beziehung auf Lanswirtschaft und Nationalökonomie (Gustav Fischer, Stuttgart).
Yamada, Y., 1934, Thünen Bunpairon no Kenkyu (Studies of Thünen's theory of distribution) (Moriyamashoten, Tokyo).

[18] See Beckmann (1987) for an entirely different but very interesting interpretation, in which the formula of natural wage is approximated by the use of specified production and utility functions.

[13]

A NOTE ON JEVONS'S LAW OF INDIFFERENCE AND COMPETITIVE EQUILIBRIUM*

by

TAKASHI NEGISHI†

University of Tokyo

I

Walras's regard for Jevons's contribution to the equilibrium theory of competitive exchange was not high since, in his letter to Jevons, Walras pointed out that Jevons had failed to derive "the equation of effective demand as a function of price, which . . . is so indispensable for the solution of the problem of the determination of equilibrium price".[1] This is no wonder. While Walras presupposed the existence of market prices which competitive traders accept as data, in his theory of general equilibrium of competitive exchange, Jevons and Edgeworth tried to justify this Walrasian supposition by explaining prices in a competitive market as ratios of exchange resulting from a process of freely competitive exchanges.

In a sense, Schumpeter recognized this difference between Walras and Jevons:

> "*The Competitive Hypothesis.* This notion had been made explicit by Cournot . . . after having started with the case of straight monopoly . . . he first introduced another seller and then additional ones until, by letting their number increase indefinitely, he finally arrived at the case of 'illimited' (unlimited) competition, where the quantity produced by any one producer is too small to affect price perceptibly or to admit of price strategy. Jevons added his Law of Indifference, which defines the concept of the perfect market in which there cannot exist, at any moment, more than one price for each homogeneous commodity. These two features—excluded price strategy and law of indifference—

---

*Manuscript received 3.3.82; final version received 25.5.82.

†The author is very grateful to an anonymous referee for valuable comments.

[1]See Walras (1965, p. 397) and Jaffé (1976). See also Walras (1954, pp. 205–206). For the assessment of Jevons by recent historians of economic thought, see Black and others (1973, pp. 98–139); Blaug (1978, pp. 324–332); Jaffé (1976); Howey (1960, pp. 39–60).

220

express, so far as I can see, what Walras meant by *libre concurrence*." (Schumpeter, 1954, p. 973).

While Walras did Jevons less than justice, Edgeworth, in a sense, did him more than justice, insofar as his concept of a trading body was generously interpreted so as to exclude the case of indeterminate equilibrium of bilateral monopoly. In our opinion, however, even Edgeworth did Jevons less than justice, since the implication of Jevons's law of indifference was not fully exploited in Edgeworth's explanation of Walrasian equilibrium of competitive exchange as a limit of the core of an exchange game, when the number of participants is infinitely large. If indivisible lump-sum transactions are ruled out and competition is assured so as to satisfy Jevons's law of indifference, it is easily seen that the Walrasian equilibrium is the only stable outcome, even in a simple four-person, two-good case of the Edgeworth game of exchange. The point is that the concept of coalition used to block allocations in an Edgeworth game is too pure from the point of view of Jevons's law of indifference.

Jevons's approach thus suggests that an infinitely large number of participants is, though sufficient, not necessary for Walrasian competitive equilibrium, a point which has been forgotten in recent studies of the large economy, in the tradition of Edgeworth.

II

Let us sketch Jevons's theory of exchange. Before giving his famous equations of exchange, Jevons discussed two concepts, i.e., the trading body and the law of indifference, both of which are very important if we are to understand the true implications of Jevons's theory of exchange.

Jevons considered exchange of goods between trading bodies.

"The trading body may be a single individual in one case; it may be the whole inhabitants of a continent in another; it may be the individuals of a trade diffused through a country in a third. England and North America will be trading bodies if we are considering the corn we receive from America in exchange for iron and other goods. The continent of Europe is a trading body as purchasing coal from England. The farmers of England are a trading body when they sell corn to the millers, and the millers both when they buy corn from the farmers and sell flour to the bakers." (Jevons, 1888, pp. 88–89).

Though some historians of economic thought are critical of Jevons's use of the trading body (see Blaug, 1978, pp. 327–328, and Howey, 1960, p. 52), similar concepts have been used very often in various fields of economic theory. For example, countries are regarded, as Jevons himself suggested, as trading bodies and the utility function, or indifference map, of a country is considered in the theory of international trade.[2] Another example concerns the models used in theories of the microeconomic foundations of macro-economics, in which the representative or aggregate household and representative or aggregate firm exchange labour services and consumers' goods (e.g., see Benassy, 1977, and Malinvaud, 1977).

The reason why Jevons uses such an artificial invention to explain exchange is that the behaviour of the aggregate or average person is much more stable than that of an individual person.

"A single individual does not vary his consumption of sugar, butter, or eggs from week to week by infinitesimal amounts, according to each small change in the price. He probably continues his ordinary consumption until accident directs his attention to a rise in price, and he then, perhaps, discontinues the use of the articles altogether for a time. But the aggregate, or what is the same, the average consumption, of a large community will be found to vary continuously or nearly so." (p. 89; see also p. 15).

Differential calculus can be used, therefore, only for the case of the aggregate or average person.

Jevons then proceeds to the discussion of the law of indifference.

"If, in selling a quantity of perfectly equal and uniform barrels of flour, a merchant arbitrarily fixed different prices on them, a purchaser would of course select the cheaper ones ... Hence follows what is undoubtedly true, with proper explanations, that in the same open market, at any one moment, there cannot be two prices for the same kind of article." (p. 91).

"It follows that the last increments in an act of exchange must be exchanged in the same ratio as the whole quantities exchanged. Suppose that two commodities are bartered in the ratio of x for y; then every m-th part of x is given for the m-th part of y, and it does not matter for which of the m-th parts ... even an infinitely small part of x must be exchanged for an infinitely small part of y, in the same ratio as the whole quantities. This result we may express by stating that the increments concerned in the process of exchange must obey the equation $dy/dx = y/x$." (pp. 94–95).

Behind this "statical view of the question" there must be a dynamic process of trading. What Jevons had in mind is a piecemeal exchange process, since "dynamically we could not treat the ratio of exchange other-

[2]See Chipman (1965, pp. 690–698), where conditions for the existence of social indifference curves are discussed. For example, homothetic utility functions are sufficient for Jevons's example given below.

wise than as the ratio of dy and dx, infinitesimal quantities of commodity" (p. 94; see also pp. 92–93).

Now we finally come across the proposition which contains "the keystone of the whole theory of exchange, and of the principal problems of economics," i.e.,

"The ratio of exchange of any two commodities will be the reciprocal of the ratio of the final degrees of utility of the quantities of commodity available for consumption after the exchange is completed."

"Let us now suppose that the first body, A, originally possessed the quantity a of corn, and that the second body, B, possessed the quantity b of beef. As the exchange consists in giving x of corn for y of beef, ... the quantities exchanged satisfy two equations, ... $F_1(a - x)/G_1(y) = y/x = F_2(x)/G_2(b - y)$." (p. 95 and pp. 99–100, respectively), where the cumbersome notations used by Jevons are replaced by ordinary ones and F_1 and G_1, and F_2 and G_2, respectively, denote A's final degrees of utility (i.e., marginal utilities) of corn and beef, and B's final degrees of utility of corn and beef.

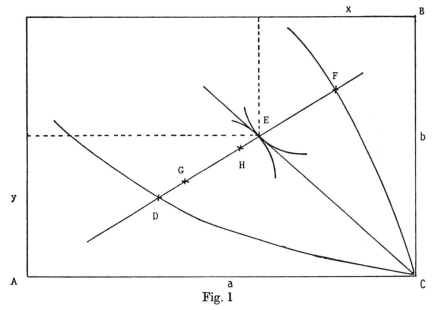

Fig. 1

III

Jevons's famous equations of exchange to determine the quantities exchanged, which are given in the previous section, are satisfied at point E in Fig. 1, i.e., the so-called Edgeworth box diagram, where the quantity of corn is measured horizontally, that of beef vertically, the quantities of commodity available to A are measured with the origin at A, those available to B, with the origin at B, curve DEF is the contract curve which is a locus of points where indifference curves of the two bodies are tangent, and point C denotes the initial allocation of commodities. If each trading body consists of only a single individual, i.e., in the case of isolated exchange or bilateral monopoly, the equilibrium is indeterminate in the sense that any point on the contract curve between D and F is a stable outcome of exchange. There is no reason why only E can be an equilibrium and Jevons's equations of exchange cannot be applied in this case.

Since Jevons said that "the trading body may be a single individual in one case", and considered the indeterminateness of equilibrium only in the case where a commodity is indivisible (pp. 88, 122–125; see also Edgeworth, 1881, p. 30), we have to admit that Jevons did not recognize the indetermin- ateness of bilateral monopoly. Edgeworth was, however, quite generous in interpreting Jevons;

> "... the Jevonian law of indifference has place only where there is competition, and, indeed, perfect competition. Why, indeed, should an isolated couple exchange every portion of their respective commodities at the same rate of exchange? Or what meaning can be attached to such a law in their case? ... This consideration has not been brought so prominently forward in Professor Jevons's theory of exchange, but it does not seem to be lost sight of. His couple of dealers are, I take it, a sort of typical couple, clothed with the property of indifference, whose origin in an open market is so lucidly described; not naked abstractions like the isolated couples imagined by a De Quincey or Courcelle-Seneuil in some solitary region. Each is in Berkleian phrase a representative particular; an individual dealer only is presented, but there is pre- supposed a class of competitors in the background." (Edgeworth, pp. 31, 109).

In view of Jevons's reason for using the trading body, i.e., the fact that the behaviour of an average person is more stable than that of a single individual, Edgeworth's interpretation of Jevons is much more reasonable and productive than those of hairsplitting historians of economic thought (see Black and others, 1973, pp. 120–121).

Edgeworth (p. 18) presupposed, however, perfect competition, where the number of participants is infinite, to justify Jevons's equations of exchange. Suppose each trading body consists of two identical (in taste and initial holding) persons, say A_1, A_2 and B_1 and B_2. It is evident that equal quantities of commodities should be allocated to identical persons in the same trading body. Allocation D can be blocked by a coalition of A_1, A_2

and either of B_1 and B_2. Thus A_1, A_2 and, say, B_1 can recontract such that, whilst B_1 remains at point D, A_1 and A_2 reach the mid-point between D and C, thereby achieving a higher level of utility than at D. Any allocation on the contract curve and close to D, say, G, can similarly be blocked by the same coalition. Similarly, allocation F or those on the contract curve and close to F can be blocked by a coalition of both B_1 and B_2 and any one of A_1 and A_2. Allocations like H, which is close to E, however, cannot be blocked in this case and belong, therefore, to the core, i.e., to the set of stable allocations which cannot be blocked by coalitions. To block an allocation like H, Edgeworth considered the case that each trading body consists of infinitely many identical persons. However close H is to E, then, it can be successfully blocked by a coalition of all persons belonging to A and some suitable number of persons belonging to B, since an identical allocation available to each person in A can be sufficiently close to H, on the line CH, that it is above the indifference curve passing through H. The only allocation to remain in the core is E, since line EC is tangent to the indifference curve passing E.[3]

In interpreting Jevons's equations of exchange, Edgeworth understood rightly the implication of Jevons's use of the trading body, but he did not perhaps fully understand the implication of Jevons's law of indifference. In our opinion, Jevons's law of indifference is so powerful that the equations of exchange hold even if the number of participants in exchange is finite.

IV

Let us return to the case of four-person, two-good exchange, where each trading body consists of two identical persons, A_1, A_2 and B_1, B_2. Fig. 2 is a reproduction of Fig. 1 and allocation H on the contract curve DEF cannot, as in Fig. 1, be blocked by the coalition of A_1, A_2 and B_1, considered by Edgeworth. We can show, however, that H is not a stable outcome of exchange, if Jevons's law of indifference and trading process are taken into consideration.

First, let us rule out the possibility of an indivisible lump-sum transaction and assume that each single transaction is divisible, so that every portion of a homogeneous commodity is treated indifferently, i.e., exchanged against the other commodity at the same rate of exchange. Since there is no Walrasian auctioneer, either of the two parties may suggest a rate of exchange, in a two individual exchange, and both parties decide what they would like to trade at that exchange rate. The resulting *provisional* contract, determined by the smaller of the two desired trades, is called a single transaction.

[3]For the original argument of Edgeworth, to which this paragraph is a simplified close substitute (I hope), see pp. 34–42. See also Hildenbrand and Kirman (1976, pp. 18–23).

In other words, the dynamic exchange process of Jevons is a piecemeal one, as was argued in Section II above, and a finite, i.e., not infinitesimal, transaction is permissible only when it is divisible.

There must be, then, at least two successive transactions and the ratio of exchange should vary in the course of exchange between C and H, if allocation H can ever be reached by exchange starting from C. Otherwise, if there is only a single transaction and the exchange ratio remains unchanged throughout the exchange process, it must be equal to the slope of line CH and exchange must proceed on line CH, starting from C and moving toward H. Such an exchange process has to be terminated at J, however, since the transaction is divisible and it is unfavourable for A to go beyond J. Further, we can see that the variable ratio of exchange between C and H must be identical to the slope of the tangent to the indifference curve passing through H, for the last infinitesimal or finite transaction arriving at H.

Suppose, therefore, that exchange proceeds like CKH, i.e., the first transaction to be done with exchange ratio favourable to B, and unfavourable to A, like CK, and the second transaction, with exchange ratio favourable to A, and unfavourable to B, like KH, though the average ratio is CH. If we suppose that this is the case, not only with exchange between A_1 and B_1 but also with exchange between A_2 and B_2, allocation H can be blocked by the following arbitrage of different exchange ratios.[4] B_1 cancels a part of the transaction with A_1, with the ratio of exchange KH, and proposes some new transaction to A_2. Suppose, for the moment, that B_1 offers A_2 the exchange ratio CK. A_2 may accept this proposal of B_1 by cancelling a part of his transaction with B_2 at the exchange ratio CK, since "provided that A gets the right commodity in the proper quantity, he does not care whence it comes, so that we need not . . . distinguish the source or destination" (Jevons, pp. 117–118). In any event, if B_1 offers A_2 an exchange ratio strictly between CK and KH, both parties can be strictly better off as a result of cancelling parts of their earlier provisional contracts. Not only B_1, but also B_2, A_1 and A_2 may take the initiative to exploit different exchange ratios.

This kind of arbitrage activity is the basis of Jevons's law of indifference and allocation E, i.e., the solution of Jevons's equations of exchange, is the only allocation which is not blocked by arbitrage leading to the law of indifference. We have to admit, of course, that we are, like Edgeworth, ruling out the possibility of collusive agreements not to engage in this type of arbitrage activity. With regard to Fig. 2, there would be an incentive

---

[4]Otherwise, A_2 and B_1 must first rearrange transactions with side-payments to A_1 and B_2 so that B_1 (A_2) can trade with A_1 (B_2) at two different rates of exchange. For the general definition of arbitrage, see Boulding (1955, p. 73).

for B_1 and B_2 to enter into a collusive agreement not to engage in any arbitrage which would undermine H and eventually result in the attainment of E.

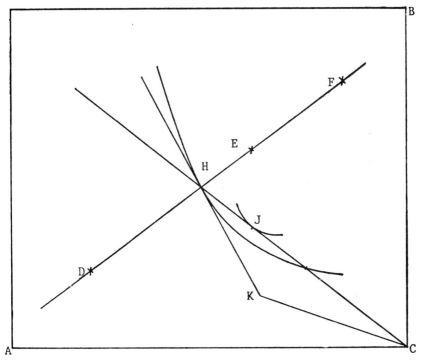

Fig. 2

The above argument for the specialized case can be generalized in several directions. First, if the exchange ratio varies, not once, but several times, we can consider that each person tries to replace a part of his transaction with an exchange ratio less favourable than the average, i.e., CH, by some transaction with an exchange ratio more favourable than the average. Secondly, the path of exchange with a varying exchange ratio may be different for different persons in the same trading body, though initial and end points are identical. Still, arbitrage is possible, since for each person some exchange transactions are with an exchange ratio more favourable than CH and some other transactions are with an exchange ratio less favourable. Thirdly, the initial point C need not be at the corner, but can be anywhere except on the contract curve. Furthermore, the initial holdings of different members of the same trading body may be different, provided that their utility functions are identical and homothetic, so that social indifference curves of the trading body can exist. Finally, the analysis extends to the case of three or more persons in each trading body.

Why can the allocation H, which cannot be blocked by Edgeworth's coalition, be blocked by Jevons's arbitrage in four-person, two-good exchange? This is because the coalition considered by Edgeworth, and in modern theory of games, is defined too stringently to be used in the theory of exchange. It is a sort of closed group of participants, in the sense that they exchange only among themselves, being completely separated from other participants who do not belong to the coalition. In the actual world, such a pure coalition is rather rare. For example, the Second World War was fought between Axis Powers (Germany, Italy, Japan, etc.) and Allied Powers (France, U.K., U.S.A., U.S.S.R., etc.), but these two coalitions were not closed and pure, since until the last moment diplomatic relations were kept open between Japan and the U.S.S.R.

In Jevons's arbitrage process described above, we may consider that B_1 and A_2 are forming a sort of coalition to block the allocation H, where the law of indifference is not established. This coalition is, however, of an impure and open kind, since B_1 cancels only a part of the transaction KH with A_1 and keeps the rest of transaction KH and the whole of transaction CK with A_1. Since the part of transaction KH to be cancelled can be very small, B_1 can safely expect that the behaviour of A_1 remains unchanged. Furthermore, by this coalition to block H, B_1 and A_2 expect to exploit others, in the sense that together they would have a larger stock of the two commodities after exchange than they had initially, i.e., before exchange at C, though these expectations are not fulfilled, in the sense that the process of arbitrage and recontracting ends up at E. Since Jevons's concept of coalition is wider than that of Edgeworth, it is no wonder that an allocation not blocked by the latter can be blocked by the former. Being dependent on expectations of the behaviour of non-members, an open coalition is certainly less stable than a closed one, though the stability of the realized coalition itself is not required to block an allocation in Edgeworth's exchange game. There is no reason, however, to exclude the possibility of open coalition, since "any individual is free to contract (at the same time) with an indefinite number" (Edgeworth, p. 18).

V

Jevons's theory of exchange is, of course, not a complete theory, as Zawadzki pointed out:

"Toutes les formules de l'auteur, qu'il s'agisse de l'échange proprement dit ou de la production, peuvent d'ailleurs être considérées beaucoup

A Note on Jevons's Law of Indifference and Competitive Equilibrium   229

plus comme des indications que comme des tentatives de solution complète."

and

"Plus spécialement en ce qui concerne l'échange de plusieurs marchandises entre elles, sa solution semble manquée, . . . Disposées comme elles sont les formules de Jevons l'obligent à comparer toujours les marchandises deux à deux; il est par suite très difficile, sinon impossible, de traiter le problème général." (Zawadzki, 1914, pp. 110–111).[5]

In the case of three or more commodities, as Walras (1954, p. 157) argued, "we do not have perfect or general market equilibrium unless the price of one of any two commodities in terms of the other is equal to the ratio of the prices of these two commodities in terms of any third commodity". According to Morishima (1977, pp. 18–19), Walras had in mind two models of general market equilibrium, i.e., the tâtonnement model with auctioneer and numéraire, and the arbitrage model without auctioneer. The latter, we may say, is similar to the one considered by Jevons, and used the theory of arbitrage which had been developed by Cournot. Morishima (p. 20) admits, however, that "in the two-commodity case the arbitrage theory is trivial, because there is, of course, no arbitrage via a third commodity". This implies that Walras considered only arbitrage among three or more commodities and did not consider arbitrage in the exchange of two commodities, which is the very problem of Jevons. In other words, he simply assumed the law of indifference, without considering how it is established through arbitrage, even in his arbitrage model.

This is also the case with Morishima and Majumdar (1978), an ingenious article which argued that the only possible outcome in a free exchange process is the Walrasian competitive equilibrium, even in a finite economy, if Cournot-Walras arbitrage behaviour is assumed. Jevons's law of indifference is simply assumed there, with the result that the only possible outcome is the Walrasian competitive equilibrium, even in an isolated exchange of two goods between two persons, i.e., even if each trading body consists of a single person. If the law of indifference itself is to be explained by arbitrage behaviour, however, the Walrasian competitive equilibrium is not the only outcome in an isolated exchange. There must be at least four persons, so that there is competition in each of two trading bodies.

What Jevons suggested to us has, therefore, not yet been fully developed by Edgeworth and his followers, let alone by Walras and his followers.

---

[5]See, however, Negishi (1962) for an attempt to solve general equilibrium on the basis of exchange of two commodities.

REFERENCES

Benassy, J. P. (1977). "A Neo-Keynesian Model of Price and Quantity Determination in Disequilibrium" in G. Schwodiauer (ed.), *Equilibrium and Disequilibrium in Economic Theory*, Dordrecht, D. Reidel.

Black, R. D. C. and others (1973). *The Marginal Revolution in Economics*, Durham, N.C., Duke University Press.

Blaug, M. (1978). *Economic Theory in Retrospect*, Cambridge, Cambridge University Press.

Boulding, K. E. (1955). *Economic Analysis*, New York, Harper and Row.

Chipman, J. S. (1965). "A Survey of the Theory of International Trade. Part 2", *Econometrica*, Vol. XXXIII, No. 3, pp. 685–760.

Edgeworth, F. Y. (1881). *Mathematical Psychics*, London, Kegan Paul.

Hildenbrand, W. and Kirman, A. P. (1976). *Introduction to Equilibrium Analysis*, Amsterdam, North-Holland.

Howey, R. S. (1960). *The Rise of the Marginal Utility School*, Lawrence, Ks., University of Kansas Press.

Jaffé, W. (1976). "Menger, Jevons and Walras De-Homogenized", *Economic Inquiry*, Vol. XIV, No. 4, pp. 511–524.

Jevons, W. S. (1888). *The Theory of Political Economy*, London, Macmillan.

Malinvaud, E. (1977). *Theory of Unemployment Reconsidered*, Oxford, Blackwell.

Morishima, M. (1977). *Walras's Economics*, Cambridge, Cambridge University Press.

——————— and Majumdar, M. (1978). "The Cournot-Walras Arbitrage, Resource Consuming Exchange, and Competitive Equilibrium" in *Hommage à F. Perroux*, Grenoble, Presse Universitaires de Grenoble.

Negishi, T. (1962). "On the Successive Barter Process", *Economic Studies Quarterly*, Vol. XII, No. 2, pp. 61–64.

Schumpeter, J. A. (1954). *History of Economic Analysis*, New York, Oxford University Press.

Walras, L. (1954). *Elements of Pure Economics*, (W. Jaffé, tr.) Homewood, Ill., Irwin.

——————— (1965). *Correspondence of Leon Walras and Related Papers, 1*, (W. Jaffé, ed.) Amsterdam, North-Holland.

Zawadzki, W. (1914). *Les Mathématiques Appliquées à l'Économie Politique*, Paris, Rivière.

5 Competition and the Number of Participants: Lessons of Edgeworth's Theorem

Takashi Negishi

1

In his *Mathematical Psychics* (1881), Edgeworth demonstrated in so-called Edgeworth equivalence theorem that the outcome of an exchange economy where traders act cooperatively is identical to the Walrasian equilibrium of perfect competition where traders act non-cooperatively as price-takers, when the number of traders of the same type is infinitely large. Certainly it clarifies an implication of Walrasian economics and is a pioneering work of the recent theory of a large economy composed of infinitely many small traders.[1] When the number of traders is limited, Edgeworth argued, traders themselves cannot determine the outcome of an exchange economy cooperatively and the utilitarian principle should be introduced to arbitrate disagreement between traders. Since the infinity of identical traders is a sufficient condition in the proof of Edgeworth's equivalence theorem, however, a natural question is whether it is also a necessary one. If it is not necesary, what is essential for Walrasian economies is not so much the infinity of the number of small traders as perfect information and no friction, also assumed in Edgeworth's theorem.

After we consider the case of infinitely many identical traders, following Edgeworth, in Section 2, we shall argue in Section 3, following Farrell (1970) and Schitovitz (1973), that the equivalence theorem holds even in the case of duopoly where there are only two suppliers of a good, though the number of demanders is infinite.[2] In Section 4, then, we shall summarize our consideration (Negishi, 1982b) in the case of four traders: that the equivalence theorem also holds if indivisible transactions are ruled out and competition is assured, so as to satisfy Jevon's Law of Indifference. Section 5 is devoted to the case of bilateral monopoly or isolated exchange between two traders, where it is argued that the equivalence theorem holds if exchanges are repeated indefinitely through time. Finally, we shall consider what lessons we learned from these considerations of the equivalence theorem from the points of view of Walrasian as well as non-Walrasian economics.

2

Edgeworth (1881, pp.34–42) demonstrated by the use of (the original form of) the Edgeworth box diagram that the only stable outcome of a pure exchange economy is the Walrasian equilibrium of perfect competition and that all the other allocations are blocked by traders cooperatively, when the numbers of traders of the same type is infinitely large.

Figure 5.1 is an Edgeworth box diagram, where the quantity of the first good is measured horizontally, that of the second good, vertically, and the quantities of goods given to trader *A*-are measured with the origin at *A*, those given to trader *B*, with the origin at *B*. Point *C* denotes the initial allocation of goods before trade, which implies that the total amount of the first good in the economy is *AC* and that of the second good, *BC*.[3] Curves I, II, etc. are indifference curves of trader *A*, curves 1, 2, etc. are those of trader *B*, and curve *DEF* is the contract curve which is a locus of points

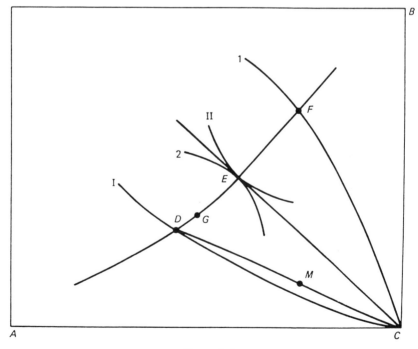

Figure 5.1

where indifference curves of two traders are tangent. Point E is the Walrasian equilibrium of perfect competition, with the common tangent to indifference curves at E passing through point C. It is clear that all the points on the contract curve between D and F are stable outcome if there are only two traders, i.e. trader A and trader B, while Edgeworth insists that all the points except E can be blocked by a coalition of some traders if there are infinitely many identical (in taste and initial holdings) traders of type A and infinitely many identical traders of type B.

Let us first consider the case where there are two traders of type A, i.e. trader A_1 and trader A_2, and two traders of type B, i.e. trader B_1 and trader B_2. It is evident that equal quantities of goods should be allocated to identical traders of the same type, so that we can still consider Figure 5.1.[4] Allocation D can then be blocked by a coalition of A_1, A_2 and either of B_1 and B_2. Suppose A_1 and, say, B_1 keep the contact D between them while A_2 cancels the contract D with B_2 and returns to C. Thus A_1, A_2 and B_1 can arrange by themselves in such a way that, whilst B_1 remains at point D, A_1 and A_2 reach the mid-point M between D and C, thereby achieving a higher level of utility than at D. With some side-payments to B_1, all the traders joining the coalition (A_1, A_2, B_1) can be better off by themselves then they are at D, and the allocation D is blocked. Any allocation on the contract curve and close to D, say, G, can be blocked similarly by the same coalition. Similarly, allocation F or those on the contract curve and close to F can be blocked by a coalition of both B_1 and B_2 and any one of A_1 and A_2. Allocations like H in Figure 5.2, however, cannot be blocked in this way and belong, therefore, to the core, i.e. to the set of stable allocations which cannot be blocked by coalitions. The reason why H cannot be blocked is that at the mid-point between H and C traders of type A cannot achieve a higher level of utility than at H.

To block an allocation like H, Edgeworth considered the case where there are infinitely many identical traders of type A and infinitely many identical traders of type B. The allocation H can then be blocked by a coalition formed by all the A traders and more than half but less than all the B traders. In the coalition some A traders still continue to trade with B traders in the coalition and are located at H, while the rest of A traders having no trade partners in the coalition are located at C. By increasing the numbers of B traders joining the coalition sufficiently and therefore increasing the number of A traders located at H, we can make the average allocation of A traders (some at H, some at C) sufficiently close to H, on the line CH, that it is located like J above the indifference curve passing through H. By reallocating among themselves, therefore, all the A traders are better off than they are at the allocation H. With some side-payments to B traders in the coalition, all the traders joining the coalition can be better off than they are at the allocation H, so that H is blocked by such a coalition. Similarly, any point between D and F where the common tangent

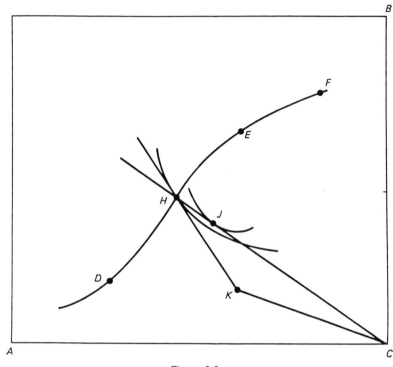

Figure 5.2

to two indifference curves does not pass through the point *C* can be blocked by a coalition of traders, if necessary, by changing the roles of *A* traders and *B* traders from those in the case of the allocation *H*. Obviously only the point *E* belongs to the core, i.e., the set of allocations which are not blocked by such a coalition.

If the number of traders of each type is infinite, therefore, the stable outcome of a pure exchange economy with perfect information and no friction (no restriction of trade, no cost of trade, no cost of organizing coalitions, etc.) can be derived as an equilibrium of perfect competition in which each trader is behaving as if taking prices (the slope of *EC*) as given. The existence of infinitely many identical traders is a sufficient condition for such an equilibrium. But, by no means is it a necessary one, as we shall see.

3

Following Farrell (1970) and Schitovitz (1973), consider next the case of duopoly where there are only two traders of another type, though the total quantities of two goods are finite in the economy. Since equal quantities of goods should be allocated to identical traders of the same type, we can still use the Edgeworth box diagrams, i.e. Figures 5.1 and 5.2, which describe the half of the economy, one of the duopolists and its infinitely many customers.

Suppose first that there are two B traders, B_1 and B_2 and infinitely many traders of type A. In Figures 5.1 and 5.2, BC is the quantity of the second good initially held by a B trader and AC is the sum of quantities of the first good initially held by the half of A traders. Curves I, II, etc. in Figure 5.1 are aggregate indifference curves of A traders, as well as individual ones, which can be constructed if the identical individual indifference curves are homothetic, so that the marginal rate of substitution between two goods depends only on the ratio of the quantities of goods and the Engel curve is a line through the origin (Chipman, 1965).

An allocation H in Figure 5.2 can now be blocked by a coalition of one B trader and more than half but less than all of infinitely many A traders. All the A traders currently trading with the B_1 trader which joins the coalition also join the coalition and keep the contract H with B_1. Some A traders currently trading with B_2 (who does not join the coalition) join the coalition and cancel the contract with B_2 to return to the initial point C. By decreasing the number of the latter type A traders joining the coalition in sufficient numbers and therefore increasing the number of A traders located at H, relative to those A traders located at C, we can make the average allocation of individual A traders in the coalition sufficiently close to that at point H, on the line CH, that it is like an allocation at J located above the indifference curve passing through H.[5] By reallocating among themselves, therefore, all the A traders in the coalition are better off than they are at the allocation H. With some side-payments to B_1 which is located at H, all the traders joining the coalition can be better off than they are at H, so that H is blocked.

Suppose next that there are two A traders, A_1 and A_2 and infinitely many traders of type B. In Figures 5.1 and 5.2, then, AC is the quantity of the first good initially held by an A trader and BC is the sum of quantities of the second good initially held by half of the B traders. Curves 1, 2, etc. in Figure 5.1 are aggregate indifference curves of B traders. In this case, an allocation H in Figure 5.2 can be blocked by a coalition of one A trader and less than half of infinitely many B traders. Suppose A_1 joins the coalition. Those B traders also joining the coalition can keep trade with A_1 unchanged so that they can maintain the same level of utility as enjoyed at allocation H. A_1 cancels trade with those B traders who are not permitted to join the coalition, so that A_1 moves on HC from H toward C. Unless it cancels too many contracts with B traders, A_1 can be located as at J above the indifference curve passing through H. By reallocating among themselves, then, all the traders joining the coalition can be made better off than they are at allocation H, so that H is blocked.[6]

Similarly, any point between D and F on the contract curve where the common tangent to two indifference curves does not pass through point C can be blocked by a coalition of traders, if necessary, by changing the roles of A traders and B traders from those in the case of allocation H. Again, it is point E only which belongs to the core allocation. In other words, even a duopoly market ends up with an equilibrium identical to that of perfect competition, if customers are infinitely many and free to organize coalitions.

4

Let us return to the case where there are two traders of type A, i.e. trader A_1 and trader A_2, and two traders of type B, i.e. trader B_1 and trader B_2. Consider the allocation H on the contract curve DEF in Figure 5.2, which, as we saw in Section 2, cannot be blocked by the coalition of A_1, A_2 and B_1, considered by Edgeworth. We can show, however, that H is not a stable outcome of exchange, if Jevons's Law of Indifference and the trading process are taken into consideration.

> If in selling a quantity of perfectly equal and uniform barrels of flour, a merchant arbitrarily fixed different prices on them, a purchaser would of course select the cheaper ones ... Hence follows what is undoubtedly true, with proper explanations, that in the same open market, at any one moment, there cannot be two prices for the same kind of article. (Jevons, 1888, p.91)

> It follows that the last increments in an act of exchange must be exchanged in the same ratio as the whole quantities exchanged. Suppose that two commodities are bartered in the ratio of x for y; then every m-th part of x is given for the m-th part of y, and it does not matter for which of the m-th parts – even an infinitely small part of x must be exchanged for an infinitely small part of y, in the same ratio as the whole quantities. This result we may express by stating that the increments concerned in the process of exchange must obey the equation $dy/dx = y/x$. (Ibid., pp.94–5)

Behind this 'statical view of the question' there must be a dynamic process of trading. What Jevons had in mind is a piecemeal exchange process, since 'dynamically we could not treat the ratio of exchange otherwise than as the ratio of dy and dx, infinitesimal quantities of commodity' (Jevons, 1888, p.94, see also pp.92–3). Let us rule out, therefore, the possibility of an indivisible lump-sum transaction and assume that each single transaction is divisible, so that every portion of a homogenous commodity is treated indifferently, i.e. exchanged against the other commodity at the same rate of exchange. In other words, the dynamic exchange process is a piecemeal one, as considered by Jevons, and finite; i.e. not infinitesimal, transaction is permissible only when it is divisible.

There must be, then, at least two successive transactions and the ratio of exchange should vary in the course of exchange between C and H, in Figure 5.2, if allocation H can ever be reached by exchange starting from C. Otherwise, if there is only a single transaction and the exchange ratio remains unchanged throughout the exchange process, it must be equal to the slope of line CH and exchange must proceed on line CH, starting from C and moving toward H. Such an exchange process has to be terminated at J, however, since the transaction is divisible and it is unfavorable for A to go beyond J. Further, we can see that the variable ratio of exchange between C and H must be identical to the slope of the tangent to the indifference curve passing through H, for the last infinitesimal or finite transaction arriving at H.

Suppose, therefore, that exchange proceeds like CKH, i.e. the first transaction to be done with exchange ratio favorable to B, and unfavorable to A, like CK, and the second transaction, with exchange ratio favorable to A, and unfavorable to B, like KH, though the average ratio is CH. If we suppose that this is the case, not only with exchange between A_1 and B_1 but also with exchange between A_2 and B_2, allocation H can be blocked by the following arbitrage of different exchange ratios: B_1 cancels a part of the transaction with A_1, with the ratio of exchange KH, and proposes some new transaction to A_2. Suppose, for the moment, that B_1 offers A_2 the exchange ratio CK. A_2 may accept this proposal of B_1 by cancelling a part of his transaction with B_2 at the exchange ratio CK, since 'provided that A gets the right commodity in the proper quantity, he does not care when it comes, so that we need not ... distinguish the source or destination' (Jevons, 1888, pp.117–18). In any event, if B_1 offers A_2 an exchange ratio strictly between CK and KH, both parties can be strictly better off as a result of cancelling parts of their earlier provisional contracts. Not only B_1, but also B_2, A_1 and A_2 may take the initiative to exploit different exchange ratios.

This kind of arbitrage activity is the basis of Jevon's Law of Indifference and allocation E; i.e. the solution of Jevons's equation of exchange (Jevons, 1888, pp.95, 99–100) is the only allocation which is not blocked by arbitrage leading to the law of indifference. Edgeworth's equivalence theorem holds if transactions are divisible and the competition between identical traders is assured so as to satisfy Jevon's Law of Indifference.

5

In the case of the bilateral monopoly or the isolated exchange where there is only one *A* trader and one *B* trader, however, Edgeworth was right to insist on the indeterminateness of the outcome of exchanges and to suggest the introduction of the utilitarian principle.

> Thus, proceeding by degrees from the case of two isolated bargainers to the limiting case of a perfect market, we see how contract is more or less indeterminate according as the field is less or more affected with the first imperfection, limitation of numbers. (Edgeworth, 1881, p.42)

> Competition requires to be supplemented by arbitration, and the basis of arbitration between self-interested contractors is the greatest possible sum-total utility. Thus the economical leads up to the utilitarian calculus. (Ibid., p.56)

The utilitarian principle can be justified by the so-called neo-utilitarian arguments which presuppose decision under uncertainty in the situation where individuals do not know what their personal positions would be, but rather have an equal chance of obtaining any of the social positions existing, from the highest down to the lowest (Harsanyi, 1955; Pattanaik, 1968; Vickrey, 1960; and Fleming, 1952).[7] Consider, for example, a prospective immigrant weighting the relative attractiveness of different communities into which he can immigrate. The immigrant is uncertain of the position that he can occupy in the various communities. Under these conditions he may

> make his decision on the basis of maximizing his expected utility, the alternative utilities in question being those of the various members of a given community ... If we identify the social welfare with the attractiveness of the various communities to this prospective immigrant, we see that the social welfare function takes the form of a weighted sum of the individual utilities. If the immigrant is completely ignorant as to what role he will find in the new community and weights the roles of all individuals equally, we get the Benthamite summation of individual utilities. (Vickrey, 1960)

Both Edgeworth and neo-utilitarians are certainly right if we are concerned with contracts which are once-for-all ones in an essentially timeless situation. If we are interested in contracts which are repeated through time, however, things are different at least in two respects. Firstly, as we argued elsewhere (Negishi, 1982a), neo-utilitarian *ex ante* arguments based on the maximization of expected utility are not applicable, since we cannot neglect the *ex post* problem of envy of the fortunate by the unfortunate. Secondly, as we shall see, it is possible to argue that the equilibrium is determinate and identical to that of perfect competition even in the case of the bilateral monopoly or the isolated exchange.

As is suggested by Walker (1973), Edgeworth himself was interested in contracts repeated through time.

> For Marshall in the passage cited has in view a market in a special sense distinguished from normal, whereas the process which I analyse has much in common with the determination of normal equilibrium. (Edgeworth, 1925, II, p.313)

> They [curves of Demand and Supply] apply also to transactions in factors of production, such as the labour-market; and not only to 'market value' in the sense of the term which refers to short periods, but also to 'natural' or normal value, provided that the periods considered are not so long but that the dispositions, and 'disponibilities' in M. De Foville's phrase, may be supposed constant. We are to conceive two groups of dealers encountering each other, not once only, but from time to time, and ascertaining by repeated tentatives a rate of exchange at which a steady flow of trade is maintained. (Ibid., p.333)

> On the first day in our example a set of hirings are made which prove not to be in accordance with the dispositions of the parties. These contracts terminating with the day, the parties encounter each other the following day, with dispositions the same as on the first day – like combatants *armis animisque refecti* – in all respects as they were at the beginning of the first encounter, except that they have obtained by experience the knowledge that the system of bargains entered into on the first occasion does not fit the real dispositions of the parties. (Edgeworth, 1925, I, p.40)

Let us now consider the problem of two good two trader exchanges which are repeated through time indefinitely. This is done by assuming that the original exchange, say, for a year, is perfectly divisible into exchanges in infinitely many short periods. Initial holdings given at the beginning of the year like manna are assumed to be distributed by traders uniformly over periods, and the unit period utility function as a function of consumed quantities of goods in the period are assumed to be unchanged through time and independent of consumption in other periods so that we can still use Figures 5.1 and 5.2. It is assumed that initial holdings are transferable through periods in either direction with no cost while goods acquired through exchange are storable through periods with no depreciation.

Let us assume that marginal utility is decreasing in the sense that the unit period utility function is concave. Formerly, if c_i is the consumption of the i-th good and $c = (c_1, c_2)$, then the unit period utility function u satisfies

$$a\ u(c^1) + (1 - a)\ u(c^2) < u(a\ c^1 + (1 - a)\ c^2)$$

for any given a such that $0 \leq a \leq 1$, where c^1 and c^2 are different consumption vectors. When $a = 1/2$, this implies that the average of utilities of different consumption vectors is smaller than the utility of the average consumption vector. By assuming away time preference so that multiperiod utility is the simple non-weighted sum of unit period utilities, it is assured that an equilibrium series of exchange must be stationary in the sense that each trader consumes unchanged quantities of goods through periods. This is because a contract with non-stationary consumptions is not Pareto-optimal and blocked by two traders cooperatively.[8]

Therefore, we have to consider only contacts between D and F on the contract curve in Figures 5.1 and 5.2, where AC is the amount of the first good given to trader A as the initial holdings and distributed to a unit period, and BC is the amount of the second good initially given to trader B and distributed to the period. Now a stationary contract like H in Figure 5.2 can be blocked by trader A who keeps the trade with trader B unchanged and stays at H in earlier periods and cancels the trade with B and returns to C in later periods. By choosing properly the length of earlier and later periods, transferring the first good (initial holdings) from later periods to earlier periods, and storing the second good (acquired through exchange) from earlier periods to later periods, trader A can locate his stationary consumption at J and be better off than at H. Similarly, any stationary contract between D and F on the contract curve except E can be blocked either by trader A or by trader B. The only maintainable stationary contract is, therefore, E which is identical to the equilibrium of perfect competition even in the case of the bilateral monopoly or the isolated exchange.

6

Edgeworth demonstrated that the existence of infinitely many identical traders is a sufficient condition for the equivalence of the core allocations and Walrasian equilibria of perfect competition for an exchange economy. We have argued above that ,though sufficient, it is not a necessary condition. This suggests that what is essential for perfect competition is not so much the number of traders or the scale of traders relative to that of the economy, as perfect information and no friction which are also explicitly assumed in the proof of Edgeworth's theorem. Let us consider what lessons we can learn from these considerations, not only from the point of view of Walrasian economics but also that of non-Walrasian economics.

In Walrasian economics it is usually assumed that traders are price-takers and prices are 'cried' by auctioneers. Although such auctioneers often exist in organized exchanges, it is highly unrealistic to assume that they exist in all the markets in the economy. Furthermore, in general it is not rational to assume that all the traders are price-takers, since a trader can gain by price-making behavior, i.e. by reducing its supplies to raise prices and by reducing its demands to reduce prices, if all the other traders are price-takers (Roberts and Postlewaite, 1976). To get rid of this difficulty, we have to assume the existence of infinite traders or negligible scale of traders relative to that of the economy, so that the possibility of such gains from price-making behavior can safely be ignored. It must be emphasized, however, that following Edgeworth we are not assuming the price-taking behavior of traders and the existence of an auctioneer. In our cooperative games of exchange, there is no possibility of the price-making behavior of some traders taking advantage of the price-taking behavior of other traders, a problem which may appear in the case of decentralized, i.e. non-cooperative, games of exchange like the Walrasian one.

In a sense Walrasian assumptions are justified by our considerations of Edgeworth's cooperative game of exchange through the equivalence theorem, since the effectiveness of assumptions in a theory should be judged not by the realism of the assumptions themselves, but by the outcome of the theory derived from them. The outcome of a theory of exchange without Walrasian assumptions, i.e. core allocations, is equivalent to the outcome of Walrasian economics, i.e. equilibria of perfect competition. Even though traders are actually not price-takers and there are no auctioneers, we may assume that traders are price-takers and there are auctioneers, provided that information is perfect and there are no frictions.

If information is not perfect and there exist such frictions as cost of organizing coalitions, cost of trade, etc., however, things are quite different. In Walrasian economics, price-taking suppliers perceive infinitely elastic demand curves. Since information is perfect, demand can be increased infinitely by a slight reduction of the price. If information is not perfect, an increase in demand is limited, since a lower price asked by a supplier may not be fully informed to customers who are currently buying from other suppliers. Even if it is informed, some of such customers, who are not informed of the quality of the product of a price-cutting supplier, may not shift their demand to the supplier, unless the reduction of price is considerable. Suppliers have to perceive, then, downward sloping demand curves for the reduction of prices. On the other hand, a higher price charged by a supplier necessarily induces present customers to leave in search of lower priced suppliers, even if such search activities involve some costs. Suppliers have to perceive, therefore, fairly elastic demand curves which are due to the asymmetric behavior of customers (Negishi, 1979, pp.36, 87; Scitovsky, 1976; Reid, 1981, p.97). As in the case of kinked demand curves due to the asymmetric behavior of rival firms (Sweezy, 1939) price rigidity may appear, which can be a microeconomic foundation of Keynesian fix-price economic theory (Negishi, 1979, pp.89–90; Reid, 1981, pp.65–6; Cuddington, Johansson and Löfgren, 1984, pp.41–4).

Notes

1. See, for example, Debreu and Scarf (1963), Hildenbrand (1974) and Hildenbrand and Kirman (1976). See also Negishi (1985) for Cournot's theory of oligopoly which is another pioneering work on the theory of a large economy.
2. Following Edgeworth like us, Farrell used the Edgeworth box diagram, while Schitovitz takes a measured theoretic approach which is certainly more general but has no intuitive appeal like the Edgeworth diagram. See also Negishi (1985) for the Bertrand model of duopoly which generates a perfectly competitive equilibrium.
3. Of course, this is a simplifying assumption and in general C can be anywhere in the box.
4. Otherwise, such an unequal allocation can be blocked by a coalition of the least favored type A trader and the least favored type B trader or a coalition of two equally favored traders with unequal allocations, so that they can be better off by themselves.
5. Though H and J are allocations to half of the traders in the economy, they can be considered as allocations to an A trader, since indifference curves are homothetic. Alternatively, we can argue more generally by the use of Scitovsky indifference curves.
6. This argument is due to Farrell (1970), though he seems to be concerned not so much with the oligopoly with a finite number of firms as with the case of an infinite number of firms. See, however, Friedman (1977), pp.283–5.
7. Creedy (1984) pointed out that Edgeworth himself had the same idea.
8. Since marginal utility is diminishing, the optimal path of the utility of a trader must be stationary through time, while the corresponding consumption stream must be stationary in view of the convexness of indifference curves to the origin.

References

Chipman, J. S. (1965) 'A Survey of the Theory of International Trade', 2, *Econometrica*, 33: 685–760.

Creedy, J. (1984) 'Edgeworth: Utilitarianism and Arbitration', *History of Political Economy*, 16: 609–18.

Cuddington, J. T., P. O. Johansson and K. G. Löfgren (1984) *Disequilibrium Macroeconomics in Open Economies* (Oxford: Blackwell).

Debreu, G. and H. Scarf (1963) 'A Limit Theorem on the Core of an Economy', *International Economic Review*, 4: 235–46.

Edgeworth, F. Y. (1881) *Mathematical Psychics* (London: Kegan Paul).

Edgeworth, F. Y. (1925) *Papers Relating to Political Economy* (London: Macmillan).

Farrell, M. J. (1970) 'Edgeworth Bounds for Oligopoly Prices', *Economica*, 37: 342–61.

Fleming, J. M. (1952) 'A Cardinal Concept of Welfare', *Quarterly Journal of Economics*, 66: 366–84.

Friedman, J. W. (1977) *Oligopoly and the Theory of Games* (Amsterdam: North Holland).

Harsanyi, J. C. (1955) 'Cardinal Welfare, Individualistic Ethics and Interpersonal Comparisons of Utility', *Journal of Political Economy*, 63: 309–21.

Hildenbrand, W. (1974) *Core and Equilibria of a Large Economy* (Princeton: Princeton University Press).

Hildenbrand, W. and A. P. Kirman (1976) *Introduction to Equilibrium Analysis* (Amsterdam: North Holland).

Jevons, W. S. (1888) *The Theory of Political Economy* (London: Macmillan).

Negishi, T. (1979) *Microeconomic Foundations of Keynesian Macroeconomics* (Amsterdam: North-Holland).

Negishi, T. (1982a) 'Edgeworth's *Mathematical Psychics* Considered from the Point of View of Fair Distribution' (in Japanese), *Mita Gakkai Zasshi*, 75–1: 27–38.

Negishi, T. (1982b) 'A Note on Jevons's Law of Indifference and Competitive Equilibrium', *Manchester School*, 50: 220–30.

Negishi, T. (1985) 'Non-Walrasian Foundations of Macroeconomics', in G. R. Feiwel (ed.) *Issues in Contemporary Macroeconomics and Distribution* (London: Macmillan).

Pattanaik, P. K. (1968) 'Risk, Impersonality and the Social Welfare Function', *Journal of Political Economy*. 76: 1152–69.

Reid, G. C. (1981) *The Kinked Demand Curve Analysis of Oligopoly* (Edinburgh: Edinburgh University Press).

Roberts, D. J. and A. Postlewaite (1976) 'The Incentives for Price-Taking Behavior in Large Exchange Economies', *Econometrica*, 44: 115–27.

Schitovitz, B. (1973) Oligopoly in Markets with a Continuum of Traders, *Econometrica*, 41: 467–501.

Scitovsky, T. (1976) 'Asymmetries in Economics', *Scottish Journal of Political Economy*, 25: 227–37.

Sweezy, P. M. (1939) 'Demand under Conditions of Oligopoly', *Journal of Political Economy*, 47: 568–73.

Vickrey, W. (1960) 'Utility, Strategy and Social Decision Rules', *Quarterly Journal of Economics*, 74. 507–35.

Walker, D. A. (1973) 'Edgeworth's Theory of Recontract', *Economic Journal*, 83: 138–49.

[15]

Vol. 40 No. 3·4   OSAKA ECONOMIC PAPERS   March 1991

Bertrand's duopoly considered as an Edgeworth's game of exchange

Takashi Negishi

(1)

Among many important contributions of Professor Hirofumi Shibata to the development of economic theory, certainly we can find several seminal articles on the various problems of welfare economics. According to the so-called fundamental theorem of welfare economics, a perfectly competitive allocation is Pareto optimal and any Pareto optimal allocation can be achieved through the perfect competition and a proper income redistribution. Roughly speaking, this implies that the perfect competition is a sufficient condition for optimal allocation. It does not mean, however, that the price-taking-behavior is necessary for optimal allocation. In this occasion to congratulate Professor Shibata for his sixtieth birthday, we discuss a small problem in welfare economics, i.e., that of an optimal allocation achieved by non-price-taking behavior.

Bertrand's model of duopoly suggested by his criticism of Cournot's model of duopoly has been traditionally considered, like Cournot's one, as a non-cooperative game between duopoly firms.[1] The aim of this note is, however, to consider it as an Edgeworth's game of exchange (or more exactly as an Edgeworth-Farrell game) among duopoly firms and consumers.

In section (2), we sketch Cournot's and Bertrand's models of duopoly and suggest the possibility to consider Bertrand's model as an Edgeworth's game of exchange. An Edgeworth box diagram is constructed in section (3) to analyze the exchange between consumers' money and the product of firms. Section (4) is devoted to show that the equilibrium of Bertrand duopoly is the core of such a game, which is identical to the competitive (marginal cost pricing) equilibrium.

(2)

Consider a case of a duopoly industry dominated by two firms. The demand function for the product of duopolists, called as the demand function for the industry, is an aggregate of the demand functions of infinitely many individual consumers. If we assume that the demand function for the industry has the downward sloping demand curve,

(1) $q = D(p)$, $dq/dp < 0$,

where p is the price consumers take as given and q is the aggregate quantity demanded by them. Then, the inverse demand function

(2) $p = p(q)$, $dp/dq < 0$

---

1) See Cournot (1987), pp.79-84 and Bertrand (1883).

is obtained from (1). The condition for the equality of demand and supply in the industry is $q_1 + q_2 = q$, where q_1 and q_2 are respectively quantities to be supplied from the first and second firms. The profit of the first firm is

(3) $p(q_1 + q_2)q_1 - cq_1$

and that of the second firm is

(4) $p(q_1 + q_2)q_2 - cq_2$

where c denotes the identical marginal cost assumed to be constant. In words, the profit of a firm is a function not only of its own supply but also of the supply of the other firm.

As is well known, Cournot considered the Nash solution that each firm will independently maximize its profit with respect to its own supply, assuming that the supply of the other is unchanged. The condition for it are obtained by the differentiation of (3) and (4) respectively with respect to q_1 and q_2,

(5) $p(q_1 + q_2) + q_1p'(q_1 + q_2) - c = 0.$

and

(6) $p(q_1 + q_2) + q_2p'(q_1 + q_2) - c = 0$

where p' denotes the derivative of p. By solving (5) for q_1, we have the reaction function of the first firm, $q_1 = R_1(q_2)$. Similarly, the reaction function of the second firm is obtained from (6) as $q_2 = R_2(q_1)$. If we draw reaction curves of two firms corresponding respectively to reaction functions R_1 and R_2 in a $q_1 - q_2$ diagram, the Cournot-Nash solution $(\overline{q_1}, \overline{q_2})$ is obtained at the intersection of two reaction curves.

Suppose now, following Bertrand, that each duopolist assumes that the other will keep its price (not supply) unchanged. If the price is higher than c, i.e., the identical marginal (as well as average) cost, each firm will undercut its rival by a very small margin because it will monopolize the market and obtain maximum profit by undercutting infinitesimally. This process continues until the price is equalized to the marginal cost c. The reaction function of the first firm is given for $p_2 \geqq c$ as

(7) $p_1 = R_1(p_2) = a(p_2 - c) + c$

where p_1 and p_2 are respectively prices charged by the first and second firms and a is a positive constant infinitesimally smaller than 1. Similarly, the reaction function of the second firm is given as

(8) $p_2 = R_2(p_2) = a(p_1 - c) + c$

for $p_1 \geqq c$. Figure 1 shows reaction curves of two firms corresponding respectively to reaction function R_1 and R_2 defined in (7) and (8). The equilibrium of Bertrand duopoly is given at the intersection B of two reaction curves R_1 and R_2, $(p_1, p_2) = (c, c)$.

The equilibrium of Cournot duopoly $(q_1, q_2) = (\overline{q_1}, \overline{q_2})$ is a Nash solution which satisfies

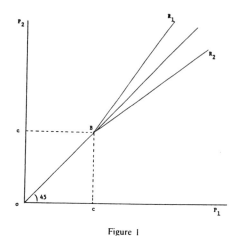

Figure 1

(9) $M_1(\bar{q}_1, \bar{q}_2) \geqq M_1(q_1, \bar{q}_2)$, $M_2(\bar{q}_1, \bar{q}_2) \geqq M_2(\bar{q}_1, q_2)$

where M_1 and M_2 are respectively profits of the first and second firms. Similarly, the equilibrium of Bertrand duopoly $(p_1, p_2) = (c, c)$ is a Nash solution which satisfies

(10) $M_1(c, c) \geqq M_1(p_1, c)$, $M_2(c, c) \geqq M_2(c, p_2)$.

If Bertrand duopoly is seen, like Cournot duopoly, as a non-cooperative game between two firms, then, Bertrand equilibrium is formally identical to Cournot equilibrium as a Nash solution of such a game. Only difference between them is that strategies for firms are quantities of supply in Cournot duopoly, while they are prices charged by firms in Bertrand duopoly. It rusults, however, in an economically important difference, since $p(\bar{q}_1 + \bar{q}_2) > c$ in view of (5) and/or (6).

In the traditional interpretation of Bertrand duopoly, like in Cournot duopoly, only firms are considered as players of games, whose profits depend, not only on their own actions, but also on actions of other players, and who might act strategically, taking repercussions between players into consideration. In other words, consumers are not regarded explicitly as such players in these games of duopoly. They are considered rather as a part of environment in which games are played by players. Certainly it is true that the role of consumers in Cournot duopoly is very limited, since they merely adjust their demand to prices given by the auctioneers who change prices so as to equate such a demand with the supply determined by firms. In Bertrand duopoly, however, consumers are more active, since they not only adjust their demand continuously to prices but also drastically shift their demand from one firm to another. In other words, consumers join to a coalition with a firm so as to block the current condition and to improve their position in the market. This may suggest the possibility to see Bertrand duopoly from the point of view of a Edgeworth game among consumers and firms.

By the use of Edgeworth box diagram, Edgeworth considered games of exchange between two types of traders. An equilibrium of Edgeworth game of exchange is called a core and is defined as a distribution of goods among traders, which cannot be blocked by any coalition of a subset of players formed so as to improve by themselves the position of at least some of the members and not to worsen the position of any of them. As is well known, Edgeworth showed that the core of such a game is equivalent to the competitive (price-taking) equilibrium of exchange if the number of traders of each type is infinitely large. This equivalence theorem was then extended by Farrell to the case of duopoly in which there are only two traders of one type and infinitely many traders of another type.[2]

(3)

Now let us consider Bertrand duopoly as a game among two identical firms having the same constant unit cost c and infinitely many identical consumers having the same taste and the same quantity of money. It is convenient to use an Edgeworth box diagram of exchange between the product to be supplied by a firms and the money to be spent by a half of infinitely many consumers. In figure 2, the quantity of the product is measured horizontally, and that of money, vertically. The quantity of the product and that of the money to be distributed to all the customers of the firm (a half of all the consumers) are measured from the origin A, while the quantity of money to be distributed to the firm and that of the product to be produced by it are measured from the origin B. The vertical distrance between A and B represents the quantity of money initially held by all the customers of the firm, while the horizontal distance between B and C is the quantity of the product, the cost of which is equal to AB. In other words, AB = c × BC.

Curves in Figure 2 drawn convex to the origin A are indifference curves of consumers. We assume that identical indifference curves of infinitely many consumers are homothetic so that the marginal rate of substitution between the product and money depends only on the ratio of the quantities of the product and money, as is shown in Figure 3. Since the slope of indifference curves are identical at A and B, and at C and D, in Figure 3, we can aggregate indifference curves I of two identical consumers into aggregate indifference curve II which is also an indifference curves of individual consumer when quantities of the product and money are doubled. In general, homothetic indifference curves of infinitely many identical consumers can be interpreted as aggregate indifference curves as well as indifference curves of individual consumers.

In Figure 2, downward sloping parallel lines are equi-profit lines of the firm, since identical slope of these lines represents the average (as well as marginal) cost c of the firm. The line BD indicates the distributions with zero profit while the profit corresponding to the line FG is indicated by BF. If there is any equilibrium in Bertrand duopoly, the corresponding point of distribution after the exchange cannot be located above the line BD in Figure 2, since the profit of the firm should be non-negative. In the terminology of an Edgeworth game, a distribution above the line BD is blocked by a coalition composed only by a firm, since it can increase its profit to zero at B. Similarly, the equilibrium point cannot be located below the in-

---

2) See Edgeworth (1881), pp.16-56, Farrell (1970), and Negishi (1989), pp.330-343.

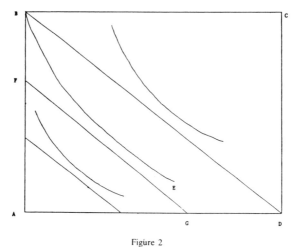

Figure 2

difference curve BE. since there must be consumers' surplus from the exchange. Otherwise. the distribution is blocked by a coalition composed only by consumers.

(4)

Since there are two identical firms in the industry, we have two identical box diagrams, i.e., the one for the first firm and its customers (a half of all the consumers) and the other for the second firm and its customers (another half of all the consumers). The equilibrium points, however, should be with the same average price of the product in two box diagrams. Suppose not. In Figure 4, which is a reproduction of Figure 2. point I represents the equilibrium of the first firm and its customers, and point II, the equilibrium of the second firm and its customers. Note that the second firm charges lower average price indicated by the slope of BB" than the the first firm which charges average price indicated by the slope of BB'. Such a distribution, however. cannot be the equilibrium of duopoly, since it can be blocked by a coalition of a firm and some consumers.

If the utility of point II is higher than that of point I, and the profit is also higher at II than at I. consider a coalition of the first firm. i.e., the higher pricing firm and its customers (a half of all the consumers). By reducing the price to BB" and changing the distribution between them to point II, both the profit of the firm and the utility of consumers are increased in the coalition. so that the distribution (I, II) is blocked by the coalition. i.e., by the price reduction of the higher pricing firm and adjustments of consumers to it. If the profit is higher at I than at II, however. consider a coalition of the second firm charging lower price and the customers of the first firm. By raising the price to BB' and choosing a point between G and I, both the profit of the firm and the utility of consumers can be increased in the coalition. so that the distribution (I, II) are again blocked by the coalition. i.e., by the price advance of the lower pricing firm and adjustments of consumers.

If the utility of point I is higher than that of point II in Figure 4, but profit is higher at II than at I, consider a coalition of the first firm charging higher price and the customers of the second firm. By reducing the price to BB" and choosing a point between F and II, both the profit of the firm and the utility of consumers are increased in the coalition, so that the distribution (I, II) is again blocked by the coalition, i.e., by the price reduction of the higher pricing firm and adjustments of consumers. Finally, if the profit is higher at I than at II, consider a coalition of the second firm and its customers so as to change the distribution between them to point I. The distribution (I, II) is blocked by the price advance of the lower pricing firm and adjustments of consumers.[3]

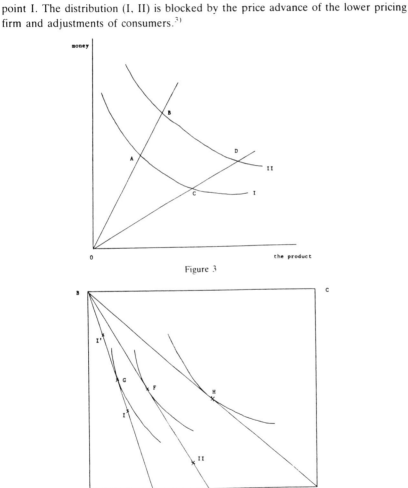

Figure 3

Figure 4

---

3) The limiting case, where both utility and profit are identical at I and at II, can also be blocked either by the price reduction and expansion of the lower pricing firm or by the price advance and contraction of the higher pricing firm.

Since we have considered all the possible cases, it is demonstrated that the equilibrium points of Bertrand duopoly, if any, must have the identical average price of the product in two box diagrams. Suppose, in the Figure 4, such a price is indicated by the line BB' and I and I' are equilibrium points, respectively, of the exchange between the first firm and its customers, and that between the second firm and its customers. The distribution (I, I'), however, can be blocked by a coalition of a firm and some consumers. Suppose that the utility is higher at I than at I'. The coalition of the second firm and its customers block I' and move to I, since the profit is also higher at I than at I'. Suppose next that the utility is higher at I' than at I. Consider a coalition of the second firm and the customers of the first firm. The second firm expands its output to a point between I' and I so that its profit is increased and so does the utility of consumers in the coalition. The equilibrium of Bertrand duopoly must, then, be identical in two box diagrams.

We can consider, therefore, only one box diagram to find the equilibrium for a Bertrand duopoly. Suppose that it is on the price line BB' in Figure 4. If it is like I' located between B and G, it is blocked by a coalition of any one firm and its customers (i.e., half of all the consumers), since both the profit and the utility can be increased by moving to point G. In other words, such a distribution is blocked by the expansion of any firm and the adjustments of its customers. If it is located like I between G and B', including G, consider a coalition of any one firm, all of its customers and some of the customers of the other firm. By expanding its output (moving I downward on BB'), the firm can increase its profit. While the customers of the firm are located, then, at such a new position of I, those of the other firm, who join the coalition, are at B, since the latter cancelled the exchange with the other firm. The average position of consumers in the coalition, then, can be located at G, so that they are better off (or not worse off) than at the old position of I, if the number of the customers of the other firms to join the coalition is properly chosen.[4] By reducing the price slightly (turning BB' to the right around B), all the consumers in the coalition can be made better off than at the old I. Thus, a distribution with the price higher than the marginal cost c can be blocked by the slight reduction of price and the expansion of output of a firm and by the consumers' adjustment to the lower price, including the selection of the firm (from which to buy) as well as that of the quantity. This is, however, exactly the process of adjustments suggested by Bertrand.

Now, only points on the line BD with the slope c remain to be considered. If it is between B and H, it can be blocked by the expansion of any firm and the adjustments of its customers. Points between H and D cannot be blocked by a coalition to expand output and to reduce the price. Since the profit is zero at such points, however, they can be blocked by the reduction of output of a firm and adjustments of its customers to it. Then only the distribution H remains unblocked by coalitions. It is the core of Bertrand duopoly considered as an Edgeworth game.[5] The equilibrium price in Bertrand duopoly has to be equal to the marginal cost c.

---

4) In the case of the constant marginal cost, the number of consumers need not be infinite, since we can make the new position of I such that BG = GI, so that all the customers of the other firms join the coalition. In the case of the increasing marginal cost, however, equi-profit curves are convex to the origin C in Figure 4 and the output might not be increased so much.

OSAKA ECONOMIC PAPERS   Vol. 40 No. 3·4

(Professor, Faculty of Economics, University of Tokyo)

References

1) Bertrand, J. Review of Walras: *Théorie mathématique de la richesse sociale* and Cournot: *Recherches sur les principes mathématiques de la théorie des richesse*, Journal des Savants, 1883, 499-503.
2) Cournot, A., *Researches into the Mathematical Principles of the Theory of Wealth*, N.T. Bacon tr., Macimillan, 1897.
3) Edgeworth, F.Y., *Mathematical Psychics*, Kegan Paul, 1881.
4) Edgeworth, F.Y., *Papers Relating to Political Economy*, I, Macmillan, 1925.
5) Farrell, M.J., "Edgeworth Bounds for Oligopoly Price," *Economica* 37 (1970), 342-361.
6) Negishi, T., *History of Economic Theory*, North-Holland, 1989.

---

5) Edgeworth (1925, p.118) came very close to this conclusion, but was prevented from reaching it, possible because he was more interested in the case with no equilibrium due to the existence of capacity limits, and because he might not realize fully the possibility of extending his limit theorem to the case of duopoly.

5 Non-Walrasian Foundations of Macroeconomics*

TAKASHI NEGISHI

MICROECONOMICS OF ALTERNATIVE MACROAPPROACHES

The aim of macroeconomics is, particularly after Keynes's *General Theory*, to explain changes in the aggregate output or employment as well as those in the price level.

The explanation of these changes in the macroeconomics of the so-called monetarism is well founded on the traditional Walrasian microeconomics, that is, the determination of the price by the equilibrium of demand and supply. Friedman (1968) describes the effects of an increase in the rate of growth of money supply at the long-run equilibrium where prices have been stable. Because prices of products typically respond to an unanticipated rise in nominal demand faster than the prices of factors of production, real wages received go down — though real wages anticipated by employees go up since at first they are likely to evaluate the wages offered at the unchanged price level, with the result that in the short-run equilibrium both demand and supply of factors of production are equally larger than those in the long-run equilibrium. This 'simultaneous fall *ex post* in real wages to employers and rise *ex ante* in real wages to employees is what enables employment to increase'. But soon employees begin to realize that prices are rising and they demand higher nominal wages. To keep the supply of labour larger than the equilibrium long-run supply, real wages

*The author is grateful to Professors Shigeo Akashi, Shozaburo Fujino, Kotaro Suzumura, Kiichiro Yagi, and Messrs Asaji Hirayama and Takashi Oginuma for their comments on the earlier versions, though they are not responsible for any remaining flaws.

169

now have to be higher than the long-run equilibrium ones. Any rise in real wages, however, decreases the demand for labour and tends to return employment to its former long-run equilibrium level.

'Temporary increase in employment comes not from inflation *per se*, but from unanticipated inflation', and exists only so far as inflation is not fully anticipated even though the rate of money growth and price rise continue to be higher than the initial long-run equilibrium rate.

This is quite a contrast to the quantity theory of money before Keynes. Even in the discussion of transition period, Fisher (1918) admitted that

> the amount of trade is dependent, almost entirely, on other things than the quantity of currency, so that an increase of currency cannot, even temporarily, very greatly increase trade. In ordinarily good times practically the whole community is engaged in labor, producing, transporting, and exchanging goods. The increase of currency of a boom period cannot, of itself, increase the population, extend invention, or increase the efficiency of labor. These factors pretty definitely limit the amount of trade which can be reasonably carried on.

In other words, pre-Keynesian quantity theory of money considered that any changes in the supply of money are absorbed in changes in the price level, with the level of employment unchanged even in the short-run.[1] The hard core of Walrasian paradigm or research programme, that is, the determination of short-run equilibrium by the equality of demand and supply, is shared by both pre-Keynesian and post-Keynesian quantity theories of money. The former cannot explain the changes in the level of employment in the short run whereas the latter, equipped with a new protective belt, does so by means of the discrepancy between anticipated and realized changes in real wages that changes both demand and supply of factors of production in the same direction.[2]

In the so-called fixprice model of macroeconomics considered by Barro and Grossman (1976), Benassy (1982), Malinvaud (1977), and others, on the other hand, demand and supply do not have to be equalized by changes in prices and the level of output or that of employment is determined by the short-side principle that either demand or supply, whichever is smaller, is realized. Fixprice implies that prices are independent of the relation between demand and supply. Since prices rise naturally in the face of excess demand unless they are controlled institutionally, we are mainly concerned with the fixprice model in the Keynesian case where prices are not reduced in the face of excess supply rather than in the case of suppressed inflation where prices cannot rise in the face of excess demand. The Keynesian case in the fixprice model is more Keynesian than the *General Theory*, since excess supplies exist not only in the labour market but also in the goods market. In other words, the first postulate of classical economics, that is, the equality of price and marginal cost, is also discarded so that firms wish to sell more, if they can, at the current price or even at a price slightly lower. In a depression, certainly, it is more realistic to suppose excess or idle capacities and unintended inventories as well as involuntary unemployment rather than to assume away, as in the *General Theory*, the former and to concentrate the analyses on the latter.

Keynesian or fixprice macroeconomics, however, has not been so well founded on microeconomic theory. Unlike the macroeconomics of the quantity theory of money, it cannot be founded on traditional Walrasian microeconomic theory, since we have to explain why price is not reduced in the face of excess supply or why price changes so slowly that it remains practically unchanged in the short run. We have to, therefore, develop a non-Walrasian microeconomic theory. In the next section, we argue that Carl Menger, who shared with Walras the honour of being one of the founding fathers of the marginal revolution, is the earliest and the greatest non-Walrasian economist. We can start our consideration of non-Walrasian economics from the microeconomics of Menger who pointed out that the price or the ratio of exchange is not the only important factor in the theory of exchange and emphasized the asymmetry between demand (offer of money, the most liquid commodity) and supply (offer of other commodities), that is, the former is easily realized while the latter is not. As a matter of fact, Fujino (1982a) pointed out (based on his (1978, 1980 and 1982b)), referring to Menger, that such an asymmetry always exists in a monetary economy, irrespective of the existence of excess supply or excess demand, because money is superior in liquidity to goods. In the next section however, our argument is more limited and is confined only to the Keynesian case of excess supply. Then in the third section, we summarize our own argument on the microeconomic foundations of Keynesian macroeconomics, based on the theory of kinked demand curves that are perceived, not by oligopolistic firms as in Sweezy (1939), but by more competitive firms. The final section is devoted to arguing that traditional Walrasian theory of perfect competition does not need to be based on the theory of the large economy and to examine the essential difference between Walrasian and non-Walrasian economics.

MENGERIAN MARKETS AND EXCESS SUPPLY

Unlike Walras who considered ideally well-organized markets, Menger is mainly interested in more realistic markets where we observe 'that it does not lie within our power, when we have bought an article for a certain price, to sell it again forthwith at that same price. . . The price at which anyone can at pleasure buy a commodity at given market and a given point of time, and the price at which he can dispose of the same at pleasure, are two essentially different magnitudes' (Menger, 1892). To explain these market-phenomena, Menger introduces the concept of *Absatzfaehigkeit der Waaren*, that is, saleability or marketability of commodities, and considers that the smaller the difference between the higher buying price and lower selling price, the more marketable the commodity usually is.

We must note, at first, that Menger distinguishes the commodity from the goods and has a separate chapter on the theory of commodity in his *Grundsaetz* (1871). He defines 'commodities as (economic) goods of any kind that are intended for sale', and explains as follows the relation between goods and commodities:

> Commodity-character is therefore not only not property of goods but usually only a transitory relationship between goods and economizing individuals. Certain goods are intended by their owners to be exchanged for the goods of other economizing individuals. During their passage, sometimes through several hands, from the possession of the first into the possession of the last owner, we call them commodities, but as soon as they have reached their economic destination (that is, as soon as they are in the hands of the ultimate consumer) they obviously cease to be commodities and become consumption goods in the narrow sense in which this term is opposed to the concept of commodity. But where this does not happen, as in the case very frequently, for example, with gold, silver, etc., especially in the form of coins, they naturally continue to be commodity as long as they continue in the relationship responsible for the commodity-character.[3]

But why do some goods cease to be commodities quickly while coins never cease to be commodities? In other words, why can little metal discs, apparently useless as such, be commodities and exchanged against useful things that can become consumption goods? This is because of the different degrees of saleability or marketability of commodities. Money is the most saleable or marketable of all commodities. 'The theory of money necessarily presupposes a theory of saleableness of goods'.[4] Degree of saleability or marketability is defined by Menger as 'the greater or less facility with which commodities can be disposed of at a market at any convenient time at current purchasing prices, or with less or more diminution of the same' (Menger, 1892).

Although Menger described in detail the circumstances upon which the degree of saleability or marketability of commodities depends, from our point of view the interesting fact is that it depends on whether the relevant market is well organized or poorly organized.

> If the competition for one commodity is poorly organized and there is danger therefore that the owners will be unable to sell their holdings of the commodity at economic prices, at a time when this danger does not exist at all, or not in the same degree, for the owners of other commodities, it is clear that this circumstance will be responsible for a very important difference between the marketability of that commodity and all others. . . Commodities for which an organized market exists can be sold without difficulty by their owners at prices corresponding to the general economic situation. But commodities for which there are poorly organized markets change hands at inconsistent prices, and sometimes cannot be disposed of at all (Menger, 1871, pp. 248-9).

Since the Walrasian model concentrates on a well-organized market, Menger's theory of commodity for which the market is poorly organized and whose marketability is not high suggests to us a non-Walrasian theory of the market. Menger's criticism of pre-Mengerian economics that 'investigation into the phenomena of price has been directed almost exclusively to the quantities of the commodities exchanged, and not as well to the greater or less facility with which wares may be disposed of at normal prices' (Menger, 1871, p. 242; see also Menger, 1892), can also be applied to Walrasian economics. In other words, Menger's theory of marketability of commodities is a first attempt of non-Walrasian economics.

Fixprice models of recent studies of macroeconomics are based on the short-side principle that in disequilibrium, transaction realized equals the minimum of supply and demand. From the point of view of Menger's marketability, the short-side principle can be interpreted to imply that commodities are highly marketable when their suppliers are on the short-side of the relevant market and not so marketable when they are on the long-side of the market. We can argue, however, that in the type of markets considered by Menger suppliers of commodities other than money are generally likely to be on the long-side of the market in the sense that they wish, if they can — that is, if there is enough demand — to sell more at the current price. This is so because, unlike the Walrasian markets where all the commodities are as marketable as money is, in Mengerian markets there is asymmetry between demand that is to offer money, the most marketable commodity, and supply that is to offer less marketable commodities.

In Figure 5.1, we consider the case of a typical supplier of a commodity,

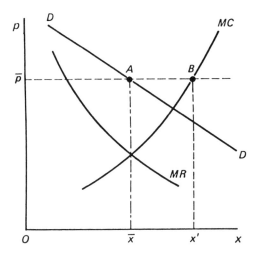

FIGURE 5.1

that is, a firm that produces it, and the level of output x is measured horizontally, and price p and cost vertically. A downwardly sloping demand curve $D\,D$ is perceived by this firm, not especially because it is a monopolist, nor because its product is differentiated, but more fundamentally because the market in which the commodity is exchanged for money is poorly organized, so that the larger amount of the commodity can be disposed of in the market only at a less favourable ratio of exchange. The equilibrium of the firm is shown to be at A, or $(\bar{p}, \bar{x})$, with the marginal revenue MR equalized with marginal cost MC at $\bar{x}$. At the current price $\bar{p}$, the firm wishes to sell as much as x', but is quantitatively constrained at $\bar{x}$, since there is not enough demand. There exists an implicit excess supply AB or $x' - \bar{x}$, and the commodity is less marketable than the money.

There are two kinds of demand and supply, that is, regular, stable demand and supply and irregular, casual demand and supply. For example, the demand curve in Figure 5.1 is concerned with regular demand that is perceived by a regular supplier. When A and B do not coincide and the regular suppliers possess excess supply, casual demand will be easily satisfied by regular suppliers at the current price $\bar{p}$. Casual supply has to compete with regular excess supply to catch casual demand and will not be easily satisfied, unless the price is reduced. The marketability of the relevant commodity is low and the resale price of those casual suppliers who want to get rid of the commodity they have just bought will be much lower than the price at which they bought as regular demanders.

PRICE RIGIDITY AND KINKED DEMAND CURVES

As we saw in the preceding section, Menger's theory of commodity suggests that demand and supply are asymmetric and competitive suppliers perceive downwardly sloping demand curves in non-Walrasian markets. In our arguments on microeconomic foundations of Keynesian economics, however, we have been insisting that in a Keynesian situation competitive suppliers perceive demand curves that are not only downwardly sloping, but also flatter to the left than to the right, having an upward-pointing kink in the middle. Such a kinked demand curve was used by Sweezy (1939) to explain observed price rigidity in oligopolistic industries.[5] Although the reasons for the existence of a kink in the demand curve perceived in a Keynesian situation is different from the one given by Sweezy in the case of oligopoly, our explanation of why the price is not reduced in the face of excess supply is, at least in formal aspects, very similar to Sweezy's explanation of oligopolistic price rigidity.

Sweezy insisted that the perceived demand curve, which he called the imagined demand curve, can only be thought of with reference to a given starting point, that is, a price-output combination that depends upon the history of the case. In Figure 5.2, where the quantity q is measured horizontally and the price p vertically, the point P is such a starting point, that is, the point of currently realized price and the sale of output of an oligopolistic firm. The firm perceives a subjective demand curve from this

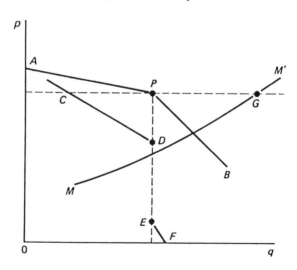

FIGURE 5.2

starting point. Sweezy pointed out that rival firms react asymmetrically according to whether a price change is upward or downward. If the firm raises its price it must expect to lose business to its rivals who will not raise their price, while if the firm cuts its price it has no reason to believe it will succeed in taking business away from its rivals who will retaliate by cutting their prices so as to avoid the loss. The perceived demand curve tends to be elastic going up and inelastic going down from the starting point P. In other words, it has a corner or a kink at P, like APB in Figure 5.2.

The marginal revenue curve derived from APB is $CDEF$, which has a discontinuity at the level of output where the perceived demand curve has a kink. If the marginal cost curve MM' passes, as in Figure 5.2, between the two parts of the discontinuous marginal revenue curve, the starting point P is also the point of profit maximization. Sweezy pointed out that any disturbance that affects only the position of the marginal cost curve may leave the equilibrium price and output entirely unaffected. More important for oligopolistic price rigidity is, however, the fact that, as Sweezy stated, any shift in demand will clearly first make itself felt in a change in the quantity sold at the current price. In other words, a shift in demand changes the position of the starting point P at which the kink occurs to the right or left without affecting the price. If the marginal cost is not increasing rapidly, the equilibrium price remains unchanged while shifts in demand are absorbed by changes in the level of output.

While the kinked demand curve in Sweezy's theory of oligopoly is the result of the asymmetric reaction of rival firms, in our case of competitive firms in a Keynesian situation it is considered to be the result of asymmetric reaction of customers. 'Lower prices asked by a supplier may not be fully advertised to customers currently buying from other suppliers who are maintaining their current price, while a higher price charged by the same supplier necessarily induces present customers to leave in search of lower price suppliers' whom they easily find, since in the Keynesian situation there are many other firms that wish to supply more at the current unchanged price.[6] In Figure 5.2, therefore, AP is horizontal and CD coincides with AP for a competitive firm in a Keynesian case. In Keynesian terminology, we may call the determination of the level of output at which the expected profit is maximized with given marginal revenue and marginal cost curves as the problem of the short-term expectation. Since short-term expectation is assumed to be realized by Keynes,[7] such a level of output must coincide with the level of output corresponding to the given starting point P in Figure 5.2. Although it wishes to supply at the current price up to the level of output corresponding to point G where the current price and the marginal cost are equalized, the firm is trapped at the level of output corresponding to *P*, with no incentive to reduce price to increase demand. There exists an implicit excess supply or idle capacity *GP* owing to the deficiency of the aggregate effective demand. Any shift in the aggregate effective demand changes the position of *P* horizontally, with price unchanged. If the marginal cost is not increasing rapidly, shifts in the aggregate demand are entirely absorbed by changes in the level of output.[8]

It is encouraging that Scitovsky (1978) also emphasized the possibility of asymmetric behaviour of customers which renders results in a kinked demand curve:

> A price increase causes those who have previously bought to buy less or stop buying altogether; a price reduction prompts previous buyers to buy more and some people who previously bought nothing to start buying. Now that last group of people are in a very different position from all the others, in that most of them learn about the price change only if the producer goes to the trouble and expense of advertising it. The others are already established customers, who learn about the price change automatically, in the course of their routine purchases and at no cost to the seller. In other words, the whole market responds to a price increase but only part of it responds to a price reduction, unless the seller advertises it.[9]

THE LARGE ECONOMY AND MARKET IMPERFECTIONS

We argue in our non-Walrasian microeconomics that even a perfectly competitive supplier cannot perceive an infinitely elastic demand curve for his product and has to admit that to increase sales the price must be reduced. By perfect competition we mean that suppliers are supplying a homogeneous good (the product is not differentiated) and they perceive infinitely elastic demand curves only in a well-organized market where the information is perfect. The most often raised objection to this argument is that even in non-Walrasian situations a single supplier can perceive an infinitely elastic demand curve, since his size is infinitesimally small relative to the market, and a relatively infinitely large market can absorb any changes in the supply of a single supplier without any change in the price. In a Walrasian tâtonnement market, the number of suppliers can be finite and a not infinitesimally small supplier can safely assume an infinitely elastic demand curve since his assumption is justified and he can sell the amount of his product that he wished to sell at the price cried by the auctioneer when the tâtonnement is finished, while no actual trade is carried out until the tâtonnement is finished. Certainly, however, there are other non-Walrasian justifications of infinitely elastic demand curves, which presuppose the existence of infinitely many suppliers whose size is infinitesimally small.

An example is Cournot's theory of oligopoly without product differentiation, in which oligopolistic firms non-co-operatively compete with each other under the assumption that other firms do not change their level of output.[10] Suppose, for the sake of simplicity, that the demand function for the industry as a whole is linear and is given in its inverse form as

$$p = A - B \sum_{i=1}^{i=n} X_i \tag{5.1}$$

where A and B are positive constants and X_i is the level of output of the i-th firm, $i = 1, \ldots, n$. The inverse demand function for a single firm, say the first firm, is also perceived as linear, that is:

$$p = A - B \sum_{i \neq 1} X_i - B X_1 \tag{5.2}$$

since X_i's, $i \neq 1$, are regarded as constants by the first firm. The condition for the equilibrium of the first firm, that is, the equality of the marginal revenue and the marginal cost is:

$$A - B \sum_{i \neq 1} X_i - 2 B X_1 = C \tag{5.3}$$

where the positive constant C denotes the marginal cost. If we suppose all the firms are identical, $X_1 = X_2 = \ldots = X_i = \ldots = X_n$, at the equilibrium, we can see from (5.3) that:

$$X_i = (A - C)/B (n + 1), \text{ for all } i. \tag{5.4}$$

Then by substituting (5.4) into (5.1), we have:

$$p = (A + n C)/(n + 1). \tag{5.5}$$

If the number of firms, n, get infinitely larger, we can see from (5.5) that the price p converges to the marginal cost C, which is equal to the marginal revenue. In other words, an infinitesimally small firm perceives an infinitely elastic demand curve.

We have to admit, therefore, that the existence of infinitely many firms is a sufficient condition for the perfect competition in which a single firm perceives an infinitely elastic demand curve. It is, however, by no means a necessary condition. Even for the case of $n = 2$, that is, a duopoly, Bertrand

and Fellner argued that the price will be equalized to the marginal cost if each duopolist assumes that the other will keep his price (not output) unchanged and average as well as marginal costs are constant.[11] If the price is higher, each firm will undercut its rival by a very small margin because it will obtain maximum profits by undercutting infinitesimally. In other words, a Bertrand-type duopolist behaves as if he perceived an infinitely elastic demand curve. Bertrand's assumption can be critized, of course, since duopolists will know, when they are out of equilibrium or when they decide to test their assumption, that their assumptions are incorrect; their rivals do not keep their prices constant. But Cournot's assumption is also subject to the same criticism, and we cannot accept Cournot and at the same time reject Bertrand.[12]

We can slightly generalize the case for Bertrand when the number of firms are increased. Suppose the marginal cost function, though still identical for all firms, is not constant but is increasing, though not continuously but stepwise. When *n* is large but still finite, there is an equilibrium where the price is equalized with the marginal costs, and no oligopolists have the incentive to reduce the price to increase the sale, assuming that others keep their price unchanged. Under the same assumption, there is also no incentive to raise the price, since in general other firms can increase their sales without increasing marginal costs. At least at equilibrium, therefore, each oligopolist perceives an infinitely elastic demand curve. In this case, unlike that of constant marginal cost, the equilibrium profit can be positive for each identical firm.

Another example is Edgeworth's demonstration that the only stable outcome of a pure exchange economy is the perfectly competitive equilibrium and all the other allocations are blocked by traders co-operatively when the number of traders is infinitely large. Figure 5.3 is an Edgeworth box diagram, where the quantity of the first good is measured horizontally, that of the second good, vertically, the quantities of goods given to trader *A* are measured with the origin at *A*, those given to trader *B*, with the origin at *B*, curve *DEF* is the contract curve which is a locus of points where indifference curves of two traders are tangent, point *C* denotes the initial allocation of goods before trade, and point *E* is the perfectly competitive equilibrium with the common tangent to indifference curves at *E* passing through point *C*. It is shown that all the points on the contract curve between *D* and *F* are stable outcomes if there are only two traders *A* and *B*, while Edgeworth insists that all the points except *E* can be blocked by a coalition of some traders if there are infinitely many identical (in taste and initial holdings) traders *A* and infinitely many identical traders *B*.[13]

Since an identical amount of goods must be allocated to the identical

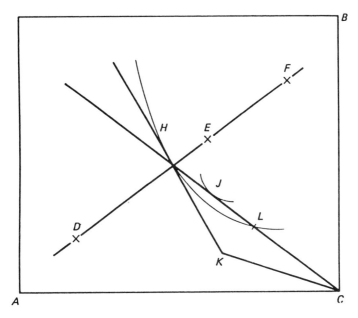

FIGURE 5.3

traders after trade, the Edgeworth box diagram can still be used to consider exchanges among infinitely many traders. Consider point H. This allocation can be blocked by a coalition formed by all the A traders and more than half but less than all of the B traders. In the coalition some traders A still continue to trade with B traders and are located at H, while the rest of the A traders who have no trade partners are located at C. By increasing the number of B traders that join the coalition sufficiently, therefore increasing the number of A traders located at H, we can make the average allocation of A traders (some at H, some at C) J located on CH between L and H. By reallocation among themselves, therefore, all the A traders are better off than they were at the allocation H. With some side-payments to B traders in the coalition, all the traders joining the coalition can be better off than they were at H, and the allocation H is blocked by such a coalition. Obviously only the point E belongs to the core, that is, the set of allocations that are not blocked by such a coalition.

If the number of traders is infinite, therefore, stable outcome of a pure exchange economy with perfect information and no friction (no restriction of trade, no cost of trade, no cost of organizing coalitions, etc.) can be derived as an equilibrium of perfect competition in which each trader is behaving as if he were taking the price ratio (the slope of *EC*) as constant. In this sense, the existence of infinitely many traders is a sufficient condition for perfect competition. But again it is not necessary, since, as we argued elsewhere, only *E* belongs to the core when there are only two *A* traders and two *B* traders if we rule out lump-sum transaction, assume the divisibility of transaction and take arbitrages leading to the law of indifference into consideration.[14]

Consider point *H* in Figure 5.3, which cannot be blocked by a coalition of two *A* traders and one *B* trader in a way suggested by Edgeworth, since *L* is located nearer to *H* than to *C*. We note that there must be at least two successive transactions like *CK* and *KH* and the ratio of exchange should vary in the course of exchange between *C* and *H*, if allocation *H* can ever be reached by exchange starting from *C*. Otherwise, that is, if there is only a single transaction and the exchange ratio remains unchanged throughout the exchange process, it must be equal to the slope of *CH* and exchange must proceed on *CH*, starting from *C* and towards *H*. Such an exchange process has to, however, be terminated at *J*, since it is unfavourable for *A* to go beyond. Suppose, therefore, A_1 trader exchanges with B_1 trader, firstly along with *CK* and then along with *KH*, and A_2 trader exchanges with B_2 trader similarly. Then the allocation *H* can be blocked by arbitrages of different exchange ratios. B_1 proposes to A_2 some new *CK* transaction or a slightly less favourable (to B_1) one, so that B_1 can be better off than at *H*. On the other hand, A_2 accepts this proposal of B_1 by cancelling a part of his *CK* transaction with B_2, so that A_2 is indifferent to or better off than at *H*. Since B_2 is not the only supplier of the second good, A_2 expects that the rest of his transaction with B_2 would not be cancelled by B_2. Not only B_1, but also B_2, A_1, and A_2 will do similarly to take advantage of different exchange ratios. The only allocation that can be blocked neither by Edgeworth coalitions nor by arbitrages is point *E*, even if there are only two *A* traders and two *B* traders.

In view of the arguments in this section, it is now clear that the difference between Walrasian economics and non-Walrasian economics lies not in whether the number of traders is assumed to be infinite or finite but in whether or not the market is perfect in the sense that the information is free and perfect, there is no cost to organize coalitions, and so on.

NOTES

1. See Fisher, 1918, pp. 55–73. Discussion with Professor Hirotaka Kato was highly useful and appreciated.

2. For the concepts of research programmes, hard core, and protective belt, see Lakatos, 1970.
3. See Menger, 1871, pp. 239, 240–1 (page numbers refer to English translation).
4. See Menger, 1892, where *Absatzfaehigkeit* is translated into saleableness. See also Menger, 1871, p. 242, where *Absatzfaehig* translated into liquid and *Absatzfaehigkeit* into marketability.
5. For the significance of the theory of kinked demand curve, see Reid, 1981, and Negishi, 1979, pp. 79–81.
6. See Negishi, 1979, pp. 36, 87.
7. See Negishi, 1979, pp. 28–9, 90. It is interesting, on the other hand, to note that short-term expectations are assumed not to be realized in the modern quantity theory as was shown in the first section of this chapter.
8. See Negishi, 1979, pp. 89–90, and Reid, 1981, pp. 65–6.
9. See also Reid, 1981, p. 97.
10. See Cournot, 1838, pp. 79–98 (page numbers refer to English translation). See also Fellner, 1965, pp. 56–69.
11. See Bertrand, 1883, and Fellner, 1965, pp. 77–86. Discussion with Professor Yoshihiko Otani was highly useful and appreciated.
12. Edgeworth, 1925, pp. 111–42, and Fellner, 1965, pp. 79–82, introduced different cost functions for different firms and/or upper limits on the amount firms produce, and argued that price oscillation appears. We disregard, however, these complications, since we are considering the possibility of perfect competition with a finite number of firms and different costs and capacity limits imply essentially the imperfectness of the competition.
13. See Edgeworth, 1881, pp. 34–42, and Negishi, 1982.
14. See Negishi, 1982, for details, and see also Akashi, 1981, for a closely related and more rigorous demonstration.

REFERENCES

Akashi, S. (1981) 'Price Competition and Competitive Equilibrium in an Economy with a Finite Number of Agents', Hitotsubashi University (mimeo).

Barro, R. J., and H. I. Grossman (1976) *Money, Employment and Inflation*, Cambridge: Cambridge University Press.

Benassy, J. P. (1982) *The Economics of Market Disequilibrium*, London: Academic Press.

Bertrand, J. (1883) 'Review of Théorie mathematique de la richesse sociale and Recherches sur les principes mathematiques de la théorie des richesses', *Journal des Savants*, 499–508.

Cournot, A. (1838) *Recherches sur les principes mathematiques de la théorie des rechesses*, Hachette, (*Researches into the Mathematical Principles of the Theory of Wealth*, trans. Bacon, London: Macmillan, 1897).

Edgeworth, F. Y. (1881) *Mathematical Psychics*, London: Kegan Paul.
Edgeworth, F. Y. (1925) *Papers Relating to Political Economy*, vol. I, London: Macmillan.
Fellner, W. (1965) *Competition Among the Few*, New York: Kelley.
Fisher, I. (1918) *The Purchasing Power of Money*, London: Macmillan.
Friedman, M. (1968) 'The Role of Monetary Policy', *American Economic Review*, 58: 1–17.
Fujino, S. (1978) 'Keynes Keizaigaku no Saikochiku (A Reconstruction of Keynesian Economics)', *Contemporary Economics*, 32 (Autumn): 50–67.
Fujino, S. (1980) 'A Microeconomic Reconstruction of Keynesian Economics: A Theory of Effective Demand-Supply and Involuntary Unemployment', Discussion Paper Series, 28, Institute of Economic Research, Hitotsubashi University, March.
Fujino, S. (1982a) Book Review of T. Negishi's *Microeconomic Foundations of Keynesian Macroeconomics*, *Economic Review*, 33: 94–6.
Fujino, S. (1982b) 'Kahei Keizai no Ronritekikozo (The Logical Structure of a Monetary Economy)', Discussion Paper Series, 52, Institute of Economic Research, Hitotsubashi University, February.
Lakatos, I. (1970) 'Falsification and the Methodology of Scientific Research Programmes', in I. Lakatos and R. Musgrave (eds), *Criticism and the Growth of Knowledge*, Cambridge: Cambridge University Press.
Malinvaud, E. (1977) *The Theory of Unemployment Reconsidered*, Oxford: Blackwell.
Menger, C. (1871) *Grunsaetze der Volkswirthschaftslehre*, Braumeller, (*Principles of Economics*, trans. Dingwall and Hoselitz, New York: Free Press, 1950).
Menger, C. (1892) 'On the Origin of Money', *Economic Journal*, 2: 239–55.
Negishi, T. (1979) *Microeconomic Foundations of Keynesian Macroeconomics*, Amsterdam: North-Holland.
Negishi, T. (1982) 'A Note on Jevons's Law of Indifference and Competitive Equilibrium', *Manchester School of Economics and Social Studies*, 50: 220–30.
Reid, G. C. (1981) *The Kinked Demand Curve Analysis of Oligopoly*, Edinburgh: Edinburgh University Press.
Scitovsky, T. (1978) 'Asymmetries in Economics', *Scottish Journal of Political Economy*, 25: 227–37.
Sweezy, P. M. (1939) 'Demand Under Conditions of Oligopoly', *Journal of Political Economy*, 47: 568–73.

[17]

History of Political Economy 14:3
© 1982 by Duke University Press

Wicksell's missing equation: a comment

Takashi Negishi

I

Sandelin in his 1980 article[1] rightly argued that we should find the missing equation and consider the value of capital as an endogenous variable in the Wicksellian model of capital, i.e., the famous wine-storage problem. He extended the Wicksellian constant-returns model into a variable-returns model and introduced one additional equation which describes the condition for an optimal amount of labor. The aim of this note is to point at another way of closing Wicksell's model; we shall suggest that the missing equation in the original Wicksellian constant-returns model is the one which describes the savers' decision.

II

The modified Wicksellian point-input/point-output model of Sandelin 1980 consists of

$$Q = f(t, L) \tag{1}$$
$$Q = wLe^{rt} \tag{2}$$
$$\partial f/\partial t = fr \tag{3}$$
$$K = Lw \int_0^t e^{rx}dx \tag{4}$$
$$L = \bar{L} \tag{5}$$
$$\partial f/\partial L = f/L \tag{6}$$

where Q is the value of the wine sold, t is the storage time, L is the labor input, w is the wage rate, r is the rate of return, K is the value of wine capital, $\bar{L}$ is the given supply of labor. The modifications due to Sandelin are (1) and (6), i.e., the production function $f(t, L)$ is not of constant returns, i.e., not $Lf(t)$, and r, derived from (1) and (2), is maximized with respect to L. Six equations can determine six variables, i.e., $Q, t, L, r, w,$ and K.

Correspondence for the author may be sent to Professor Takashi Negishi, Faculty of Economics, University of Tokyo, Bunyo-Ku, Tokyo 113 JAPAN.

1. Bo Sandelin, Wicksell's missing equation; the production function and the Wicksell effort, *History of Political Economy* 12(1980): 29–40.

310

III

In the original Wicksellian constant-returns case, (1) is replaced by

$$Q = L f(t) \qquad (7)$$

where $f(t)$ is the price of wine determined on the world market and is an increasing function of its age t.[2] The economy is the small-country one which exports wine and imports other goods, say wheat, whose price p is also given in world market. Since the country "is a closed economy as far as its land, labor and capital are concerned," the capitalist who advances wage income has to postpone his consumption, i.e., to save for the period of production t, when the firm determines the period of production, i.e., plans to invest wL for t. Suppose the postponed consumption of wheat out of net income obtained from the advance of wage income wL after t periods yields utility

$$U = a(t)wL \, (e^{rt} - 1)/p \qquad (8)$$

since wL grows to wLe^{rt}, where $a(t)$ is a decreasing function of t which signifies the time preference of the capitalist. By maximizing U with respect to t, we see that the capitalist agrees to do required saving if

$$-a'(t)/a(t) = re^{rt}/(e^{rt} - 1) \qquad (9)$$

is satisfied. Now we have six equations, (2), (3), (4), (5), (7), and (9), to determine six variables, Q, t, L, r, w, and K. In this model, Wicksell's 'missing equation' is (9), which describes the saving decision of the capitalist.

I am grateful to a reader for valuable comments.

2. See K. Wicksell 1934. *Lectures on political economy*, vol. 1, trans. Classen, p. 172.

[18]

Vol. 42 (1982), No. 2, pp. 161—174

Zeitschrift für
Nationalökonomie
Journal of Economics
© by Springer-Verlag 1982

Wicksell's Missing Equation and Böhm-Bawerk's Three Causes of Interest in a Stationary State

By

Takashi Negishi, Tokyo*

(Received March 10, 1981; revised version received November 11, 1981)

(1)

It is well-known that Böhm-Bawerk [3] adduced three causes of the existence of interest, i. e., a premium (agio) attached to the present consumers' goods in the exchange against the future consumers' goods. They are (1) better provision for wants expected in the future than in the present, (2) undervaluation of future wants, and (3) the superiority of more roundabout or more protracted method of production[1].

The mutual relation, however, among these three causes has not been clearly recognized in recent literature, which is, in our opinion, the reason why the present state of capital theory is confused with respect to whether the rate of interest can be positive in a stationary state. As Orosel [10] rightly pointed out, the distinguishing characteristic of the Austrian school is that the time structure of primary inputs plays a central role in the theory of production. Standard interpretation seems to be, furthermore, that Böhm-Bawerk himself tried to show that the third cause is capable of producing interest by itself even if operating in the absence of the first two

---

* I am indebted to Professors D. Bös, M. Faber, G. O. Orosel, M. Yano, Mr. K. Matsuyama and Mr. T. Mizuno for helpful comments and encouragements. See footnotes 4, 6, 19, 20 and 22 below.

[1] Böhm-Bawerk [3], pp. 259—289, especially 283. Schumpeter [13], pp. 927—930.

11*

0044-3158/82/0042/0161/$ 02.80

causes[2], since Wicksell [14], following Böhm-Bawerk developed a stationary state model in which a positive rate of interest is explained by the marginal productivity of the period of production[3]. In such a one-sided productivity model, however, there is one equation missing[4]. This problem was solved by Hirshleifer [7] by introducing time-preference relation, i. e., the second cause of Böhm-Bawerk. Although this solution may not be unanimously acknowledged yet[5], Bernholz [2] and Faber [5] seem also to show the positive rate of interest in a stationary state on the basis of the second and third causes of Böhm-Bawerk. What has become of the first cause?

Our aim is firstly to show that the first cause is more important than the second cause in the sense that Böhm-Bawerk [3], [4] admitted that the most important third cause generates and works through the first cause. Since the first cause is independent of the second cause, this implies that the third cause alone, without the help of the second cause, can cause a positive rate of interest in a stationary economy, in spite of Hirshleifer [7] and many other recent writers. As was already pointed out by Arvidsson [1], however, the consideration of the first cause in a stationary state requires a life-cycle model in which people live for finite periods, have rising incomes, and consume their life-incomes[6]. Our second aim is, therefore, to justify such an explanation of a positive rate of interest on the basis of the third cause by constructing a stationary two-period life-cycle model in which younger savers can have larger consumptions when they are old.

---

[2] Schumpeter [13], p. 930. However, Schumpeter's argument on the relation between the second cause and other causes is confused. Nor his assertion that "Böhm-Bawerk himself tried to show that the two first reason will not necesssarily produce a premium without the third" is warranted.

[3] See Böhm-Bawerk's numerical example of the third cause ([3], pp. 351—365) and Wicksell [14], pp. 172—184. See also Lutz [9], pp. 25—36, 186—187 (Japanese Translation, pp. 42—61, 340—342).

[4] Hirshleifer [7], Pasinetti [11], Sandelin [12] and Lutz [9], pp. 34—36 (Japanese Translation, pp. 58—60). I am grateful to Mr. T. Mizuno for calling my attention to Hirshleifer [7].

[5] Pasinetti [11] and Sandelin [12].

[6] I am indebted to Professor G. O. Orosel for the suggestion that the life-cycle model should be used, while I owe to Professor M. Faber the reference to Arvidsson [1], an important article which discussed the mutual relations among Böhm-Bawerk's three causes of interest.

(2)

Let us first see how an equation was missing in Wicksellian model where only the third cause of Böhm-Bawerk, i. e., superiority of roundabout method of production, is considered and how the problem was solved in Hirshleifer [7] by introducing the second cause of Böhm-Bawerk, i. e., time preference. For the sake of convenience to consider a life-cycle model later, let us develop a discrete, period analysis version[7].

A point input-point output production function of the representative firm is

$$Y = f(t) L \tag{1}$$

where Y is the volume of output of a consumers' good, L is labor input, t is the period of production (non-negative integer) and $f(t)$ is an increasing[8] concave function. Rate of return or rate of interest r is defined by

$$pY = (1+r)^t wL \tag{2}$$

where p is the price of consumers' good and w is the rate of wage. Given p and w, we can solve for r as a function of t. The maximization of r with respect to t, i. e., $r(t-1) \leqq r(t)$, $r(t) \geqq r(t+1)$, requires that

$$f(t)/f(t-1) \geqq 1 + r \geqq f(t+1)/f(t). \tag{3}$$

Finally, the assumption of full employment gives

$$aL = \bar{L} \tag{4}$$

where $\bar{L}$ denotes the total available labor, a given constant, and a is the given scale ratio of the representative firm and the total economy. We can make consumer's good numeraire, i. e., $p = 1$. To determine Y, t, L, w and r, one equation is still missing, unless we do assume that the value of capital

$$K = \sum_{s=0}^{s=t-1} awL (1+r)^s \tag{5}$$

---

[7] Böhm-Bawerk [3], pp. 351—365, Wicksell [14], pp. 172—184, Hirshleifer [7], Lutz [9], pp. 25—36, 186—187, (Japanese Translation, pp. 42—61, 340—342). Pasinetti [11] and Sandelin [12].

[8] Kuenne [8], p. 282, was right here to point out the role of capital scarcity to assure that f is increasing with respect to t. His argument was, however, confusing, since he did not make a clear distinction between the first and second causes. See also Faber [5], p. 133.

is given, as W i c k s e l l actually did. It is clear, however, that to give K exogeneously is quite unsatisfactory, since capital here is not homogeneous but heterogeneous and its composition should be determined endogeneously[9].

To supply a missing equation, S a n d e l i n [12] extended the production function (1) into a more generalized one,

$$Y = F\,(L, t) \tag{6}$$

where F is increasing and concave with respect to both L and t, i. e., not linear with respect to L. From (2) and (6), then, r is a function of not only t but also L. The maximization of r with respect to L requires

$$\partial F/\partial L = F/L. \tag{7}$$

S a n d e l i n claimed that this is the missing Wicksellian equation, since Y, L, t, w and r can be determined by (2), (3), (4), (6) and (7). It may seem that positive interest as well as capital to be maintained [from (5)] are determined by a one-sided productivity model, since (3) implies $r > 0$. The third cause alone may seem to generate positive interest in a stationary state, even if there exist no first and second causes. What will happen, however, if capitalists do not agree to maintain such an amount of capital at such a rate of interest? Our solution of this over-determinancy problem is as follows. If the production function (6) is not linear with respect to L, there must be an implicite factor of production besides labor, say, land. In the long run, then, the market for it is created and rent is established. The production function is now

$$Y = F\,(L, T, t) \tag{8}$$

where $a\,T$ is the total amount of land available, and F is linear homogeneous with respect to L and T. If we denote land rent by v, wL in (2) and (5) should be replaced by $wL + vT$. Because of the new variable v, an equation is still missing, even if T is given.

To maintain the amount of capital stationary, capitalists have to maintain the level of consumption unchanged, i. e., neither save

---

[9] This corresponds to Y a s u i's [15] correction of the Walrasian system. See also G a r e g n a n i [6], part 2, chapter 2. Even if one consider subsistence fund and make capital homogeneous, i. e., $K = awLt/2$, furthermore, one has to explain endogenously why such an amount of fund is maintained, in other words, why it is neither accumulated further nor consumed away. See B ö h m - B a w e r k [3], pp. 351—365.

nor dissave. Hirshleifer [7] introduced a utility function of the representative household of capitalists,

$$U = U(c_1, c_2) \tag{9}$$

where c_1 and c_2 are the levels of consumption in any two consecutive periods. From the maximization of (9) being subject to the budget constraint, the condition for the stationary consumption is

$$U_1(aY/b, aY/b)/U_2(aY/b, aY/b) = 1 + r \tag{10}$$

where U_1 and U_2 are partial derivatives of U with respect to c_1 and c_2, and b is the given scale ratio of the representative household and the total economy. Eq. (10) is the missing equation found by Hirshleifer, since we can determine Y, L, t, w and r from (1), (2), (3), (4) and (10).

Since r is positive from (3), this implies that a positive rate of interest is demonstrated in a stationary economy. From the point of view of Böhm-Bawerk's three causes of interest, second and third causes are utilized in this demonstration, since (10) implies the undervaluation of future wants, while the superiority of more roundabout method of production is represented by the assumption that $f(t)$ is an increasing function in (1). What has become of the first cause, the better provision for wants in the future than in the present, which, in our opinion, Böhm-Bawerk considered more important than the second cause, in its relation to the third cause? Since the first cause has not been much discussed in the recent literature, let us see how it is explained by Böhm-Bawerk himself.

(3)

Böhm-Bawerk's first cause runs as follows. "A first principal cause capable of producing a difference in value between present and future goods is inherent in the difference between the relation of supply to demand as it exists at one point in time and that relation as it exists at another point in time". "If a person suffers in the present from appreciable lack of cetrain goods, or of goods in general, but has been reason to be more generously provided for at a future time, then that person will always place a higher value on a given quantity of immediately available goods than on the same quantity of future goods. This situation occurs with very great frequency in our economic life". Of course, "it must be admitted that the counterpart is no rarity in economic life. There are people who at the moment are relatively well provided for and for whom there will presumably be less provision in the future". However, "most goods are durable, especially money, which with its aspect of non-particularization is capable of representing all classes of goods, hence they can be reserved for the service of the future"[10]. On the average, therefore, people expect to be better provided for their wants in the future than in the present.

The situation can be shown in Fig. 1. Present goods are measured horizontally, and future goods, vertically. Line Oa has slope 1 and indicates the equal provision for wants in the present as well as in the future. If a person is provided with Od amount of present goods and expects to be provided with Oe amount of future goods, the indifference curve passing point b which has slope -1 at f (no undervaluation of future goods) has slope less than -1 at b indicating the positive rate of interest, since marginal utility of future goods is less than that of present goods.

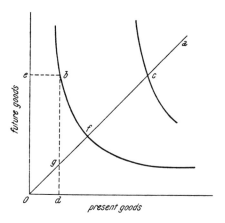

Fig. 1

The situation where the second cause of Böhm-Bawerk exists can be seen at the point c in Fig. 1. Since future wants are systematically undervalued, the slope of the indifference curve at point c is less than -1. The rate of interest is positive even if there exists no "difference between the relation of supply to demand as it exists at one point in time and that relation as it exists at another point in time". The second cause is independent of the first cause and can explain by itself a positive rate of interest. It is also clear that

---

[10] Böhm-Bawerk [3], pp. 265—268.

the first cause is independent of the second cause and can explain by itself a positive rate of interest. Furthermore, "it can be easily demonstrated that this phenomenon (second cause) necessarily contributes to enhance the effectiveness of our first principal cause of the lesser valuation of future goods", since the slope of the indifference curve at b is all the more steeper if its slope at f is steeper[11]. The first and second causes "work cumulatively"[12].

(4)

It is clear that the third cause, i. e., the technical superiority of present goods, is independent of the second one, since (10) is an independent condition from the specification of $f(t)$ in (1). The relation to the first cause is, however, more subtle. The third cause is independent of the first one only in the sense that firstly the first cause can be created by other factors than the third cause and that secondly the third cause, without the help of such other factors, can alone create the first one.

Indeed, Böhm-Bawerk [3] argued for the latter as follows.

"As for the difference in provision for wants in different periods of time, elimination of that factor would give the situation an appearance lacking every semblance of verisimilitude. It would, in fact, be a thorough contradiction of itself. For if the value of a unit of product were the same in all periods of time, —, if such a situation ever occurred at any time at all, it would inevitably nullify it self immediately. For if every utilization for future periods were not only technically but also economically more remunerative than utilization for the present — then people would naturally withdraw the bulk of their goods from the service of the present in order to devote them to the more lucrative service of the future. But that would immediately cause an ebb tide in provision for the present, and a flood tide in provision for the future. — As a result, the difference in the situation as to provision for wants which had momentarily been set aside, would automatically be restored"[13].

"— third cause of the higher value of present goods is completely independent of the other two previously discussed.

It is far removed any from necessity of borrowing strength and effectiveness from any difference arising out of other sources in

---

[11] For the second cause, Böhm-Bawerk [3], pp. 268—273.

[12] Böhm-Bawerk [3], p. 283.

[13] Böhm-Bawerk [3], pp. 279—280.

the situation relating to provision for wants. So far removed is it, in fact, that this cause itself is capable of creating such a difference, should that become necessary"[14].

Furthermore, Böhm-Bawerk [4] argued for the independence of the third cause from the first one in the controversy raised by Fisher and Bortkiewicz whether the third cause constitutes an independent reason besides the first one, or whether it merely constitutes a partial reason within the first one. He tried, though unsuccessfully in our opinion, to show the independence by demonstrating that the technical superiority of present goods can bring forth a value advantage, that is, interest, also if the final state of demand and supply in present and future is constant, when there is an other counteracting factor in the sense of negative first cause[15]. In our Fig. 1, the example of Böhm-Bawerk corresponds to the case where there is a debt of bg falls due. This, of course, does not deny the fact that the third cause itself works to provide future wants better than present one. Finally, however, Böhm-Bawerk admitted,

> "I could have maintained that I am correct at least formerly in my own arrangement because my third reason indubitably differs from my first reason insofar as I defined the latter as supply divergencies resulting from other sources"[16].
> "Indeed it is a trifle whether the third reason outwardly independent or must be grouped under the main heading first reason"[17].

What is important for us is, however, that the third cause creates and works through the first cause and, therefore, the reasoning used to prove positive interest by the third cause is similar to the one used by the first cause, as far as savers' decision model is concerned.

(5)

In view of Böhm-Bawerk's arguments we have just seen, it seems more natural to demonstrate positive interest in a stationary state by the combination of the third cause and the first cause

---

[14] Böhm-Bawerk [3], p. 280.

[15] Böhm-Bawerk [4], pp. 181—182.

[16] Böhm-Bawerk [4], pp. 192—193.

[17] Böhm-Bawerk [4], p. 193.

which necessarily follows from the third cause rather than by the combination of the second and the third causes whose coexistence is accidental. As was pointed out by Arvidsson, we have to consider a life-cycle model of individual members of the economy, to apply the first cause in a stationary state where the economy as a whole is equally provided in the future as well as in the present. A life-cycle model is not alien to Böhm-Bawerk, since he considered the case of "all the indigent beginners in every calling, especially the budding artist or jurist, the first year medical student, the civil servant or business man just breaking in", as examples of those who expect future wants better provided than present ones and value future goods less, and admitted also the counterpart case, "a clerk in an office, for instance, who is fifty years old and is earning sixty dollars a week must face the prospect that in ten or fifteen years he will have nothing of his own but a few hundred dollars a year from an annuity, perhaps, that he purchased from an insurance company"[18].

Let us consider an economy of stationary population, where each individual lives for two periods so that the size of young and working population and that of old and retired population are equal in each period. In the first period, each individual works for given hours but consumes less than he earns and lends his saved capital to firms, while he not only consumes the yield from his capital but also dissaves all his capital in the second period. The second cause, i. e. time preference, is assumed away, so that (10) is satisfied only when r is zero. If people consume only the produced, consumers' good, younger population cannot consume and has to save all the income in the first period, since what older population dissaved must be saved by younger population, which is equal to the wage payments advanced. To avoid this difficulty, we assume that people always consume a unit of labor service in conjunction of his consumption of a unit of consumers' good. Of course, this is a simplifying assumption to make a graphical exposition (Fig. 2) possible and we can make the ratio of consumers' good and labor service variable.

The life-time budget equation for the representative individuals is

$$(p + w)\, c_1 + (p + w)\, c_2/(1 + r) = w\bar{L}/b \tag{11}$$

where c_1 and c_2 denote respective the amount of consumption of consumers' good (and also of labor service) in the first and in the

---

[18] Böhm-Bawerk [3], p. 266.

second period, and p, w, r, $\bar{L}$, b are, as before, the price of consumers' good, wage, rate of interest, given total labor supply and
the scale ratio of representative individual and the total economy.
If the life-time utility $U(c_1, c_2)$ is maximized being subject to (11),

$$U_1(c_1, c_2)/U_2(c_1, c_2) = 1 + r \tag{12}$$

should be satisfied, where U_t denotes the partial derivative of U
with respect to c_t. Since time preference is assumed way, the left-
hand side of (12) is 1, if $c_1 = c_2$. When r is positive, therefore, c_2
should be larger than c_1 from the usual assumption of quasi-concavity of U, which implies that the future want is better provided
than the present one (the first cause). In Fig. 2, c_1 is measured
horizontally, and c_2, vertically. Budget Eq. (11) is represented by the

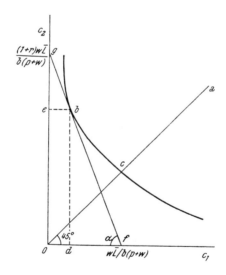

Fig. 2

line fg whose slope is such that $\tan \alpha = (1 + r)$. The condition (12)
is satisfied at b, where an indifference curve whose slope is -1
at c (i. e., when $c_1 = c_2$) is tangent to the budget line fg. As b in
Fig. 1, b in this Figure also indicates that the future want is better
provided than the present one.

The possibility for the better provision of future want is, of
course, assured by the third cause, i. e., the assumption that $f(t)$

is increasing in the production function of the representative firm

$$Y = f(t) L \tag{1}$$

though we have to assume that f is defined here only for $t=0$ and 1. If $t \geq 2$, the existing capital [defined in (5)] will exceed, as we shall see later, what the old population saved, which is impossible in a model where the problem of the inheritance is assumed away. The rate of return or the rate of interest r is defined, as before, by

$$pY = (1+r)^t wL \tag{2}$$

and the period of production t must satisfy

$$f(t)/f(t-1) \geq 1 + r \geq f(t+1)/f(t) \tag{3}$$

whenever it is applicable.

In each period, labor market must be cleared, i. e. instead of (4),

$$aL + b(c_1 + c_2) = \bar{L} \tag{13}$$

is required since bc_1 and bc_2 denote, respectively, the demand for not only consumers' good but also for labor service from young and old populations. On the other hand, the clearance of the market for consumer's good requires

$$b(c_1 + c_2) = aY. \tag{14}$$

Now, these seven conditions, i. e., (1), (2), (3), (11), (12), (13) and (14) can determine seven unknowns, i. e., w, r, c_1, c_2, L, Y and t, while $p=1$ by the choice of consumers' good as numeraire. The possible values for t are 0 and 1. Suppose $t=0$. From (3), r is positive. From (2), (13) and (14), however, we have

$$p(c_1 + c_2) + w(c_1 + c_2) = w\bar{L}/b \tag{15}$$

which is in contradiction to (11) when r is positive. Therefore, the case of $t=0$ is not possible. Suppose next that $t=1$. From (3), we see that r is positive, since $f(1) > f(0)$, i. e. the more roundabout method is superior (the third cause). Incidentally, when $t=1$, we have $pc_1 = wc_2$ from (2), (11), (13) and (14). The value of the consumer's good consumed by the younger population is equal to the value of the labor service consumed by the older population. If people consume only consumers' good and no labor service, therefore, the younger population cannot consume at all. It can be seen, furthermore, that the value of capital,

$$K = \sum_{s=0}^{s=t-1} awL \ (1+r)^s, \tag{5}$$

i. e., awL in this case, is equal to the value of the savings, $w\bar{L} - b \ (p+w) \ c_1$, in view of (11), (13) and $pc_1 = wc_2$. This justifies our assumption that $t \leqq 1$, since otherwise K exceeds the value of the savings which is impossible in a model with no inheritance.

(6)

A positive rate of interest in a stationary state is demonstrated by using Böhm-Bawerk's first and third causes, but without using the second cause. One might be, however, dissatisfied with the model given in the previous section on the ground that the length of the period of production is arbitrarily assumed not to exceed that of individual life minus one. To get rid of this assumption, we have introduce the inheritance of capital into the model so that the value of capital invested can be larger than the value of the savings. In a stationary state the representative individual cannot dissave all his capital at the end of his life but must leave the capital of equal value as he inherited at the beginning of his life. As his life-time consumption is related to the capital inherited at the beginning of his life, so the life-time consumption of the next generation is related to the capital he is going to leave at the end of his life. A positive rate of interest is, therefore, impossible in a stationary state, unless the representative individual underevaluates the consumption of the next generation in comparison with his own consumption. This seems, however, to introduce Böhm-Bawerk's second cause from the backdoor[19].

In the model given in the previous section, furthermore, the resulted length of the period of production is actually identical to the length of individual life minus one. This can be generalized, however, so that the period of production is much shorter than the individual life, if we assume that the length of the latter is more than three periods. What is needed for the model without inheritance is the assumption that the period of production is shorter more than one period than that of the individual life. The assumption in section (5) that people always consume labor service can be dropped

---

[19] The discussion with Professor M. Yano was useful.

when the period of production is more than one period shorter than that of the individual life[20].

(7)

Recapitulation. Böhm-Bawerk tried to show that the third cause, which produces the first cause and works through it, can make interest rate positive in a stationary state without any help of the second cause. This is possible only in a life-time model where individuals can consume more in the later part of their life than in the earlier part. Wicksell's missing equation should be supplied, therefore, by the consideration of the first cause and not by the introduction of the second cause, from the point of view of Böhm-Bawerk's three causes. In view of his admission that "the arrangement of reasons can be changed in such a way that the first and third reason stand combined"[21], other interpretation in recent literature, i. e., to combine the second and third causes, cannot be warranted as what Böhm-Bawerk himself had in mind[22].

References

[1] G. Arvidsson: On the Reasons for a Rate of Interest, International Economic Papers 6 (1956), pp. 23—33.

[2] P. Bernholz: Superiority of Roundabout Processes and Positive Rate of Interest. A Simple Model of Capital and Growth, Kyklos 24 (1971), pp. 687—721.

[3] E. v. Böhm-Bawerk: Positive Theory of Capital, South Holland, Illinois 1959.

[4] E. v. Böhm-Bawerk: Further Essay on Capital and Interest, South Holland, Illinois 1959.

[5] M. Faber: Introduction to Modern Austrian Capital Theory, Lecture Notes in Economics and Mathematical Systems, Vol. *167*, Berlin – Heidelberg – New York 1979.

[6] P. Garegnani: Il Capitale nelle Teorie della Distribuzione, Milano 1960.

[7] J. Hirshleifer: A Note on the Böhm-Bawerk/Wicksell Theory of Interest, Review of Economic Studies *34* (1967), pp. 191—199.

---

[20] This possibility was pointed out by Professor Orosel.

[21] Böhm-Bawerk [4], p. 192.

[22] Professor Orosel pointed out that the second cause is also necessary if the absence of the second cause is defined by *all* indifference curves being 45-degree lines.

[8] R. E. Kuenne: The Theory of General Economic Equilibrium, Princeton 1963.

[9] F. A. Lutz: Zinstheorie, Tübingen 1956 (Japanese Translation: Rishiron, Tokyo 1962).

[10] G. O. Orosel: Faber's Modern Austrian Capital Theory: A Critical Survey, Zeitschrift für Nationalökonomie *41* (1981), pp. 141—155.

[11] L. L. Pasinetti: Wicksell Effects and Reswitchings of Technique in Capital Theory, in: S. Strom and B. Thalberg (eds.): The Theoretical Contributions of Knut Wicksell, Hong Kong 1979, pp. 53—61.

[12] B. Sandelin: Wicksell's Missing Equation, the Production Function, and the Wicksell Effect, History of Political Economy *12* (1980), pp. 29—40.

[13] J. A. Schumpeter: History of Economic Analysis, Oxford 1954.

[13] K. Wicksell: Lectures on Political Economy, Vol. I, New York 1977.

[15] T. Yasui: Jikanyoso to Shihonrishi (Time-Element and Interest), Journal of Economics (University of Tokyo) 6 (1936), pp. 1332—1382.

Address of author: Professor Takashi Negishi, Department of Economics, University of Tokyo, Bunkyoku, Japan.

Printed in Austria

19

2 Economic structure and the theory of economic equilibrium

TAKASHI NEGISHI

1. Introduction

This chapter discusses the structure of Walrasian general equilibrium theory and Marshallian partial equilibrium theory, both of which form a large part of the traditional or current mainstream economics called neo-classical economics. Beyond the general exposition of these equilibrium theories, we shall particularly pursue two issues.

First, we shall try to clarify implicit dynamic concepts hidden in these theories, which are generally regarded as uni-periodal economic theories. Actually, the start of the development of modern dynamic economics was, at least partially, made possible by John Hicks (1946), who integrated Walrasian and Marshallian implicit dynamic concepts, along with more explicit Swedish ones, into a unified theory. The implications of some of these implicit dynamic concepts have, furthermore, not yet been fully and explicitly developed by modern theories of the dynamic economics.

Secondly, we shall critically compare Walrasian and Marshallian theories with Francis Edgeworth's theory of market, which succeeded William Stanley Jevons's view of market. The communication structure is different between the Walras–Marshall model of non-cooperative market games and the Jevons–Edgeworth model of cooperative market games. While the first two approaches have an identical result in the case of a large economy with infinitely many agents, the latter suggests the possibility of a quite different result in the case of competition among a few, if we can safely ignore the costs of communication, negotiation and organization. In other words, the former theories do not fully consider the implications of non-price competitions.

After this introductory section, the following two sections will be devoted to discussing the Walrasian general equilibrium theory. We shall describe how the core elements of an economic system are successively combined to form the general equilibrium models of exchange, production, credit and capital formation and, finally, money and circulation (section 2). Then, using a simplified model of credit and capital formation, we shall consider the implicit time structure of Walrasian seemingly uni-periodal theory (section 3). One possible interpretation is the stationary equilibrium, while another possibility is to consider the temporary equilibrium.

In the next two sections, the time structure of the Marshallian partial equilibrium theory will be discussed to show, first, that, unlike in the case of Léon Walras, all the core elements of an economic system are already introduced in the simplest model, the market-day model, but most of them are regarded as 'being constant' until sufficient time has past to make them adjust in the short-run or in the long-run model (section 4). Another implicit time structure to be shown in Alfred Marshall's theory is his concept of the stationary equilibrium of an industry in which individual firms are in disequilibrium, clearly a biological analogy with the case of a constant forest and its changing trees (section 5).

Though Walrasian and Marshallian theories have different time structures, they share an identical view of markets: that economic agents are isolated and communicate with each other only in terms of prices and price-related concepts like demand and supply functions. In the last two sections, we shall explain Edgeworth's view of markets, in which individual agents are free to form and block coalitions and make contracts and recontracts not necessarily in terms of the price concept. Results are compared with those of the Walras–Marshall view in the case of a large economy (section 6) as well as in the case of a duopoly (section 7).

The chapter will finish with a brief conclusion.

2.   Logical structure of Walrasian theory

Walras (1954) insisted that complicated phenomena can be studied only if the rule of proceeding from the simple to the complex is always observed. Walras first decomposes a complicated economy of the real world into several core elements like consumer-traders, entrepreneurs, consumer goods, factors of production, newly produced capital goods and money. He then composes a simple model of a pure exchange economy by picking up a very limited number of such elements, that is individual consumer-traders and consumer goods, and disregarding the existence of all other elements. Consumer goods to be exchanged among individual consumer-traders are assumed simply to be endowed to them and not considered as produced at cost. There are no production activities in this hypothetical world.

Travel from this simple model to the complex world proceeds by adding one by one those core elements so far excluded, that is first entrepreneurs and factors of production in the model of production, then newly produced capital goods in the model of credit and capital formation, and finally money in the model of money and circulation. In the model of production, capital goods are introduced as a kind of factor of production, but the investment, that is the production of new capital goods, simply does not exist. In all the Walrasian models of exchange, production and credit and capital formation, there exists no money at all; it is finally introduced in the model of money and circulation.

In this journey from the simple to the complex, each intermediate model, enlarged from a simpler one and to be enlarged into a more complex one, is still a closed and self-compact logical system. Even the simplest model, that of the exchange, is already a model of general equilibrium, in which results of interactions among the core elements introduced are to be studied fully and exhaustively. However, each of the Walrasian models is as unrealistic as the starting model of pure exchange, with the exception of the last, into which all the core elements of a real world economy have been introduced.[1]

Those unrealistic models into which have been introduced only a limited number of core elements of the economy cannot, of course, be of practical use in considering what Hicks (1934) called particular problems of history or experience. They are designed to show the fundamental significance of such core elements of the real world economy as entrepreneurs and production, investment and the rate of interest, inventories and money, by successively introducing them into simple models that are then developed into more complex ones. Walras's theoretical interest was not in the solution of particular problems but in what Hicks called the pursuit of the general principles that underlie the working of a market economy.

One can study the problem of the exchange in the most essential form when the model of exchange is abstracted from all the other complex problems. There we can see most clearly Walras's view of a well-organized, highly institutionalized market in which the specialized auctioneer determines the uniform market price and changes it according to the excess demand or supply generated as functions of the price by price-taking traders. The model of production can show the role of entrepreneurs and the mechanism of distribution among factors of production, including capital goods, without being bothered by such time-related problems as investment, saving and the rate of interest. The latter problems can, then, be studied intensively in the model of credit and capital formation, in which the complex problems of money and circulation have not yet been introduced.

If the key of our approach in this volume is the relationship between

---

[1] For a difficulty in the last model, that of money and circulation, see Negishi (1988) chapter 7, section 5.2.

production and time, then the time structure implicit in Walrasian seemingly uni-periodal theory should be found not in the model of production but in the model of credit and capital formation.

3.   Time structure of Walrasian theory

Since the original Walrasian system of equations of credit and capital formation is too complicated to describe, let us consider a drastically simplified version of a two-good (consumer and capital goods), two-factor (labour and capital) economy.[2] Two goods are produced from the input of labour service and the service of capital goods under constant returns to scale. Labour is the sole primary factor of production and there is no inventory investment, nor is there money.

Let X_1 and X_2 be the level of output of the consumer and new capital goods, respectively. The aggregate income of labourers and capitalists is

$$Y = w(a_1 X_1 + a_2 X_2) + q(b_1 X_1 + b_2 X_2) \tag{1}$$

where w denotes the rate of wage, q denotes the price of the service of capital goods, a_1 and a_2 are, respectively, the labour input coefficients in the production of the consumer and capital goods and b_1 and b_2 are, respectively, the capital input coefficients in the production of consumer and capital goods. Input coefficients are functions of factor prices, w and q.

At the general equilibrium of credit and capital formation, there is no profit left for entrepreneurs, so that

$$p_1 = wa_1 + qb_1 \tag{2}$$

$$p_2 = wa_2 + qb_2 \tag{3}$$

where p_1 and p_2 are respectively the price of the consumer and new capital goods. Since markets for two goods have to be cleared,

$$D(p_1, p_2, w, q, Y) = X_1 \tag{4}$$

$$H = X_2 \tag{5}$$

where D denotes the demand for consumer goods and H stands for the demand for new capital goods. Factor markets have also to be cleared so that

$$a_1 X_1 + a_2 X_2 = L \tag{6}$$

$$b_1 X_1 + b_2 X_2 = K \tag{7}$$

[2]   This is a simplified version of the model given by Morishima (1977, pp. 108–12). We cannot, however, agree with Morishima's interpretation of the model (1977, pp. 112–22). See footnote 3, below.

where L and K are, respectively, the given existing labour force and the given existing stock of capital goods. Since there is no money, suppose capitalists own capital goods and lend them to entrepreneurs or sell the service of capital goods to them. If gross saving is defined as the excess of income over consumption, then capitalists save in kind or purchase new capital goods with saving, so that

$$p_2 H = S(p_1, p_2, w, q, Y) \tag{8}$$

where S denotes the aggregate gross saving.

Equations (1)–(8) may be interpreted as the description of a temporary equilibrium in the sense of Hicks (1946), as was done by Morishima (1960; 1977, pp. 70–81). It is assumed that expectations on the future prices are static, that is the elasticity of expectation is 1, in the determination of consumption and saving so that D and S are functions of current prices. There are eight equations to determine seven unknowns, Y, w, q, X_1, X_2, p_2, and H, since we can choose the consumer goods as *numéraire* so that $p_1 = 1$. The eight equations are not independent, however, and one of the equations can be derived from other equations and from Walras's law,

$$Y = p_1 D + S. \tag{9}$$

In the determination of consumption and saving, capitalists assume that goods and services of factors have the same prices in the future as they have at the present moment, and the difference between resultant gross saving and the value of the depreciation of capital goods, that is the net saving, can be either positive or negative. If it is positive, we have the case of a progressive economy, which Walras (1954, p. 269) himself wished to consider. The capital stock K is larger in the next period than in the current period so that temporary equilibrium prices in the former are in general different from those in the latter, even though capitalists in the current period expected unchanged prices through periods.

The assumption of the saving in kind is not necessary if we follow Walras and introduce a commodity E consisting of perpetual net income of a unit of *numéraire*, the price of which is the inverse of the rate of perpetual net income or the rate of interest i (Walras, 1954, p. 274). If this commodity is sold by entrepreneurs or firms wishing to buy new capital goods and is purchased by capitalists wishing to save, the clearance of the market of this commodity through changes in i implies that aggregate gross saving = 'aggregate excess of income over consumption = aggregate demand for $(E) \times$ price of (E) = aggregate demand for new capital goods $\times$ price of capital goods' (Walras, 1954, p. 21). Therefore,

$$p_2 H = S(p_1, w, i, Y) \tag{8'}$$

instead of (8) since, in the determination of consumption and saving, capitalists are now concerned, not with p_2 and q, but with i. Similarly, (4) may be replaced by

$$D(p_1, w, i, Y) = X_1. \tag{4'}$$

At equilibrium, the rate of net income for capital goods has to be equalized for the rate of net income for the commodity E,

$$(q/p_2) - d = i \tag{10}$$

where d denotes the technically given rate of depreciation of capital goods. This is nothing but Walrasian implicit or degenerate investment function, derived from assumptions that investors are price takers and that expectations are static.[3] Since the introduction of a new unknown i is matched by the introduction of additional equation (10), we still have equality between the number of unknowns and the number of equations.

If the general equilibrium of credit and capital formation is interpreted as a temporary equilibrium, entrepreneurs and capitalists fail to expect future prices in a progressive economy correctly, since changes in prices are induced by changes in K in a series of successive temporary equilibria. If we wish the perfect foresight to prevail and the expectation of unchanged prices to be correct in the general equilibrium of credit and capital formation, then this should be interpreted (see Yasui, 1970, pp. 173–278) as a stationary equilibrium, where K remains unchanged through periods. The reason is that only in a stationary state do the prices of the service of capital goods remain unchanged indefinitely into the future, as Walras assumed in equation (10). Of course, the service of the factors of production can have the same prices in the future as they have at the present, not only in a stationary state but also in a progressive economy of balanced growth. As Wicksell (1967, pp. 226–7) pointed out, however, the latter case is inconceivable, 'as the sum of natural forces cannot be increased'.

The condition for the stationary state is that the aggregate gross saving is equal to the value of depreciation of capital goods, or

$$H = dK \tag{11}$$

in view of (8) or (8'). Since the number of equations are increased by the addition of (11), one more unknown should be introduced. The existing stock of capital goods K is, therefore, no longer an arbitrary given quantity and has to be solved jointly with other unknowns from equations of general equilibrium of credit and capital formation. Then, we have nine unknowns,

---

[3] It is, therefore, superfluous to introduce the Keynesian investment function. See, however, Morishima (1977, pp. 112–22).

$K, i, Y, w, q, X_1, X_2, p_2$ and H to be solved from any nine equations of ten equations, (1)–(3), (4′), (5)–(7), (8′), (10) and (11), since $p_1 = 1$ and one of the equations is not independent in view of (9). Yasui (1970) first pointed out the necessity of this modification of the original Walrasian theory of credit and capital formation.[4]

Two alternative interpretations of Walras's theory of credit and capital formation – temporary equilibrium and stationary state – correspond respectively to two methods of economic dynamics in modern economic theory: the temporary equilibrium method and the growth equilibrium method, distinguished and evaluated by Hicks (1965, p. 28). Also, it is well known that Walras's theory of capital gives the micro-economic foundation to the so-called neoclassical macro-growth theory developed by Robert M. Solow, Trevor W. Swan, James Edward Meade and Hirofumi Uzawa.

4.   Time structure of Marshallian theory

Like Walras (1954) Marshall (1921) also started with a very simple model to study complicated economic phenomena and then proceeded to more complex models. There is an important difference, however, between Walrasian general equilibrium analysis and Marshallian partial equilibrium analysis.

Unlike Walras who started with a general equilibrium model of an imaginary economy, which contains only a limited number of core elements of a real world economy, Marshall begins with the partial equilibrium analysis of a whole complex of a real world economy as such. In other words, every Marshallian model contains all the core elements of the economic system. Of course, Marshall also simplifies his study at first by confining his interest to a certain limited number of core elements of the economy. But he does it not by disregarding the existence of other elements but by assuming that other things remain unchanged. In this sense most of Marshall's models of an economy, though realistic, are open and not self-sufficient, since some endogenous variables (i.e. the 'other things') remain unexplained and have to be given exogenously.

Marshall's simplest model, which corresponds to Walras's model of exchange, is that of the market day, in which goods to be sold are, unlike in the case of Walras, produced goods, although the amount available for sale is, for the time being, assumed to be constant. Since the length of a single

---

[4]   Yasui pointed this out as early as 1936. See Yasui (1970, p. 248) and also Garegnani (1960) Part 2, chapter 2. In spite of Garegnani, however, the fact that the stock of the existing capital goods cannot be an arbitrary given is not the defect of Walrasian theory of credit and capital formation. This is also the case with the classical theory of the stationary economy.

market day is so short, the level of output cannot be changed, even though production does exist in this temporary model. Unlike in Walras's model of production investment is actually undertaken in Marshall's short-run model. The latter is also a model of production, though the amount of currently available capital is given and unchanged, since the length of the period is still not long enough to allow for adjustment in capital equipment. The effects of such adjustments can be fully considered only in the study of Marshall's long-run model.

While money is introduced only in the final model of Walrasian theory, money does exist in all Marshallian models, though its purchasing power or its marginal utility is sometimes assumed to be constant. Walras has to consider the problem of exchange without using money under the unrealistic assumption of *tâtonnement*, that no exchange transaction should be undertaken at disequilibrium prices. Since, however, money is already introduced even in the model of the market day, Marshall can consider the problem of exchange in monetary economy, that is the exchange of a commodity against money, without making any *tâtonnement* assumption. The study of such non-*tâtonnement* exchange is made easy by the assumption of constant marginal utility of money, which makes the final equilibrium price independent of exchange transactions carried out at disequilibrium prices (Hicks, 1946, pp. 127–9).

Thus each Marshallian model corresponds to a different state of the same real world economy. The market-day and short-run models are, therefore, as realistic as the long-run model. They are of practical use in considering what Hicks (1934) called particular problems of history or experience. 'Marshall forged an analytical instrument capable of easier application.' A good example is the concept of consumer surplus. Hicks concluded that Walras and Marshall differ in interest, the former being more interested in principles, the latter in practical applications.

However, even if one is interested in principles alone, Marshall's contributions are important complements to Walras's. For example, of particular and continuing interest is a dynamic element implicit in the equilibrium concept of Marshall, who regards economic biology as the Mecca of the economist (Marshall, 1961, p. xiv). Considering the relation between an industry and its firms as the relation between a forest and its trees, Marshall studied the long-run normal supply price of an equilibrium industry in the case where 'some business will be rising and others falling' (Marshall, 1961, p. 378). Marshall used this concept of equilibrium industry with disequilibrium firms to argue for the compatibility of the increasing returns to scale and competition, considering that individual firms have their life-cycles and do not have enough time to exploit the increasing returns fully.

5. Equilibrium industry with disequilibrium firms

Marshall considered the stationary state of an industry as the first 'step towards studying the influence exerted by the element of time on the relation between cost of production and value' (Marshall, 1961, pp. 315–16). He did not require, however, that every firm in the industry remain of the same size. It is supposed that firms rise and fall, but that the representative firm remains the same size. The representative firm is defined as the miniature of an industry, like the representative tree of a virgin forest. It may not be possible to pick out an actual firm as being representative of the industry. It is, however, a very convenient device in considering the normal supply price of an industry composed of firms behaving differently under different conditions.

The normal supply price of the industry is assumed to be the normal expenses of production (including normal profit) of the representative firm. It is the price the expectation of which is sufficient to maintain the existing aggregate amount of industrial production. A higher price increases aggregate production by increasing the growth of the rising firms and slackening the decay of the falling firms. A lower price diminishes industrial production, since it hastens the decay of the falling firms and slackens the growth of the rising firms.

Why do some firms rise by increasing their output while others fall by diminishing theirs? On the basis of his life-cycle theory of firms, Marshall argues that young firms, like young trees, grow, while old firms, like old trees, decay. It may be considered that a young (an old) firm increases (decreases) its output by expanding (reducing) its capacity, since its normal expenses of production (including normal profit) fall short of (exceed) that of the representative firm, that is, the normal supply price of the industry.[5] In Marshall's stationary state, of course, the condition of the long-run equilibrium is satisfied, so that the demand price equals the normal supply price of the industry, while the supply price of each firm is considered to be its normal expenses of production including normal profit.

When the amount produced is such that the demand price[6] is higher than the supply price, then sellers receive more than sufficient to make it worth their while to bring that amount of the goods to the market. There is an incentive at work to increase the amount brought forward for sale. On the other hand, when the amount produced is such that the demand price is

[5] In other words, short-run average cost including normal profit is higher (lower) than the normal supply price of the industry for the contracting (expanding) firms, while short-run marginal cost is equal to the normal supply price of the industry for all firms.

[6] The demand price for a certain amount of a good is the price that clears the market, i.e. makes the demand equal to the given amount.

lower than the supply price, sellers receive less than sufficient to make it worth their while to bring that amount of the goods to the market. There is, then, an incentive at work to diminish the amount brought forward for sale (Marshall, 1961, p. 345).

Let us denote by x the supply price of a firm and by p the supply price of the industry. A firm increases its output if p is higher than x, and decreases it if p is lower than x. It is assumed that the rate of change in output is proportional to the difference between p and x. Different firms may have an identical value of x or a different value of x. Let $y(x)$ be the total output of firms with the same value of x. Furthermore, let $D(x)$ denote changes (increases if positive, decreases if negative) in y. Then, from this assumption,

$$D(x)/y(x) = (p - x). \qquad (12)$$

Since the aggregate output of the industry remains unchanged in the stationary state, that is,

$$\int y(x)dx = \text{constant}, \qquad (13)$$

we have from (12),

$$\int D(x)dx = \int (p - x)y(x)dx = 0. \qquad (14)$$

If we define the proportion of the total output $y(x)$ of firms with the supply price x to the aggregate industrial output as

$$f(x) = y(x)/\int y(x)dx, \qquad (15)$$

we have, in view of (15),

$$p = \int xf(x)dx, \qquad (16)$$

since from the right hand side of (14)

$$p\int y(x)dx = \int xy(x)dx. \qquad (17)$$

From the definition (15),

$$\int f(x)dx = 1. \qquad (18)$$

Therefore, (16) implies that the normal supply price of the industry or its representative firm is the average supply price of individual firms in the industry.[7]

Marshall considered increasing returns in the sense of internal economy with respect to the long-run average cost of individual firms, since he

---

[7] It is interesting to see that Marx's market value (1959, p. 178) corresponds in this respect to Marshall's normal supply price of the industry. See Negishi (1988) chapter 6, section 6.

argued that short-run supply price increases with output, but an increase in demand gradually increases the size and efficiency of the representative firm (Marshall, 1961, p. 460). If there exist internal economies and if the supply price of an individual firm is a decreasing function of its output capacity, there is no limit to the expansion of a firm with the largest capacity until the whole industrial output is concentrated in its hands. To prevent concentration of the whole industrial output in the hands of a single firm, Marshall emphasized that the life span of private firms is limited and that expanding young firms with low supply prices are eventually changed into shrinking old firms with high supply prices long before such concentration is actually realized.

Marshall's life-cycle theory of firms insists that firms of the industry, like trees in the forest, have a cycle of birth, growth, decay and death. It is based on the fact that the expansion of an individual firm is eventually arrested by the decay, if not of the owner's faculties, then of his liking for energetic work, of his unabated energy and of his power of initiative (Marshall, 1961, pp. 285–6; Marshall, 1921, pp. 315–16). This life-cycle theory of firms may, therefore, give a realistic picture of nineteenth-century industry, but the question is whether it remains relevant with the development of joint-stock companies, which, as Marshall himself admitted, do not really die.

However, we may revive Marshall's biological concept of equilibrium of an industry by considering the life-cycle of technology in equilibrium growth instead of the life-cycle of firms in stationary state.[8]

6.   Edgeworth's equivalence theorem

As was pointed out in section 2, Walras's view of market is that of a well-organized market, in which individual traders do not communicate with each other but communications are exclusively made between each trader and the (perhaps fictitious) auctioneer, who acts as the incarnation of the law of supply and demand. Although Marshall paid more attention to the case of an imperfect market where connections among traders are important (Marshall, 1921, p. 182), his general view of market is still not much different from that of Walras in the sense that the leading role is played by the uniform market price and the law of supply and demand.

An alternative view of market with a completely different communication structure is that of Edgeworth. This succeeded Jevons's view of market, in which an important role is played by the arbitrage behaviour of traders in order to establish the law of indifference. Mutual communication among traders is essential, since in Edgeworth's theory of exchange they are

[8] For an example of such an attempt, see Negishi (1985) chapter 5.

expected to form and block coalitions and to make contracts and recontracts. Contracts are not made necessarily in terms of the uniform price, and supply and demand are not expected to make changes in such price.

However, in the case of a large exchange economy with infinitely many traders on both sides of the market, Edgeworth (1881, pp. 34–42) demonstrated the equivalence of the outcome of two different views of the market (the Walras–Marshall view and the Jevons–Edgeworth view) by using the so-called Edgeworth box diagram. In this section we shall sketch Edgeworth's demonstration, which forms a corner-stone of modern mathematical economics, while a more interesting case of duopoly will be discussed in the next section.

Consider an exchange economy in which two goods are exchanged between two trading bodies. Each trading body consists of infinitely many traders who are identical with respect to tastes and initial holdings of goods. The outcome of exchange can be seen by considering the exchange between the representative trader of each homogeneous trading body through the use of the Edgeworth box diagram.

In Figure 2.1, the quantity of the first good is measured horizontally, that of the second good, vertically; and the quantity of goods given to trader A are measured with the origin at A, those given to trader B, with the origin at B. Point C denotes the initial allocation of goods before trade. This implies also that the total amount of the first good to be exchanged between traders A and B is AC and that of the second good, BC.[9] Curves I, II, etc., are indifferent curves of trader A, curves 1, 2, etc., are those of trader B, and curve DEF is the contract curve, a locus of points where the indifference curves of two traders are tangent.

Point E is the equilibrium of the perfect competition, with the common tangent to indifference curves at E passing through point C. This is the outcome of the exchange if traders are price takers and demand and supply are equalized at the uniform price ratio denoted by the slope of the line EC. Edgeworth's equivalence theorem insists that point E is the outcome of the exchange even if traders are not price takers but form and block coalitions and freely make contracts and recontracts.

It is clear that all the points off the contract curve cannot be stable outcomes of the exchange, since both traders can be better off by making recontracts in order to settle down at some point on the contract curve. On the contract curve only the points between D and F can be candidates for the stable outcome of exchange, since otherwise a trader can be better off by blocking the contract and returning to point C. If A and B are only traders,

---

[9]   Of course, this is a simplifying assumption and in general C can be anywhere in the box.

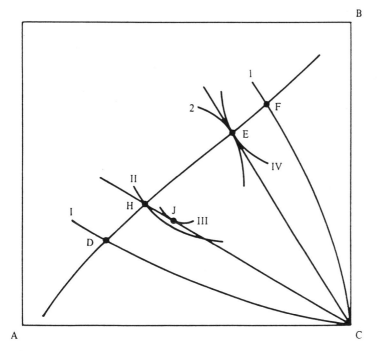

Figure 2.1   *The Edgeworth box diagram*

as in the case of isolated exchange, then all the points on the contract curve located between D and F are stable outcomes of exchange. It should be noted that such points other than point E cannot be reached through exchange with the uniform price ratio.

In the case of a large economy, however, it can be shown that all the points on the contract curve other than point E can be blocked by some coalition of traders that aims to make the participants better off. If so, only point E can be the stable outcome of the exchange, and the outcome of two different views of market are shown to be equivalent.

For example, the contract of point H in Figure 2.1 can be blocked by a coalition formed by all the A-type traders and more than half but less than all of the B-type traders. In the coalition, some A-type traders still continue trade with B-type traders and are located at H, while the rest of the A-type traders have no trade partners in the coalition and are located at C. By sufficiently increasing the number of B-type traders joining the coalition, and therefore increasing the number of A-type traders located at H, we can make the average allocation of two goods for A-type traders (some at H, some at C) so close to H on the line CH that it is located like J, above the indifference curve passing through H. By reallocating among themselves, therefore, all the A-type traders are better off than they are at point H. With some payments to B-type traders in the coalition, all the traders in the coalition are better off than they are at point H, so that an exchange contract H is blocked by a coalition of traders.

Similarly, any point between D and F on the contract curve, where the common tangent to two indifference curves does not pass through the point C, can, if necessary, be blocked by a coalition of traders by changing the roles of A-type traders and B-type traders from those in the case of point H. Obviously only the point E belongs to the core, that is the set of exchange contracts that are not blocked by coalitions of traders.

As far as the case of a large economy with infinitely many traders on both sides of the market is concerned, therefore, different views on the information structure in the market does not matter at all. By Edgeworth's equivalence theorem one may defend the unrealisticness of the neoclassical assumption of no mutual communication among traders and the existence of an auctioneer, since what matters is not the realism of the assumption but that of the outcome.

7. Communication structure of duopoly

Following the suggestion of Farrell (1970) let us now consider the case of duopoly with Edgeworth's communication structure, where there are only two traders of one type and infinitely many traders of another type, though the total quantities of two goods are finite in the exchange economy. Since equal quantities of goods should be allocated to identical traders of the same type, we can still use the Edgeworth box diagram (Figure 2.1), which now describes half of the economy, that of the duopolists and its infinitely many customers.

Suppose first that there are two B-type traders, B_1 and B_2, and infinitely many traders of type A. In Figure 2.1, BC is the quantity of the second good initially held by a B-type trader and AC is the sum of quantities of the first good initially held by half of the A-type traders. Curves I, II, etc., in Figure 2.1 are now aggregate indifference curves of A-type traders, as well as individual ones, which can be constructed if the identical individual curves are homothetic, so that the marginal rate of substitution between two goods depends only on the ratio of the quantities of goods and the Engel curve is a line through the origin.

An exchange contract H in Figure 2.1 can now be blocked by a coalition of one B-type trader (one of duopolists) and more than half but less than all of infinitely many A-type traders. All the A-type traders currently trading with the B_1 trader, who we assume joins the coalition, also join the coalition and keep the contract H with B_1. Some A-type traders currently trading with B_2, who does not join the coalition, join the coalition and cancel the contract with B_2 to return to the initial point C. By sufficiently decreasing the number of the latter group of A-type traders joining the coalition and therefore increasing the number of A-type traders located at H, relative to those A-type traders located at C, we can make the average allocation of two goods for individual A-type traders in the coalition so close to point H on the line CH that it is like an allocation J located above the indifference curve passing through H.[10] By reallocating among themselves, therefore, all the A-type traders in the coalition are better off than they are at the contract H. With some payment to B_1 located at H, all the traders joining the coalition can be better off than they are at H, so that the contract H is blocked.

Suppose next that there are two A-type traders, A_1 and A_2, and infinitely many traders of type B. In Figure 2.1, AC is now the quantity of the first good initially held by an A-type trader and BC is the sum of quantities of the second good initially held by the half of the B-type traders. Curves 1, 2, etc., in Figure 2.1 are aggregate indifference curves of B-type traders. In this case, an exchange contract H in Figure 2.1 can be blocked by a coalition of one A-type trader (one of duopolists) and less than half of infinitely many B-type traders. Then suppose A_1 joins the coalition. Those B-type traders also joining the coalition keep trade with A_1 unchanged so that they can keep the same level of utility as enjoyed at the exchange contract H. Duopolist A_1 cancels trade with those B-type traders who are not permitted to join the coalition, so that A_1 moves on the line HC from H towards C. Unless too many contracts with B-type traders are cancelled, A_1 can be located like J above the indifference curve passing through H. By reallocating among themselves, then, all the traders joining the coalition can be better off than they are at H, so that the contract H is blocked.

Similarly, any contract between D and F on the contract curve, where the common tangent to two indifference curves does not pass through the point C, can be blocked by a coalition of traders, if necessary, by changing the roles of A-type traders and B-type traders from those in the case of the contract H. Again, it is only the point E that belongs to the core. In other words, even a duopoly market ends up with an equilibrium identical to that of the perfect competition if duopolists and infinitely many customers are free to communicate to organize coalitions.

If, on the other hand, there is no such direct communication between duopolists and customers and the latter behave simply as price takers in the

---

[10] Though H and J are allocations to half of the A-type traders in the economy, they can be considered as allocations to an A-type trader, since indifference curves are homothetic. Alternatively, we can argue more generally by the use of Scitovsky indifference curves.

face of the uniform price offered by the former, it is well known that the equilibrium is in general different from that of the perfect competition, as was shown by Cournot (1897). The structure of communication is, therefore, very important in the case of the theory of duopoly and, more generally, in the case of oligopoly. In view of the prevalence of non-price competition among oligopolists, which implies the existence of direct communication between oligopolists and customers, we have to admit the unrealisticness of the assumption of the traditional theory of oligopoly, which denies the possibility of such communication.

Our consideration suggests, then, that the efficiency of an industry may depend not so much on the degree of concentration (the number of firms) as on the possibility of such direct communication and the cost of information, communication and organization.

8.   Conclusions

Implicit dynamic concepts are hidden in the time structure of Walrasian and Marshallian theories, which are generally regarded as uni-periodal economic theories. Some of them correspond clearly to the more developed concepts of modern dynamic theories. The implications of Marshall's equilibrium of industry with disequilibrium firms has, however, not yet been fully and explicitly developed by modern theories of dynamic economics. While Edgeworth's theory of exchange has generally been evaluated as an important contribution to the theory of perfect competition, the implications of its communication structure of the market are considered in the case of duopoly, and it is suggested that the efficiency of an industry depends not so much on the degree of concentration as on the communication structure.

References

Cournot, A. (1897) *Researches into the Mathematical Principles of the Theory of Wealth*, Macmillan, London (French original, 1838).

Edgeworth, F.Y. (1881) *Mathematical Psychics. An Essay on the Application of Mathematics to the Moral Sciences*, C. Kegan Paul, London.

Farrell, M.J. (1970) 'Edgeworth Bounds for Oligopoly Prices', *Economica*, 37, pp. 342–61.

Garegnani, P. (1960) *Il capitale nelle teorie della distribuzione*, Giuffré, Milan.

Hicks, J. (1934) 'Léon Walras', *Econometrica*, 2, pp. 338–48.

(1946) *Value and Capital*, Clarendon Press, Oxford.

(1965) *Capital and Growth*, Clarendon Press, Oxford.

Marshall, A. (1921) *Industry and Trade*, Macmillan, London.

(1961) *Principles of Economics*, ed. C.W. Guillebaud, Macmillan, London (1st edn 1890).

Marx, K. (1959) *Capital*, vol. III, Progress Publishers (German original 1867).

Morishima, M. (1960) 'Existence of Solution to the Walrasian System of Capital Formation and Credit', *Zeitschrift für Nationalökonomie*, 20, pp. 238–43.

(1977) *Walras' Economics*, Cambridge University Press, Cambridge.

Negishi, T. (1985) *Economic Theories in a Non-Walrasian Tradition*, Cambridge University Press, Cambridge.

(1988) *History of Economic Theory*, North-Holland Publishing Company, Amsterdam and New York.

Walras, L. (1954) *Elements of Pure Economics*, ed. W. Jaffé, Allen & Unwin, London (French original 1874).

Wicksell, K. (1967) *Lectures on Political Economy*, Kelley, New York (Swedish original 1901–6).

Yasui, T. (1970) *Walras o megutte (Essays on Walras)*, Sobunsha, Tokyo.

20

10 On the Non-existence of Equilibrium: From Thornton to Arrow

Takashi Negishi*

1 INTRODUCTION

Among the many contributions to economic science made by Arrow, one of the most important is certainly the proof of the existence of an equilibrium for a competitive economy.[1] The case where no equilibrium exists even though indifference curves, production functions, and so on, are fairly well behaved is a useful one to show the necessity of proving the existence of equilibrium. Mill (1869) indicates that one of the first examples of the non-existence of equilibrium consists of the counter examples to equilibrium theory given in W. T. Thornton's *On Labour* (1869) though Thornton himself was concerned not so much with the non-existence of equilibrium as the possibility of trade at disequilibrium prices. The Thornton-Mill examples of the non-existence of equilibrium are remarkable because they are due to the discontinuity of demand curves; other unsuccessful attempts to show the non-existence of equilibrium failed because of their assumption of continuity. The Thornton-Mill examples, as well as the example of Wald (1951), are, however, not so serious to equilibrium theory, if we consider, not the Walrasian *tâtonnement* with recontract, but the non-*tâtonnement* without recontract. From such non-*tâtonnement* point of view, a truly important example of the non-existence of equilibrium is the one given by Arrow, that is, the case where a Pareto optimal allocation cannot be viewed as a competitive equilibrium.[2]

*I must thank Professor K. J. Arrow for invaluable suggestions and warm encouragement given to my early studies of general equilibrium theory. It was in 1957 when I was a first year graduate student at Tokyo that I dared to write to him to discuss an alternative proof of the *existence* of equilibrium based on *Pareto optimality* of a competitive equilibrium, which was later published in *Metroeconomica* (1960). Subsequently, I joined the Office of Naval Research project at Stanford, where I began my studies of the *non-tâtonnement* stability problem.

2 THORNTON'S EXAMPLES

Thornton's *On Labour, Its Wrongful Claims and Rightful Dues, Its Actual Present and Possible Future* (1869) is famous in the history of economic science because it made J. S. Mill recant the wages fund doctrine.[3] It is, however, not only an attack on a specific equilibrium theory of the wages fund doctrine, but also a criticism of equilibrium theory in general. As Mill (1869) recognized, Thornton presented at least three counter examples to the theory that the equations of supply and demand determine prices.

The first example given by Thornton is that of Dutch and English auctions for fish.

> When a herring or mackerel boat has discharged on the beach at Hastings or Dover, last night's take of fish, the boatmen, in order to dispose of their cargo, commonly resort to a process called Dutch auction. The fish are divided into lots, each of which is set up at a higher price than the salesman expects to get for it, and he then gradually lowers his terms, until he comes to a price which some bystander is willing to pay rather than not have the lot, and to which he accordingly agrees. Suppose on one occasion the lot to have been a hundredweight, and the agreed price twenty shillings. If, on the same occasion, instead of the Dutch form of auction, the ordinary English mode had been adopted, the result might have been different. The operation would then have commenced by some bystander making a bid, which others might have successively exceeded, until a price was arrived at beyond which no one but the actual bidder could afford or was disposed to go. That sum would not necessarily be twenty shillings; very possibly it might be only eighteen shillings. The person who was prepared to pay the former price might very possibly be the only person present prepared to pay even so much as the latter price; and if so, he might get by English auction for eighteen shillings the fish for which at Dutch auction he would have paid twenty shillings. In the same market, with the same quantity of fish for sale, and with customers in number and every other respect the same, the same lot of fish might fetch two very different prices.[4]

Thornton's second and third examples of the failure of supply and demand as the law of price are those of horses and of gloves.

Suppose two persons at different times, or in different places, to have each a horse to sell, valued by the owner at £50; and that in the one case there are two, and in the other three persons, of whom every one is ready to pay £50 for the horse, though no one of them can afford to pay more. In both cases supply is the same, viz., one horse at £50; but demand is different, being in one case two, and in the other three, horses at £50. Yet the price at which the horses will be sold will be the same in both cases, viz., £50.

When a tradesman has placed upon his goods the highest price which any one will pay for them, the price cannot, of course, rise higher, yet the supply may be below the demand. A glover in a country town, on the eve of an assize ball, having only a dozen pairs of white gloves in store, might possibly be able to get ten shillings a pair for them. He would be able to get this if twelve persons were willing to pay that price rather than not go to the ball, or than go ungloved. But he could not get more than this, even though, while he was still higgling with his first batch of customers, a second batch, equally numerous, and neither more nor less eager, should enter his shop and offer to pay the same but not a higher price. The demand for gloves, which at first had been just equal to the supply, would now be exactly doubled, yet the price would not rise above ten shillings a pair. Such abundance of proof is surely decisive against the supposition that the price must rise when demand exceeds supply.[5]

3   MILL'S INTERPRETATIONS

Mill (1869) misinterpreted Thornton's example of auctions for fish that 'the demand and supply are equal at twenty shillings, and equal also at eighteen shillings'. Mill argued that the case may be conceived but in practice is hardly ever realized as it is an exception to the rule that demand increases with cheapness. In the second edition of *On Labour* (1870), Thornton reproduced the same example but changed prices from twenty and eighteen shillings to eight and six shillings and made a rejoinder to Mill.

In this particular case it would not be possible for supply and demand to be equal at two different prices. For the case is one in which demand would increase with cheapness. A hawker who was ready to pay 8 s. for a hundred herrings, would want more than a hundred if he could get a hundred for 6 s. There being then but a given quantity in the market, if that quantity were just sufficient to satisfy all the customers ready to buy at 8 s., it follows that it would not have sufficed to satisfy them if the price had been 6 s. If supply and demand were equal at the former price, they would be unequal at the latter.[6]

In this example, therefore, there is an equilibrium price that equalizes demand and supply, that is, the price established by Dutch auction. If English auction is adopted, however, trade takes place at a lower price with demand larger than supply and unsatisfied demand remains after trade is over. The reason is, first, that there is no competition to bid up the price since no one except the actual purchaser is willing to buy any at that price. Secondly, the actual purchaser himself would not bid up the price even though he wants to buy more than the quantity supplied since he knows that the supply will not be increased. The lesson from this example is not the possibility of the non-existence of equilibrium but the possibility that Walrasian equilibrium can be established either through Walrasian *tâtonnement* or by Dutch auction, but not by English auction, if the supply is constant. Similarly, we can construct an example where Walrasian equilibrium can be established either through Walrasian *tâtonnement* or by English auction but not by Dutch auction when demand is constant but supply increases as the price rises.

Mill (1869) correctly recognized the examples of horses and gloves, given by Thornton as counter-examples to the law of demand and supply, as those of the non-existence of equilibrium:

At £50 there is a demand for twice or three times the supply; at £50.0s. 01/4d. there is no demand at all. When the scale of the demand for a commodity is broken by so extraordinary a jump, the law fails in its application; not, I venture to say, from any fault in the law, but because the conditions on which its applicability depends do not exist.

Mr. Thornton has shown that the law is not fulfilled – namely, when there is no price that would fulfil it; either the demand or the supply advancing or receding by such violent skips, that there is no halting point at which it just equals the other element.

The reason for the non-existence of equilibrium is, of course, the discontinuity of the demand (or supply) curve, in the case of present examples, caused by the indivisibility of a horse and a pair of gloves, as was pointed out by Chipman (1979). In both examples, each identical demander wants a minimum unit of commodities, that is, a horse or a pair of gloves, so that no price rise can clear the excess demand, that is, equate demand with the given positive supply.

Although Thornton's original (1869) aim was to show the possibility of trade at disequilibrium prices by the use of all of his three examples, he later (1870) recognized that the examples of horses and gloves show also the non-existence of equilibrium.

> Mr. Mill does not deny that in every single instance in which I have represented the law of supply and demand as failing, it does actually fail. Nay, he goes so far as to admit that in one of my classes of cases 'the conditions on which the applicability of the law depends do not exist' – that, whereas in those cases the law is that the price will be one which equalises the demand with the supply, I have shown not only that the price arrived at does not equalise them, but that there is no price whatever that could. And of another set of cases he similarly admits that fulfilment of the law therein is 'in the nature of things impossible'.[7]

4   UNSUCCESSFUL EXAMPLES

Thornton-Mill examples of the non-existence of equilibrium are remarkable in the sense that they are due to the discontinuity of demand curves while other unsuccessful attempts to show the non-existence of equilibrium failed because of their assumption of the continuity of demand and supply curves derived from well-behaved indifference curves and production functions.

Henderson and Quandt (1958) considered the case of a backward-bending supply curve for a factor of production such as labour in a two-commodity system of a consumption good and labour. It is shown as curve ce in Figure 10.1 where the price p of a commodity (labour) relative to the other (consumption good) is measured vertically and the demand D and supply S of the commodity, horizontally. If the demand curve for labour is like fg, equilibrium cannot exist since 'the quantity of labor that consumers offer is less than the quantity that entrepre-

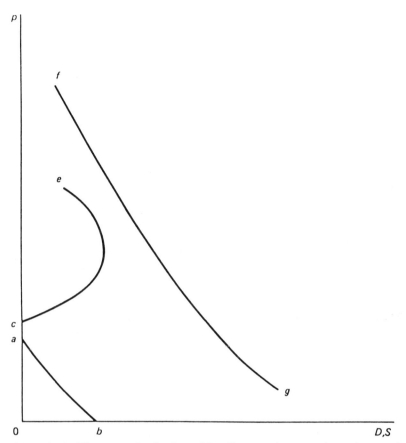

Figure 10.1   The case of a backward-bending supply curve for a factor of production in a two-commodity system of a consumption good and labour

neurs demand at every wage rate'. An example of a quadratic excess demand function for labour

$$D - S = p^2 - 14p + 53$$

is given, which has no real roots for $D = S$.[8] A backward-bending supply curve of labour can be derived from well-behaved indifference curves between leisure and consumption. Although no detailed descriptions of the behaviour of consumers and entrepreneurs and of the relations between them are given, demand and supply curves are considered as continuous and no sufficient conditions required in modern theorems of the existence of a competitive equilibrium are explicitly excluded. Henderson and Quandt's example of the non-existence of equilibrium has, therefore, no choice theoretic foundations.

According to Jaffé, Walras was aware of the possibility of non-existence of equilibrium, that is, of 'no solution' in his theory of exchange of two commodities for each other. What Walras showed is the case of a demand curve *ab* and a supply curve *ce* in Figure 10.1.[9] Chipman (1965b) correctly argued that this is a play on words, for what characterizes Walras's example is not the fact that there is no solution, but rather that there is no trade.[10] The demand curve should be considered not as *ab* but as *pab*, and the supply curve, not as *ce* but as O*ce*, so that any *p* located between *a* and *c* is a solution.

Morishima (1977) insists, however, that a no-trade equilibrium cannot be regarded as an essential equilibrium of exchange. Certainly, the essentiality of equilibrium is very important in the other three problems of Walras, that is, equilibria of production, capital accumulation, and money. If no commodity is produced at all, the equilibrium involving the possibility of production is not essential and reduced to an exchange equilibrium. Similarly, the equilibrium involving the possibility of capital accumulation is not essential and reduced to a simple production equilibrium if no net investment is made, and the monetary equilibrium is not essential and reduced to real economic equilibrium if the price of money is zero.[11] In the case of exchange equilibrium, however, the inessentiality of equilibrium (that is, no trade) is not so serious as in the case of inessentiality of other equilibria, since whether trade exists or not depends on the distribution of endowments of commodities among traders, which itself is changed through trading out of equilibria. The aim of trade is to make no further trade necessary, and no-trade equilibrium implies, not so much that no trade can take place, as that no trade is necessary, since a Pareto-optimum is already achieved, possibly through trading out of equilibria. In other words, Walras's example of the non-existence of an essential equilibrium can be important only if we stick to Walrasian *tâtonnement* which rules out any trading out of equilibria. Even then it should be noted that an essential exchange equilibrium becomes an inessential one after the equilibrium trade takes place.

5   NON-*TÂTONNEMENT* POINT OF VIEW

Not only Walras's example of an inessential exchange equilibrium, but also Thornton-Mill examples of the non-existence of equilibrium are not serious from the point of view of non-*tâtonnement* theory which introduces trading out of equilibria.[12] As a matter of fact, the original intention of Thornton's attack on equilibrium theory is to demonstrate not so much the non-existence of equilibrium, as the possibility (in the case of auctions for fish) or the necessity (in the cases of horses and gloves) of trading out of equilibria, that is, at disequilibrium prices.

Certainly £50 is not an equilibrium price of a horse, since only a horse is supplied while two or three horses are demanded. If a horse is sold at this disequilibrium price of £50, however, a Pareto-optimum is achieved, since unsatisfied demander(s) and the supplier do not evaluate a horse at more than £50 while the satisfied demander does not agree to sell back the horse just bought at £50. Even though there still remains excess demand of one or two horses at £50 after this trading, both demand and supply can be made zero by a slight rise of price from £50, so that an inessential exchange equilibrium is achieved. In the case of gloves, similarly, a Pareto optimal inessential exchange equilibrium is established at a price slightly higher than 10 shillings for a pair, after 12 pairs are sold to 12 persons at 10 shillings for a pair, even though another 12 persons remain unsatisfied.

If we stick to Walrasian *tâtonnement* where trading out of equilibria is ruled out, neither an essential nor inessential equilibrium exists in the examples of horses and gloves. In the case of fish, however, there exists an essential equilibrium at the price of 20 shillings (or 8 *s.*) which can be achieved through Walrasian *tâtonnement*. Even then, such an equilibrium cannot be established if we adopt the English auction. Suppose, as in the example of Thornton, the single person who is prepared to pay 20 shillings (or 8 *s.*) is the only person prepared to pay 18 shillings (or 6 *s.*) which is arrived through the English auction. At the latter price there is an excess demand, since this person wants more fish than at the former price. If fish are sold to this person at the latter price, however, the result is a Pareto-optimum which can be made an inessential equilibrium by raising the price up to 20 shillings (or 8 *s.*) after trading.

If, unlike in Thornton's examples, commodities are divisible, the result of trading out of equilibria can even be an essential equilibrium in the sense that at least the last step towards a Pareto optimum is an equilibrium trade. This can be seen by considering an example of the non-existence of equilibrium constructed by Wald (1951). Wald considered an exchange economy of three persons and three commodities. Marginal utilities of the j-th commodity for the i-th person U_{ij}:

$i = 1, 2, 3, j = 1, 2, 3$, are given as

$$u_{11}(x_{11}) = 1/x_{11},$$

$$u_{12}(x_{12}) = (b - x_{12})/x_{12}^2 \qquad \text{for } x_{12} \leq b$$
$$\qquad\qquad = 0 \qquad\qquad\qquad \text{for } x_{12} > b$$

$$u_{13}(x_{13}) = 2(c - x_{13})/x_{13}^2 \qquad \text{for } x_{13} \leq c$$
$$\qquad\qquad = 0 \qquad\qquad\qquad \text{for } x_{13} > c$$

$$u_{21}(x_{21}) = 1/x_{21}^2$$

$$u_{22}(x_{22}) = 1/x_{22}$$

$$u_{23}(x_{23}) = 0$$

$$u_{31}(x_{31}) = 1/x_{31}^2$$

$$u_{32}(x_{32}) = 0$$

$$u_{33}(x_{33}) = 1/x_{33}$$

where x_{ij} signifies the amount of the j-th commodity held by the i-th person, and the initial holding a_{ij} of the i-th person of the j-th commodity is given as

$$a_{11} = a, \quad a_{12} = 0, \quad a_{13} = 0,$$
$$a_{21} = 0, \quad a_{22} = b, \quad a_{23} = 0,$$
$$a_{31} = 0, \quad a_{32} = 0, \quad a_{33} = c,$$

where a, b, c are given positive constants.

Wald skilfully demonstrated that no Walrasian equilibrium exists in this economy. Suppose, however, that trading out of equilibria is possible provided that it is Pareto improving, that is, no one's utility is decreased and someone else's utility increased by such a trade.[13] Since only the first and second persons are interested in the second commodity, and only the first and third persons are interested in the third commodity, and clearly the initial distribution of commodities (a_{ij}'s) is not Pareto optimal, the first and second commodities are exchanged between the first and second persons, and the first and third commodities are exchanged between the first and third persons, until a Pareto optimum is reached. The last (possibly infinitesimal) trade towards a Pareto optimum is an equilibrium trade at prices proportional to the first person's marginal utilities at the Pareto optimum, in the sense that demand and supply are equalized for each commodity at such prices, provided that the Pareto optimum is an inessential equilibrium. In this case, the Pareto optimum achieved is an inessential equilibrium. If $x_{12} = b$ and $x_{21} = 0$ at such Pareto optimum, then $u_{11} > 0$, $u_{12} = 0$ while u_{21} is positive but finite and u_{22} is infinitely large so that conditions for a Pareto optimum are not satisfied. Therefore, $x_{12} < b$ and $x_{22} > 0$. Similarly, $x_{13} < c$ and $x_{33} > 0$. Then, positive (x_{11}, x_{12}, x_{13}) is the most preferred among the commodity bundles equally or less valuable at positive prices proportional to marginal utilities, u_{11}, u_{12} and u_{13}. Since $u_{11}/u_{12} = u_{21}/u_{22}$ and $u_{11}/u_{13} = u_{13}/u_{33}$, positive (x_{21}, x_{22}) and (x_{31}, x_{33}) are also the most preferred respectively among the commodity bundles equally or less valued.

Thornton seemed to admit these arguments, though he insisted that the law of demand and supply can then be applicable only in a trivial sense.

> it would be but a mere fraction of the whole stock of goods that would be sold at equation price, by far the greater part being sold at prices at which supply and demand were unequal ... the price at which the last lot of any commodity is sold must be one at which supply and demand are equal – one at which, there being of course but one customer desirous of purchasing left, that last customer could get as much of the commodity as he desired – the truth might be rather worth knowing than not; still, seeing that every lot of the commodity except the very last would have been sold at prices at which supply and demand were not equal, it is not easy to conceive a piece of knowledge more barren of practical utility.[14]

6 ARROW'S EXAMPLE

Our considerations suggest that an example of the non-existence of equilibrium which does really matter for the equilibrium theory is the one of Pareto optimum, either given as the initial distribution of commodities or achieved as a result of trading out of equilibria, which is not an inessential equilibrium. Such is the celebrated example given by Arrow.[15]

Figure 10.2 is the so-called Edgeworth box diagram, where the first commodity is measured horizontally, and the second commodity

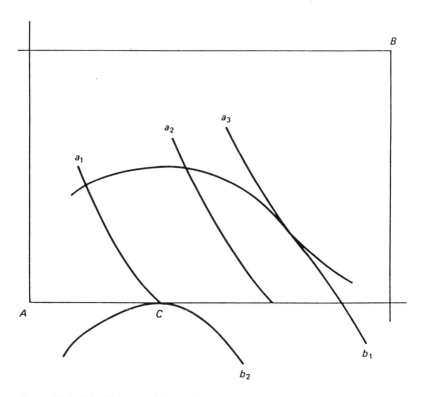

Figure 10.2 The Edgeworth box diagram

vertically. Commodities allocated to person A are measured from the
origin A, and those allocated to person B, from the origin B. Curves a_1,
a_2, a_3 are indifference curves of person A and curves b_1, b_2 are those of
person B. Point C is clearly a Pareto optimum where the marginal
utility of the first commodity is zero for person B. If the first
commodity is free, the price line through C is horizontal and A
demands an infinitely large amount of the first commodity while B does
not supply any of the first commodity, so that C is not an equilibrium.
If the first commodity is not free, the price line through C is not
horizontal and B demands more of the second commodity while A does
not supply the second commodity, or even demands it, so that again C
is not an equilibrium.

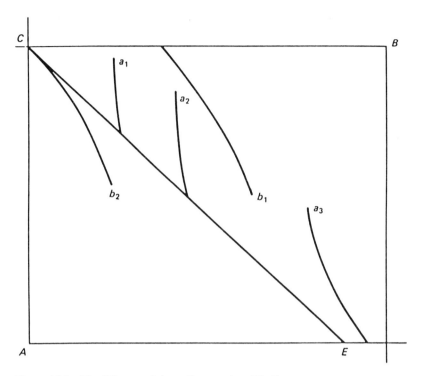

Figure 10.3   The Edgeworth box diagram (modified)

In Arrow's example, the demand curve for the first commodity is discontinuous when its price is zero, since the demand is infinitely large when the price is zero while the demand is zero when the price is even infinitesimally positive. Similar discontinuity exists also in Wald's example. This is partly the reason for the non-existence of equilibrium. An example of a demand curve discontinuous at some positive price can be constructed by a slight modification of Arrow's example. Figure 10.3 is an Edgeworth box diagram similar to Figure 10.2, except that the area ACE does not belong to the consumption set of A.[16] Suppose the first commodity is a consumption good and the second commodity is labour. A has AC of the maximum amount of labour to be supplied and B has BC of consumption good. To supply labour it is physiologically necessary to consume the consumption good and the line CE

indicates the minimum necessary consumption required by A to supply different amounts of labour. When the price of the consumption good in terms of labour is AC/AE or lower, A demands AE or more of the consumption good while A does not supply labour and does not demand the consumption good when the price is higher than AC/AE. The demand curve for the first commodity is discontinuous at the price of AC/AE and a Pareto optimum C is not an equilibrium, since B does not supply the consumption good when its price is AC/AE or lower and demands labour when the price is higher than AC/AE.

NOTES

1. See Arrow and Debreu (1954); Arrow and Hahn (1971), pp. 107–28.
2. See Arrow (1951). Chipman (1965b) gave an interesting interpretation with references to classical debates on the possibility of glut.
3. Mill (1869); see Negishi (1985) for Mill's recantation of wages fund theory.
4. Thornton (1869), pp. 47–8, quoted from Mill (1869); see also Thornton (1870), pp. 56–7.
5. Thornton (1869), pp. 49, 51–2, quoted from Mill (1869); see also Thornton (1870), pp. 59, 61–2.
6. Thornton (1870), pp. 57–8; see also p. 60.
7. Thornton (1870), p. 68. 'One of my classes of cases' is the case of horses and 'another set of cases' is the case of gloves.
8. Henderson and Quandt (1958), pp. 155–7. Fortunately, this example was withdrawn in the subsequent editions.
9. Walras (1954), pp. 108, 502.
10. Chipman (1965a) argued, however, that Walras 'seems to assume that both traders start out with more of everything than they want, so that there is really no economic problem', which is clearly not the case, since the price is positive and finite.
11. See Morishima (1977), pp. 17–18; Hahn (1965).
12. See Arrow and Hahn (1971), pp. 324–46, and Negishi (1972), pp. 207–27.
13. This seems to be the most plausible rule for trading out of equilibria in a moneyless model of an economy; see Hahn (1962); Morishima (1964), pp. 43–53; Uzawa (1962). For the so-called Hahn rule which is applicable to monetary economy, see Arrow and Hahn (1971), pp. 337–45.
14. Thornton (1870), p. 65. See also Thornton (1869), p. 53.
15. See Arrow (1951), Figure 2 and Quirk and Saposnik (1968), p. 133, Figure 4.8. In the latter figure, however, the contract curve is wrongly drawn.
16. For the definition of consumption set which is independent of preference, see Debreu (1959), p. 51.

REFERENCES

Arrow, K. J. (1951) 'An Extension of the Basic Theorems of Classical Welfare Economics', in J. Neyman (ed.) *Proceedings of the Second Berkeley Symposium on Mathematical Statistics and Probability* (Berkeley: University of California Press) pp. 507–32.

Arrow, K. J. and G. Debreu (1954) 'Existence of an Equilibrium for a Competitive Economy', *Econometrica*, 22: 265–90.

Arrow, K. J. and F. H. Hahn (1971) *General Competitive Analysis* (San Francisco: Holden-Day).

Chipman, J. S. (1965a) 'The Nature and Meaning of Equilibrium in Economic Theory', D. Martindale (ed). *Functionalism in the Social Sciences* (Philadelphia: American Academy of Political and Social Science) pp. 35–64.

Chipman, J. S. (1965b) 'A Survey of the Theory of International Trade, Part 2', *Econometrica*, 33: 685–760.

Chipman, J. S. (1979) 'Mill's "Superstructure": How well does it stand up?' *History of Political Economy*, 11: 477–500.

Debreu, G. (1959) *Theory of Value* (New Haven: Yale University Press).

Hahn, F. H. (1962) 'On the Stability of Pure Exchange Equilibrium', *International Economic Review*, 3: 206–13.

Hahn, F. H. (1965) 'On Some Problems in Proving the Existence of Equilibrium in a Monetary Economy', in F. H. Hahn and F. P. R. Brechling (eds) *The Theory of Interest Rates* (London: Macmillan) pp. 126–35.

Henderson, J. M. and R. E. Quandt (1958) *Microeconomic Theory* (New York: McGraw Hill).

Mill, J. S. (1869) 'Thornton on Labour and Its Claims', in *Collected Works of John Stuart Mill*, vol. V (Toronto: University of Toronto Press) pp. 631–68.

Morishima, M. (1964) *Equilibrium Stability and Growth* (Oxford: Oxford University Press).

Morishima, M. (1977) *Walras' Economics* (Cambridge: Cambridge University Press).

Negishi, T. (1972) *General Equilibrium Theory and International Trade* (Amsterdam: North-Holland).

Negishi, T. (1985) 'Comments on Ekelund "Mill's Recantation of the Wages Fund",' *Oxford Economic Papers*.

Quirk J. and R. Saposnik (1968) *Introduction to General Equilibrium Theory and Welfare Economics* (New York: McGraw-Hill!)

Thornton, W. T. (1869) *On Labour, Its Wrongful Claims and Rightful Dues, Its Actual Present and Possible Future* (London: Macmillan).

Thornton, W. T. (1870) ibid, 2nd edn (London: Macmillan).

Uzawa, H. (1962) 'On the Stability of Edgeworth's Barter Process', *International Economic Review*, 3: 218–32

Wald, A. (1951) 'On Some Systems of Equations of Mathematical Economics', *Econometrica*, 19: 368–403

Walras, L. (1954) *Elements of Pure Economics*, translated from the definitive (1926) edn by W. Jaffé (1st edn 1874–7) (London: Allen & Unwin).

[21]

Comment

Takashi Negishi

Let me begin by emphasizing that I am not a typical member of the Society for the History of Economic Thought in Japan, which was founded in 1950, started to publish its *Annual Bulletin* in 1963, and has now 808 members. Unlike myself, many of its members are trained in Marxist economics and have no training or research experience in neoclassical economics. They seem to be happy by themselves and to have no interest in seeking recognition from mainstream economists, or in joining with historians of science, since the history of economic thought is still firmly established in the university curriculum, and typically a large university has several historians of economics in its economics department. Rather they share their interests with historians of philosophy, ethics, jurisprudence, and social and political thought, since some of them belong as well to such societies as the Japan Society of British Philosophy.

As a mainstream economic theorist who has made some contributions to the areas of general equilibrium, international trade and neo-Keynesian economics and who is much interested in the history of economics, I do argue that economists will always need historians of economics, even if in the near future the latter will no longer worry about the approval of the former. Economics cannot dispense with its history. The newest version of macroeconomics, for example, had to characterize itself as new *classical,* while there are many "neo-" or "post-" schools in the current theory like neo-Austrian, neoclassical, neo-Ricardian, neoinstitutionalism, neo-Walrasian, post-Keynesian, and so on; the implications of which cannot be fully understood without a proper knowledge of the history of economics.

Correspondence may be addressed to the author, Faculty of Economics, University of Tokyo, Bunkyo–ku, Tokyo 113, Japan.
History of Political Economy 24:1 © 1992 by Duke University Press. CCC 0018-2702/91/$1.50

With an ever-growing emphasis on formal techniques in mainstream economics, however, many economic theorists are not any more likely to develop their interest in the history of their science than are the natural scientists. This is very unfortunate. To develop our science in the right direction, I believe more theoretical resources should go into the study of the history of economics from the point of view of the current theory.[1] This of course does not mean to cut or stretch a past theory into a Procrustean bed for the current theory. The history of our science should be used as a mirror in which the current theory reflects the knowledge of how it failed to succeed in the past. To learn from past theories does not impede the progress of our science. Progress often means, however, sacrificing something old. To make sure that we are going in the right direction, it is always necessary to see whether we have sacrificed something in error.

Consider the case of international trade theory. From the point of view of the two commodity two factor two country model of the neoclassical theory of international trade, the model of Ricardo's numerical example of comparative advantage has been regarded as the special case where labor is the single factor of production. This is a Procrustean bed, since labor, capital and land all exist in Ricardo's model. England has more capital and labor relative to land, and the marginal labor productivity is lower than Portugal's even though her technology is as advanced as Portugal's. If England's subsistence level is not lower than Portugal's, furthermore, it is the rate of profit which is lower in England than in Portugal. Another Procrustean bed interpretation is that the Ricardian theory of international trade cannot determine the terms of trade unless the reciprocal demands of countries are taken into consideration. Since wage costs of products are determined by subsistence wages in Ricardo's model, the terms of trade can be inferred from the rate of profit ratio. International capital mobility is assumed implicitly in classical economics, since it emphasized, unlike neoclassical economics, the role of importers and exporters, whose capital replaces, as Adam Smith pointed out, the capital of domestic and foreign producers. Capital moves from England to Portugal until the ratio of the rate of profit satisfies the required risk premium for investments in foreign trade and in foreign countries. The relative price of cloth and

1. It is interesting and encouraging, however, to see that more than half of the graduate students in U.S. elite schools are moderately interested in history of economics, although less than twenty percent of them have great interest. See Klamer and Colander (1990, 17).

wine is, then, determined by the risk premium, which Ricardo emphasized, and changes in reciprocal demands are absorbed into changes in the labor population. One lesson of this brief study is the importance of the role of exporters and importers in international trade and investment, which modern theory failed to learn from classical theory, but which is very important from the point of view of Keynesian economics (see Negishi 1982, 199–210; Gandolfo 1986, 28–31; Itoh and Negishi 1987, 89–93).

It may certainly be fruitful for historians of economics to do comparative studies of the development of the various sciences, but it is also their duty to criticize and advise economists so that the latter can develop economics in the right direction. Historians do not need the approval of economists. It is the latter who should ask the approval of the former.

References

Gandolfo, G. 1986. *International Economics*. Vol. 1. Berlin: Springer-Verlag.

Itoh, M., and T. Negishi. 1987. *Disequilibrium Trade Theories*. Chur, Switzerland: Harwood.

Klamer, A., and D. Colander. 1990. *The Making of an Economist*. Boulder, Colo.: Westview Press.

Negishi, T. 1982. The Labor Theory of Value in the Ricardian Theory of International Trade. *HOPE* 14.2:199–210.

Author Index

Subject Index

Economists of the Twentieth Century

Monetarism and Macroeconomic Policy
Thomas Mayer

Studies in Fiscal Federalism
Wallace E. Oates

The World Economy in Perspective
Essays in International Trade and European Integration
Herbert Giersch

Towards a New Economics
Critical Essays on Ecology, Distribution and Other Themes
Kenneth E. Boulding

Studies in Positive and Normative Economics
Martin J. Bailey

The Collected Essays of Richard E. Quandt (2 volumes)
Richard E. Quandt

International Trade Theory and Policy
Selected Essays of W. Max Corden
W. Max Corden

Organization and Technology in Capitalist Development
William Lazonick

Studies in Human Capital
Collected Essays of Jacob Mincer, Volume 1
Jacob Mincer

Studies in Labor Supply
Collected Essays of Jacob Mincer, Volume 2
Jacob Mincer

Macroeconomics and Economic Policy
The Selected Essays of Assar Lindbeck, Volume I
Assar Lindbeck

The Welfare State
The Selected Essays of Assar Lindbeck, Volume II
Assar Lindbeck

Classical Economics, Public Expenditure and Growth
Walter Eltis

Money, Interest Rates and Inflation
Frederic S. Mishkin

The Public Choice Approach to Politics
Dennis C. Mueller

The Liberal Economic Order
Volume I Essays on International Economics
Volume II Money, Cycles and Related Themes
Gottfried Haberler
Edited by Anthony Y.C. Koo

Economic Growth and Business Cycles
Prices and the Process of Cyclical Development
Paolo Sylos Labini

International Adjustment, Money and Trade
Theory and Measurement for Economic Policy, Volume I
Herbert G. Grubel

International Capital and Service Flows
Theory and Measurement for Economic Policy, Volume II
Herbert G. Grubel

Unintended Effects of Government Policies
Theory and Measurement for Economic Policy, Volume III
Herbert G. Grubel

The Economics of Competitive Enterprise
Selected Essays of P.W.S. Andrews
Edited by Frederic S. Lee and Peter E. Earl

The Repressed Economy
Causes, Consequences, Reform
Deepak Lal

Economic Theory and Market Socialism
Selected Essays of Oskar Lange
Edited by Tadeusz Kowalik

Trade, Development and Political Economy
Selected Essays of Ronald Findlay
Ronald Findlay

General Equilibrium Theory
The Collected Essays of Takashi Negishi, Volume I
Takashi Negishi

The History of Economics
The Collected Essays of Takashi Negishi, Volume II
Takashi Negishi

Studies in Econometric Theory
The Collected Essays of Takeshi Amemiya
Takeshi Amemiya

Exchange Rates and the Monetary System
Selected Essays of Peter B. Kenen
Peter B. Kenen

Econometric Methods and Applications (2 volumes)
G.S. Maddala